Design to Thrive

In Praise of Design to Thrive: Creating Social Networks and Online Communities that Last

"Tharon Howard's experienced and reflective account of how to develop social networks and online communities is remarkable because it puts the social experience first. Technology can improve as well as kill social experience. Howard's theoretical stance is firmly grounded in a lifetime of practical experience which makes fascinating and sometimes very amusing reading. Have you ever wondered why some networks and communities thrive and others fail? Read this book and find out."

–Jurek Kirakowski, Ph.D., Senior Lecturer, Human Factors
Research Group, Cork, Ireland

"A must read for anyone who wants to create social networks and online communities that are truly useful. It provides practical and well researched techniques that can be applied to design of web sites, consumer applications, and enterprise applications."

–Scott Isensee, User Experience Lead Architect, IBM Corporation

"If you are planning to jump on the social networking bandwagon, then this book is for you. Design to Thrive *sets forth a blueprint that will help make your online community engaging, useful, usable, viable, and sustainable. This book lays out a set of principles and practices, grounded in both theory and practical experience in an accessible, easy to grasp format. Replete with examples,* Design to Thrive *can take your social network from a fad to a truly valuable resource for its members."*

–Carol Righi, Ph.D., President, CarolRighi.com

"Dr. Howard addresses the history, creation, care, and feeding of online communities and social networks with the thoroughness of the academic he is. He illustrates his points with a rich collection of real-world examples from a longtime community and network designer, which he also is. With his "RIBS" – Remuneration, Influence, Belonging, and Significance, the four elements necessary for the long-term success of online communities and social networks – Dr. Howard puts plenty of meat on the bone."

–Randolph G. Bias, Ph.D., Associate Professor, School of Information;
Director, Information eXperience Lab, University of Texas at Austin

"Tharon has distilled his vast knowledge into an accessible discussion of why people join and take part in online communities and social networks, giving simple tips for setting up and supporting electronic social structures along the way."

–Dana Chisnell, co-author of *Handbook of Usability Testing, Second Edition*

"Kudos to Professor Tharon Howard for writing an insightful and entertaining guide to designing and sustaining social networks and online communities. Design to Thrive *is that rare book that melds personal wisdom, built from years of working with a wide range of online networks and communities, with solid design principles that software companies, moderators, and online community leaders can apply to make better products and more vibrant communities. Tharon presents a powerful model for stimulating ideas about designing and maintaining online communities called RIBS – Remuneration, Influence, Belonging, and Significance. The RIBS model can serve as a source of inspiration for both designers who are building the infrastructure for communities and the leaders who want their communities to thrive."*

–Chauncey E. Wilson, Senior Manager, Autodesk AEC User
Research and Adjunct Lecturer, Bentley University

Design to Thrive

Creating Social Networks and Online Communities that Last

Tharon W. Howard

AMSTERDAM • BOSTON • HEIDELBERG • LONDON
NEW YORK • OXFORD • PARIS • SAN DIEGO
SAN FRANCISCO • SINGAPORE • SYDNEY • TOKYO
MORGAN KAUFMANN PUBLISHERS IS AN IMPRINT OF ELSEVIER

ELSEVIER

MORGAN KAUFMANN PUBLISHERS

Morgan Kaufmann Publishers is an imprint of Elsevier.
30 Corporate Drive, Suite 400, Burlington, MA 01803, USA

This book is printed on acid-free paper.

Notices

Knowledge and best practice in this field are constantly changing. As new research and experience broaden our understanding, changes in research methods, professional practices, or medical treatment may become necessary.
Practitioners and researchers must always rely on their own experience and knowledge in evaluating and using any information, methods, compounds, or experiments described herein. In using such information or methods they should be mindful of their own safety and the safety of others, including parties for whom they have a professional responsibility.
To the fullest extent of the law, neither the Publisher nor the authors, contributors, or editors, assume any liability for any injury and/or damage to persons or property as a matter of products liability, negligence or otherwise, or from any use or operation of any methods, products, instructions, or ideas contained in the material herein.

Library of Congress Cataloging-in-Publication Data
Application submitted

British Library Cataloguing-in-Publication Data
A catalogue record for this book is available from the British Library.

ISBN: 978-0-12-374921-5

For information on all Morgan Kaufmann publications,
visit our Web site at www.mkp.com or www.elsevierdirect.com

Printed in China
09   10   11   12   13   5   4   3   2   1

Table of Contents

CHAPTER 4 • Remuneration

CHAPTER 5 • Influence

CHAPTER 6 • Belonging

CHAPTER 7 • Significance

CHAPTER 8 • Technology Changes Rapidly; Humans Don't

Communities don't happen by accident, although you'd never know it from the haphazard way most companies go about trying to create them.

I've worked for software development tool vendors for more than two decades, and everywhere I've gone, the company has tried to create a community among our customers. For some companies the motivation was a straightforward desire to reduce support costs by getting customers to answer each others' questions. Others saw it as a low-cost channel to educate and enable users, reasoning that a successful customer was more likely to remain a customer. A select few were sophisticated enough to realize that an active community would help bind customers to their products: if they contemplated switching vendors they might view losing their investment in the community as a greater loss than their investment in the product. One saw it as a contest in bragging rights with its biggest competitor and was able to prove that, with a sufficiently large marketing budget, it is actually possible to persuade programmers to exchange their e-mail addresses for free vendor-logo'ed tee-shirts and trial software. (This is not, you understand, considered a breakthrough discovery in the annals of software marketing.)

The most confusing element of my two decade random walk through the user group landscape was the pattern of success and failure—or rather, lack thereof. One group I was lucky enough to be a part of, a handful of disparate European distributors for an American software vendor, thrived despite—or perhaps because of?—our mutual struggles to customize for our various local markets a product ill-fitted to such ambitions. At times our meetings had more of an atmosphere of a support group for a rare and unpronounceable illness than a user group. I've seen other communities experience exhilarating initial success only to stagnate and wither away, dead for all practical purposes long before the last professional administrator turns out the lights on the Web forums' server for the final time. I've even witnessed at least two user groups not merely fail but actually take up torches and pitchforks against the parent company (fortunately, neither was at companies where I worked) in debates over control, sponsorship, and censorship. (In some ways, these uprisings presaged recent furors in the social networking world over issues such as privacy and content ownership.)

With the benefit of Tharon Howard's book and the insights he describes here, a pattern begins to emerge. All of these companies had at least some idea of what was in it for them in building a community. *Few had any idea of what would be in it for the participants.* In fact, I still get e-mail invitations from startup companies that aim to be the next LinkedIn.com, with no explanation of how they plan to be different from the *current* LinkedIn.com in a way that matters to me. Saddest of all to watch are companies that thought they had cracked the code and could incent participation by handing out "points" for various activities. The points in turn meant, well, nothing because nobody else cares how many points you have. These companies learned the hard way that you can't fake authentic peer recognition.

This book provides the necessary antidote to the thoughtless, random, and, in too many cases, desperate nature of many of today's attempts to build online communities. It replaces the typical "build it and they will come" and "go big or go home" mentality with a systematic analysis of what *really* motivates people to join, remain, and grow within a community; of the importance of giving as well as getting; and of where the all-important sense of belonging comes from. With the knowledge in these pages you'll understand how to nurture and nourish a community rather than helplessly watch it wither and fail. This book will tell you what actually makes communities work, both for the people who make up the life of the community and for the companies that support them. Read it and implement it before your online community dies.

Carl Zetie
Waterford, VA

WHERE DID THIS BOOK ORIGINATE?
Fortunate to be Stuck in Cars

You'd think that a book about social networking and online communities would start off with a celebration of Internet technologies and that, as an author, I would want to thank all of the people in online communities who have taught me so very much about what it takes to make communities and social networks great. And of course, I *do* want to thank them, and I will for they certainly do warrant special recognition. However, as I thought about where this book came from and who needed to be acknowledged as being most influential in terms of my thinking about building sustainable communities and networks, I realized that much of the knowing, making, and doing that made this book possible was a result of automobile technologies rather than wide-area networking technologies. The story of this book is, somewhat ironically, the result of being stuck in automobiles on long highway expeditions with some of the best colleagues anyone could hope to have.

I owe a tremendous debt to Rocky Gooch and am grateful for all the time he and I spent together driving all over the states of New Mexico, Vermont, and South Carolina throughout the 1990s meeting with rural K-12 teachers in those states and helping them get connected to the BreadLoaf Rural Teacher Network (BLRTN). Rocky, who was taken from us by cancer a few years ago, was the director of the BLRTN, and part of his charge as a community manager was to provide technical support that enables rural teachers who really do live on dirt roads to find a way to connect to the information superhighway. I particularly remember times when Rocky and I would drive out into the deserts of New Mexico—traveling up to 30 miles on dirt and gravel roads that almost certainly violated the contracts on the rental cars we were driving—in order to meet with a K-12 teacher who, even today, no Internet service provider would ever consider sending a service truck out to support.

More than anything else, I remember how Rocky and I felt when we would get a particular teacher connected to BLRTN on some crotchety old 2400 baud modem, and she would be so grateful that she would shower us with hugs, sometimes a lavish home-cooked meal, or tokens of gratitude obtained from the local pueblo. For a community manager, there's nothing quite like meeting face to face with a member of a network you manage and having that person convince you with *prima facie* evidence that your network impacted their professional lives profoundly. The feeling you get when you're in the presence of the naked, unencumbered joy people feel about being reconnected to the communities upon which they depend is more powerful and far more addictive than any drug. You can't be human, feel that joy as a community manager, and not get hooked on social media. You know—without the need for false humility or jaded cynicism—that you mattered; that you made a difference. And once you're hooked, you spend all your time, as Rocky and I did on those long drives, talking about how to make your network better so that you could have an even greater impact on the lives of those members you serve. I owe Rocky a great deal because this book began with those car rides where Rocky and I got hooked and asked ourselves how to make the BLRTN social network and its communities better spaces for our members.

The second way car rides have had an impact on this book came about as a result of a conversation I had with Dr. Greg Hawkins driving through the "corridor of shame" in South Carolina to consult with folks from the Centers for Neighborhood and Family Life in Hilton Head about ways that they could leverage work Greg and I had accomplished designing a social network for the Boys and Girls Clubs of America (BGCA) with funding we had received from the U.S. Bureau of Justice Assistance back in 2003. Since the goal of our presentation to the folks in Hilton Head was to help them understand what made our social network a success, our conversation during that long drive across the state naturally dealt with factors that any community manager might be able to use to build successful communities.

Initially, we talked about things like how to get funding, what kinds of server and bandwidth needs had to be met, what kinds of staffing were necessary, and, of course, what interface technologies needed to be developed and whether to use open source systems or work with a third-party vendor. However, what really clicked for me that day was when we ostensibly stopped talking about building social networks and when Greg told me about his dissertation research on what was necessary for someone to develop a psychological sense of community in real towns and urban communities. As Greg, who is a specialist in public policy, talked about the positive benefits that small towns and urban communities realized when their citizens had a strong sense of community, I realized that all the ink we'd spilt on talking about server requirements, staffing needs, and software packages had blinded me to the real role networking technologies play in the design of social networks. I guess you could say that I gave myself permission to think about online communities in a completely different way after that, and the RIBS heuristic that serves as at the basis for this book eventually resulted. For that, I'm truly grateful to Greg, as well as Ashley Cowden, Brian Verhoeven, Kathy Pringle, Eric Rogers, and all the other MA in Professional Communication graduate students who worked on the Virtual Conferencing Center we created for the BGCA movement.

Although I haven't been stuck in cars with them, I have been fortunate to have wonderful colleagues over the years who have helped me both by counseling me on the best ways to maintain professional communities online and as readers who responded to early drafts of chapters for this book. I owe particular thanks to Chauncey Wilson for introducing me to Denise Penrose and Mary James from Morgan Kaufmann at the UPA Conference in Baltimore, but I also want to thank him for his long service to a private, online community of usability testing professionals we maintain. Thanks also to Laurie Gray, Jurek Kirakowski, Dick Miller, and Maggie Reilly who continue to serve with Chauncey and who have given me such terrific advice over the years as members of that community's advisory council. Thanks also to former members of the council, Steve Krug, Larry Marine, Whitney Quesenbery, Mary Beth Rettger, and Larry Wood. I also need to acknowledge the efforts of Caroline Jarratt, Ginny Redish, Carol Righi, and Carl Zetie who not only served as council members and as community leaders with me, but also suffered through and responded to early draft versions of chapters of the book. And they really did suffer because I started writing the book in the middle with Chapter 4 and initially worked without using subheads, case studies, marginal notes, sidebars, or any other support for the basal text. Yet, despite the often inchoate thinking, they hung in there with me and gave me good advice. Indeed, in addition to their electronic reviews, Carl and Ginny spent several hours with me on the phone, taking time from their families in order to help me simplify and organize the chaos.

Many of the stories of communities and social networks in this book are based on my personal experience, but I've also had the good fortune to hang out (sometimes in cars and sometimes online) with other community managers who have graciously allowed me to share at least a small portion of their stories here. Stacy Sisson and Rachael Luxemborg from Adobe Systems, Inc. were extremely supportive and, even though much of the community building work they do with Adobe Group Managers is covered by nondisclosure agreements, they went above and beyond to help get legal permission so I could share a small glimpse of the forward-thinking work they do. Similarly, I owe a debt of gratitude to my Clemson colleagues Dr. Cynthia Haynes and Dr. Jan Holmevik for sharing their experiences managing MOOs, Second Life properties, and, most particularly, a role-playing World of Warcraft guild. Because I was aware of Cynthia's expertise as a result of our participation in the Serious Games Colloquium she and Jan organized for our Rhetoric(s), Communication, and Information Design doctoral program here at Clemson, I asked Cynthia for help finding examples of *mythos* as a community-building device. Within hours she had me connected with Paul Gorton in the United Kingdom. Without batting an eye, Mr. Gorton graciously gave permission to share his wonderfully creative and entertaining story about worgen and warriors that appears in Chapter 6. I also owe a similar debt of gratitude to my colleague and mentor here at Clemson, Dixie Goswami. Dixie's collaboration with me for more than two decades now building communities for BreadLoaf, various National Endowment for the Humanities grants, several South Carolina Department of Education projects, and other local programs simply can't be ignored, even though I can't adequately list or describe all the projects here. I also need to acknowledge Laura Coaty, who generously allowed me to call on her extensive marketing expertise in Chapter 7.

While I have had the good fortune to be stuck in cars with excellent colleagues, my sons have had the misfortune of being stuck in cars with me, where they had to listen to me blather on about all sorts of ways to design online communities and social networks and even humored me by connecting the techniques I was describing with experiences they had in the world of online games. Since both Logan and Bryce are avid gamers and are officers in World of Warcraft guilds, they've allowed me to watch how those types of gaming communities have evolved, and I owe both a great deal for demonstrating to me that business leaders, educators, and industry professionals have much to learn from gaming communities. I particularly owe Logan a big thank you, as many of the epic mounts and Level 60 characters used in this book came from screen captures he made on my behalf. I also need to thank several long-suffering graduate students who also helped me by making connections they found in the concepts I was discussing with experiences they had. Alicia Hatter and Nicole Snell read early drafts of chapters and not only provided invaluable copyediting, but also shared examples from communities they use regularly. Rita Howard and Amanda Gold also provided invaluable support by tracking down the contact information we needed in order to secure permission to reproduce screen captures, copyediting, and providing feedback on chapters. Special thanks also need to go to Heather Scherer, Nate McFadden, and Mary James from Morgan Kaufman. They didn't just edit the book for grammatical errors, but they took the time to work with me on the content development and allowed me to use our collaboration as grist for the mill when I needed examples to illustrate a technique or concept.

There's one final person with whom I've been stuck in cars who needs to be recognized since, without her, this book would never have been attempted. Much of this book was actually drafted in the car. Wendy—who is my first and best colleague, critic, and collaborator—would take notes on a laptop while we drove from South Carolina to Maryland in order to visit our oldest son or to work with one of our clients in a neighboring state. For almost a year, she sacrificed her evenings and weekends to help me organize the content and, after I rewrote the material we had compiled, to be the Hemingway who forced me to eradicate bovine scatology, to chop unnecessary stories, and to clarify when passages were obscure. She is the *sine qua non* of this book, and there's no doubt that this is a better book and I am a better person because of her gentle hand and unwavering support.

CHAPTER 1
Why Design to Thrive?

WHY?

BUZZ—WHY SHOULD YOU BE INTERESTED?

Social networks and online communities are very much in the popular consciousness these days. Second Life, Facebook, MySpace, LinkedIn, Twitter, Digg.com, Yahoo! groups—everywhere you look on the Net, there are new "communities" or social spaces popping up, clamoring for your attention. Forrester Research reported that four out of five online adults visited a social media site at least once a month in 2009 [1]. Second Life, a popular three-dimensional social network, reported that it had over 14 million registered users in June 2008, users who completed $19 million in "Linden dollar" transactions during the month of May 2008. By April of 2009, Second Life's total transactions had grown to $27 million Linden dollars [5].

Obviously, social networks and online communities are big business—or at least the successful ones are. Facebook, which was started by 20-year-old Harvard undergraduate Mark Zuckerberg as a means for college students to keep up with the dating games among friends, sold Microsoft a 1.6% interest in the company for $240 million. This kind of rags-to-riches story has become a meme with social networks and has garnered a lot of attention in the popular press. As a result, it has also gotten the attention of many young entrepreneurs, marketing directors, PR specialists, and Web consultants—all of whom are seeking to cash in on the Web 2.0 revolution.

The problem is that while online communities are extraordinarily powerful and useful, the rags-to-riches mythology that surrounds many of them belies the tremendous amount of work and rigorous thinking that goes into their design. This has resulted in what I like to call the "field of dreams" approach to designing social networks and electronic communities. The attitude here is "if you build it, they will come." That may have worked for Kevin Costner and baseball fields in Hollywood's version of an Iowa cornfield, but it doesn't ensure success when you're designing the architecture for an online community. As Carl Zetie, formerly of Forrester Research and now a senior marketing strategist for a major technology company, points out here, we may be facing a situation like the dot-com bubble of 2001:

> I'm baffled to be receiving invitations from numerous brand new sites who all seem to think they have identified some unique niche in the market. The worst of them are "targeted at professionals" (oooh, good thing nobody else thought of that!), the best have some unique aspect that can be easily imitated if it catches on. It's a profound mystery to me why anybody or their V[enture] C[apitalist] backer thinks they can jump into the Social Network game at this point without some radically better idea, and it's oddly reminiscent of the late stages of the Dotcom bubble when every VC seemed to think that their portfolio was incomplete without an online medical site. What happened to the good old days of VCs who would dismiss these things with a curt "that's not a business plan, it's a feature"?
>
> **[7], personal e-mail**

You can avoid the problems Zetie describes. And you can avoid the consequences associated with building a failed internal social network or online community for your own organization. Whatever background you come from (Web designer or developer, information architect, content manager, usability or user-experience specialist, PR, or marketing professional), this book will help you build successful and sustainable social networks and online communities.

WHAT EXPERIENCE HAS TAUGHT ME

I've tried to take an approach in this book that shares both my successes and my failures building these online communities and networks for more than 20 years now. My experience with online communities goes all the way back to the "bad old BITNET days" when e-mail distribution lists were all the rage. Back then as a graduate student in the 1980s, I had the opportunity to work in a natural language processing laboratory at Purdue University where a team of computational linguists were working with industry professionals across the country to try to figure out ways to make computers understand human communication.

Of course, despite the best efforts of natural language processing professionals, we *still* haven't figured out how to talk to our computers and get intelligible answers the way that Captain Kirk or Commander Spock could talk to computers on the TV show *Star Trek*. Still, what I learned from my experiences watching those early efforts to smash geographical and temporal barriers to online collaboration was that although we couldn't talk to the computers, we absolutely could use computers *to transform the ways we talked to each other*. I discovered the power of online communities through those e-mail lists and anonymous FTP sites. I became fascinated with the impact, even then, that these early social tools were having on the ways that knowledge was being made among academics and researchers on the one hand and revolutionizing business practices on the other. I recognized that, as Clay Shirky so aptly put it, "Whenever you improve a group's ability to communicate internally, you change the things that it is capable of" ([6], 171).

As an educator, I realized that I needed to start preparing my students to work in a radically different world than I had been trained for. I realized that my students were soon going to be working on cross-functional teams solving business and industry problems for multinational corporations. So in the late 1980s and early 1990s, I began experimenting with like-minded colleagues at universities in France, Germany, Japan, and Spain, where we would connect our students in virtual teams and have them work on solving real-world business problems. These pre-worldwide Web international exchanges gave students who had never experienced any cultures beyond those you could find in the cornfields surrounding West Lafayette, Indiana, an opportunity to have something like a study-abroad experience without having to give up a whole semester and paying the travel expense to do so.

During this period, I also found colleagues in industry who were willing to form academic–industry partnerships that allowed students to use online communities and social networking tools to collaborate with corporate professionals on real research projects—projects that were important to the organization but that the company was forced to abandon for some reason.

For example, during the mid-1990s my students in South Carolina collaborated with Time Warner's team of New Media Editors in New York. At the time, women didn't feel compelled to connect to the Internet and were an underserved market on the Web. As a result, the students conducted usability testing research and wrote recommendation reports aimed at helping Time Warner better understand how to meet the needs of women through a portal called "Pathfinder," which the company was launching as an experiment in online publishing. Everyone benefited from these experiences—the companies benefited from the time they invested in the students' education and the students developed hands-on experience with solving problems in online environments.

Not only did the students learn from these "service learning" projects, but I personally gained invaluable experience building social collaboration spaces. In addition to learning how to build "safe" spaces where my students would and could collaborate with other students and/or industry professionals, I also learned to design spaces where my colleagues and I could meet in order to plan the work that the students would do. In these groups, my colleagues from industry and education began talking about our shared passion for understanding what makes for successful online collaborative projects, and I got a reputation for being able to build successful communities. As a result, I began to consult on projects where managers recognized that—if they could figure out how to design them effectively—they could also

WEB LINK
Pathfinder: Your Guide to the Web Sites of Time, Inc.
http://www.pathfinder.com/ pathfinder/index.html

profit from online communities and social networks the way my students were benefitting.

FIVE TYPES OF ONLINE GROUPS CLIENTS SEEK

What I've discovered through my consulting work is that my clients and volunteer projects tend to fall in five groups, and it's these five groups upon which I base most of the experiences I share in this book.

Internal project and professional development teams

In the first group, there are clients who want to build internal groups of project teams or departments in order to promote collaboration and professional development. For example, the manager of an end-user support department recently contacted me. She wanted to connect all the information product developers who create user-support manuals and training materials for the mainframe computer software that her company sells. Her staff members were all busy professionals assigned to work on different product teams and were located at different sites throughout the $1.6 billion corporation, so they rarely had time to meet, socialize, and share ideas as a department. She wanted to have her staff meet online in order to share new ideas and techniques. She was concerned that her department was still cranking out the same old print-based documentation they had been writing for the past 20 years (which is why I'm not using her name) and she wanted her people to start considering alternative distribution media such as video tutorials, wikis. She thought that maybe, by pulling her folks together into an online community, they could support each other and think creatively about ways to enhance the ways they deliver user support and training to their customers.

Communities of practice

The second type of social group with whom I have worked extensively involved professionals working for lots of different companies who come together in order to enhance what Etienne Wenger calls their "community of practice." These groups are primarily made of practitioners in a field or profession who are passionate about the work that they do. For example, one of the online communities I've successfully maintained since 1993 is made up of professionals in the usability and user experience design field who—even though they work for competing companies—come together to help each other better understand the best practices and latest techniques being used in that community of practice.

Networks across disciplinary boundaries

The third type of social groups with whom I've worked have been large-scale social networks where people were working across disciplinary and functional boundaries in order to share information. For example, I worked with the Breadloaf Rural Teacher Network (BLRTN) where middle school and high school teachers in rural states such as Vermont, Alaska, New Mexico, and South Carolina could find other teaching professionals and collaborate. Despite differences in the grades they teach or their disciplines, BLRTN teachers are able to find support from colleagues who also have the same educational "dirt under their fingernails" and can sustain their peers.

Diane Waff, a member of BLRTN, describes her experience this way:

> Moving out from the isolation of the classroom to the shelter of inquiry communities that provide safe spaces for real dialog, the sharing of stories, relationships with colleagues, and reflection helped me to develop a critical reflective stance with regard to my own teaching and school reform efforts.

[3], 70–71

Similarly, I also worked with an organization that had 35,000 employees with different job titles, different responsibilities, different skill sets, and different educational backgrounds who nevertheless needed to share information across those boundaries in order to help the organization achieve its goals. Like the BLRTN network, a primary goal of these types of clients is their interest in retaining employees by providing them with the social support of peers.

Brand communities and user group communities

The fourth group with whom I've worked are either public relations and marketing specialists or user support professionals who are caught up in the buzz about social networking and what are often called "brand communities." They see the success that Apple or Adobe Systems has had at building a loyal group of customers who are so passionate about their experience with these companies' products that they want to share their experiences with other customers. Typically, these clients end up wanting to build online "user group" communities where their customers can go to share ideas about ways to use their products. These clients hope that these communities will reduce their customer support costs by getting users to support each other and that they will build greater customer loyalty.

Gaming communities

The last group that I've studied closely and learned a great deal from may, at first, strike some as odd. However, my experiences with online gaming communities have actually provided some of the best techniques for designing strong, sustainable communities that I've found. Indeed, as James Paul Gee has also argued in his book, *What Video Games Have to Teach Us about Learning and Literacy*, I discovered that the problem-solving behaviors that gamers use translate perfectly into strategies that both educators and business professionals can leverage [2].

Over 50% of teachers leave the profession within their first 5 years, and this failure to retain teachers costs U.S. school systems more than $7 billion per year [4]. Social networks such as BLRTN cut that cost by improving retention.

This is particularly the case in what are called "Massively Multiple Online Role Playing Games" (MMORPGs). The most popular of these today is Blizzard's World of Warcraft, which, as of 2009, boasted over 11.5 million online gamers. Affectionately known as "WoW" by players, this game is an incredibly valuable tool for understanding communities and social networks because WoW is a three-dimensional world where players are required to build and join communities in order to enjoy success in the game. In other words, just like many competitive business ventures, WoW players have to learn to build strong, successful communities or they will fail. Unlike business, however, if you fail to design an effective community in WoW, you don't get fired or lose all your investors. In MMORPGs, you have the opportunity to restart and you get to try again—only this time having the benefit of learning from your previous mistakes. This makes games such as WoW, Everquest, America's Army, Halo 3, and other MMORPGs perfect test beds for learning how to be a successful community designer.

TECHNOLOGICAL TESTOSTERONE POISONING

Working with social technologies for more than two decades now has taught me that success isn't determined by technology alone. My diverse experiences working with the five types of groups listed above have given me the opportunity to work with a number of different software packages: Listserv, Listproc, major-domo, Lyris, PostNuke, Geeklog, Cascade, Druple, FirstClass, phpBB, Wikimedia, Lamba-MOO, IRC, and many, many others. The list of "killer apps" that could be used for community building and social networking these days is obscenely large. And I'll admit it—I do suffer from a kind of technological testosterone poisoning, which makes me want to play with them all. What's more, I find that many of my clients also suffer from this same poisoning.

> **TIP**
> The likelihood of success or whether or not your community or social network will still be around in 6 to 8 months, depends on factors beyond the particular engine you're using … It's about the design of the community and four core principles, which I call **RIBS.**

However, working with all these different tools has made me keenly aware of the fact that it doesn't matter what technology you're talking about—the likelihood of success or whether or not your community or social network will still be around in 6 to 8 months depends on factors beyond the particular engine you're using. I still have online communities functioning today that are tremendously successful and recognized as the go-to places in their respective fields—and yet these communities continue to run on technologies that were created in the 1980s. Online communities that have been in existence for going on two decades now have taught me that it's not about technology. It's about the design of the community and four core principles, which I call RIBS.

RIBS: THE FOUR ELEMENTS NECESSARY FOR LONG-TERM SUCCESS

This book describes four elements necessary for the long-term success of online communities. I call these four elements the RIBS of online communities and social networks. "RIBS" stands for

- Remuneration
- Influence
- Belonging
- Significance

The bulk of this book is dedicated to explaining what each of these elements means, and the book is designed so that approximately one-half of each chapter that describes one of the RIBS elements is dedicated to specific design techniques that you can use in your social network or community. Furthermore, each technique is exemplified with an actual example drawn from a social network or online community that I have built or from a popular system with which you're likely to be familiar.

However, before we can talk about RIBS, we need to be clear about how "social networks" and "online communities" differ from each other, as well as how they differ from other Web 2.0 technologies. As we will discover, social networks are very good at supporting certain kinds of tasks, whereas online communities are better at supporting other activities. These differences are described in Chapter 2, and Chapter 3 then offers 10 more specific ways that building social networks and online communities can provide additional benefits to an organization depending on whether you are building them for use internally by members of your organization or for external use by the public.

After describing what we're talking about and why you might want to build them, we will then be able to turn to a discussion of *how to build them well*, and that's where the RIBS heuristic comes into focus.

Remuneration

Chapter 4 deals with *Remuneration*. This principle is—at least on the surface—probably the best understood characteristic necessary for the construction of successful online communities and social networks. Its simplest formulation basically says that people need to believe that they will obtain some positive return on the investment of their time and energy in order to be attracted to participation in a community. Individuals will not become members of a social network unless there is a clear benefit for doing so.

Influence

Chapter 5 addresses the *Influence* criterion. Influence in a community is, in my opinion, the most important and most overlooked area for community managers and designers. Far, far too many "communities" have been started and then fail because the architects or leaders in the community overlooked and failed to provide structures that allow the members to have influence in the community. Essentially, influence means giving the members of the community a clear sense that they have a voice in the community and control over how their voice will be heard.

Belonging

Chapter 6 addresses *Belonging*, which is yet another area of community development and design that, at least in the electronic world, is all too often ignored. Successful communities have secret handshakes, special languages, icons, colors, and symbols that (1) help members identify each other and (2) cultivate that strong emotional attachment to others in the community, that strong feeling of belonging. Chapter 6 discusses specific strategies you can use to encourage the strong sense of belonging and presence your users will need.

Significance

Chapter 7 deals with the criterion of *Significance*, which is essentially saying that in order for a community to be successful it has to be seen as significant. It has to be respected. This chapter discusses public relations, marketing, policy making, and other strategies that designers can use to enhance the significance of their communities and networks for users.

WHAT ARE RIBS GOOD FOR?

The RIBS are intended to be a means of generating and provoking design ideas. The RIBS model can certainly be used as an analytical tool that can help people better understand how communities and social systems work. Indeed, I hope that part of the fun of this book is that you'll see techniques you recognize from popular systems such as Facebook, Twitter, and LinkedIn and will enjoy a new appreciation for their design. However, that's not the main goal of this book. Instead, the RIBS construct is intended primarily to be a means for designers to envisage new ideas and to think proactively about the communities they are either building or maintaining.

In order to build and/or maintain Web 2.0 interfaces, what today's designers need is something to help guide their thinking in creative, productive ways. RIBS is a model that does that, and as such it is a "heuristic" in the original sense of the word, i.e., an invention strategy. It will help you make informed decisions about where the design of a community does or does not need attention. RIBS, as a heuristic, will help point you in the direction you need to go.

The four chapters on each element of RIBS are full of strategies and tactics. You're still going to have to think creatively about which to use for your social network or online community—how to combine strategies and tactics or come up with different ones based on what you learn about each element. You're still going to have to do the hard work of development, but it should be easier with RIBS as the roadmap.

Each social network and online community is different. There are no simple algorithms or "one solution fits all" for building sustainable social networks or online communities. But there are lots of important points to keep in mind, strategies to develop, and tactics to use. RIBS organizes all this into a useful heuristic, and that's what the rest of this book is about.

WORKS CITED

[1] Corcoran S. The broad reach of social technologies. Forrester. 20 March 2009. 29 August 2009. http://www.forrester.com/Research/Document/Excerpt/0,7211,55132,00 .html?cm_mmc=google-_-Recent_Documents-_-The_Broad_Reach_Of_Social_ Technologies-_-social_network_statistics|-|100000000000000002263&cm_guid=1-_- 100000000000000002263-_-3107558978.

[2] Gee J.P. What Video Games Have to Teach Us about Learning and Literacy Revised and Updated Edition. New York: Palgrave Macmillan; 2007.

[3] Goswami D., Lewis C., Rutherford M., Waff D. On Teacher Inquiry: Approaches to Language and Literacy Research. New York: Teacher College Press; 2009.

[4] Hernandez N. Teacher turnover costs systems millions, study projects. Washingtonpost .com. 21 June 2007. 16 May 2009. http://www.washingtonpost.com/wp-dyn/content/ article/2007/06/20/AR2007062002300.html.

[5] Second life economic stats. Secondlife.com. 28 August 2009. 29 August 2009. http:// secondlife.com/whatis/economy_stats.php.

[6] Shirky C. Here Comes Everybody: The Power of Organizations Without Organizations. New York: Penguin; 2008.

[7] Zetie C. LinkedIn group for UT. E-mail to the author. 26 June 2008.

CHAPTER 2
The Nature of the Beasts

WHAT ARE WE TALKING ABOUT?

SYNOPSIS

What distinguishes a social network from an online community and why would you choose to build them? This chapter differentiates between these two types of social structures by comparing them in terms of the issues shown in Table 2.1 below.

Table 2.1 Comparison of Social Networks and Online Communities

A social network:	An online community:
■ has an organizational structure focused around an individual user's one-to-one relationships	■ has an organizational structure focused around a shared purpose rather than one-to-one relationships
■ has weak secondary connections between members	■ has strong, predictable secondary relationships among members
■ allows its users to be members of many communities in the network at the same time	■ is distinct from other communities because of differences in purpose, policies, and computing environment
■ is good for sharing activities	■ is good for activities requiring sharing and cooperating
■ is less effective at activities requiring cooperation and collective action	■ is effective at providing the framework for activities requiring collective action
■ makes it easier for users to build communities	■ should not be confused with "adhocracies," "discussion groups," "forums," or "lists"

Since many people are interested in building social networks or online communities in order to accomplish specific types of activities for companies and professional organizations, the chapter examines the complexity required to complete different kinds of collaborative activities. It will illustrate why building a social network is probably going to be less effective than an online community if your goal is, say, to pull together a group of people for the purpose of cooperating on the design, build, and launch of a new product in a company.

In order to compare and contrast social networks and online communities, the chapter will begin by examining some popular definitions of these systems, starting with social networks and then moving to online communities. Then once we have made clear what we are discussing in this book, we'll conclude the chapter with a discussion of terms like "groups," "forums," and "lists" which are often erroneously and inappropriately used as synonyms of communities and social networks.

WHAT IS A SOCIAL NETWORK (COMPARED TO AN ONLINE COMMUNITY)?

Because of the tremendous advantages and the explosive growth of social networks and online communities, the desire to capitalize on the "Web 2.0" bandwagon has encouraged many people to become pretty sloppy with the terms "social networks" and "online community." Indeed, Bill Eager makes the point that sites have begun calling themselves "social networks" so that they can ride on the marketing coat tails of social networking gorillas such as Facebook, LinkedIn, and Second Life [6]. After all, if advertisers are looking to spend their dollars on social networks and communities, then why would anyone be surprised that many webmasters and electronic entrepreneurs should choose to characterize their sites as social networks or communities?

Confusing social network with community

In their book *Online Communities Handbook*, Anna Buss and Nancy Strauss state that they define "online communities as Web sites where user relationships develop. By this definition, **social networks** are online communities in their purest form" ([2], 16).

Now, it's unlikely that anyone would disagree with Buss and Straus about the fact that forming and sustaining relationships with others is at the core of both online communities and social networks. However, their definition fails to distinguish between social networks and communities and is symptomatic of many who have overemphasized the "Web" in Web 2.0. There is a great deal more to both online communities and social networks than is offered by this definition. For example, when Buss and Strauss limit the distribution medium online communities can use to "Web sites" only, they eliminate the possibility that social networks and online communities can exist as:

- bulletin boards
- Listserv groups
- USENET groups
- Second Life communities
- FirstClass forums
- World of Warcraft "guilds"
- MOO or MUD sites
- IRC (Internet Relay Chat) channels

In other words, these Web 2.0-biased definitions do violence to online communities, which have been around and accepted since the 1980s, and they ignore the future possibility that social networks and online communities may grow around software clients that people use that are not Web based. There are over 11.5 million people who have purchased and installed the software World of Warcraft (better known as WoW), and they use WoW to connect to other people in the virtual world created by the game in order to collaboratively solve problems presented by the game and to form relationships with other players.

Similarly, Second Life users, who also connect to one another without Web-based software, spent over 400 million hours logged into the 3D virtual world in 2008, and they spent over $100 million in user-to-user transactions in the fourth quarter of 2008 alone [3]. It seems inappropriate and myopic to ignore these kinds of numbers just because they didn't occur within a Web framework.

Social networks put individuals at center of relationships

However, the larger problem with Buss and Strauss's definition is that it fails to recognize that the organization of "relationships" in social networks is fundamentally different than online communities. In social networks such as LinkedIn or Facebook, the *individual user* is at the center of the network.

A leading scholar on social networks, danah boyd, doesn't capitalize her name.

The nature of the relationships is direct, one to one, and dyadic. The definition of a social network that boyd and Ellison offers begins to capture this concept:

> We define social network sites as web-based services that allow individuals to (1) construct a public or semi-public profile within a bounded system, (2) articulate a list of other users with whom they share a connection, and (3) view and traverse their list of connections and those made by others within the system. The nature and nomenclature of these connections may vary from site to site.

In addition to providing one of the best definitions of "social networks" currently available, boyd and Ellison also have compiled a useful timeline of launch dates for major social networking sites, which is shown in Figure 2.1. The timeline helps reinforce just how quickly and explosively social networking has grown, and it also shows the beginnings of social networks, which most researchers agree began with Six Degrees.com, up through the introduction of Twitter and the date Facebook became available for any user rather than college and high school students.

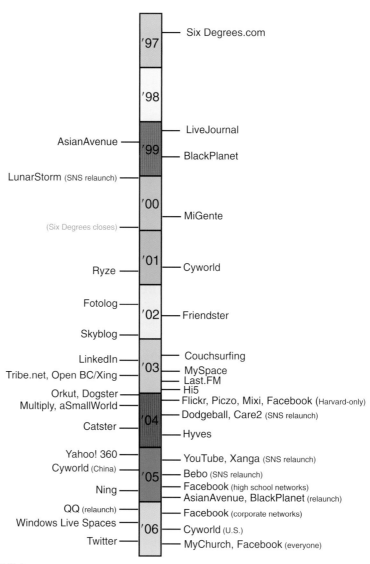

FIGURE 2.1
boyd and Ellison's timeline of major social network launch dates.

In terms of distinguishing between communities and social networks, it's important to recognize that the "profile" users created inside the boundaries of a social network are unique to each individual. The networks may display my connections to others in the network because I may share "mutual friends" with someone on Facebook or, in the case of LinkedIn, I can view "shared connections" that already exist with someone (as Figure 2.2 illustrates). However, the point is still that the view of the network which I see and the basis upon which the connections are built is *entirely unique to me.*

See the Significance chapter for a discussion of how Six Degrees .com got its name as well as Facebook's choices regarding the exclusivity of its user base.

Communities are different. The individual isn't at the center of relationships in a community; instead, an individual's relationship to others in the community is secondary. The primary focus in a community is on the user's commitment to a core set of interests, values, and communication practices. The individual makes a commitment to the group as a whole before other individual members, but paradoxically, this commitment means that the contacts that I have with the other members of a community is richer, more complex, and more predictable than the contacts I can make in a social network.

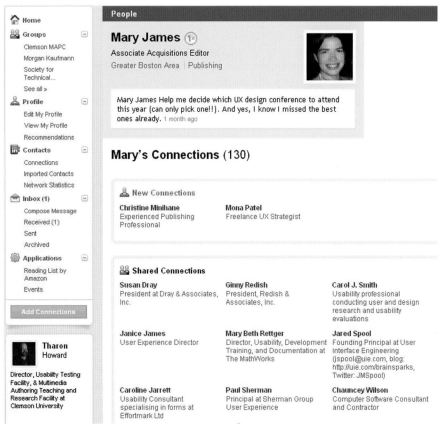

FIGURE 2.2
Example of shared connections.

Note that, throughout this book, I use the term "group" to refer to collectives, which are neither communities nor social networks. Some potential examples of these are discussed at the end of this chapter.

We can begin to see why potential relationships in online communities are more predictable (and therefore more exploitable) when one considers that another distinguishing characteristic between networks and communities is that several groups and communities can exist within a single network.

Because the individual is at the center of social networks, it's possible for users to belong to multiple groups and communities on the same network. As the "Groups" column in Figure 2.2 illustrates, I'm a member of the Clemson MAPC group on LinkedIn, which allows me to keep in contact with graduate students, alumni, and other faculty in the MA in Professional Communication program. I'm also a member of the Society for Technical Communication group on LinkedIn, which allows me to send announcements to and ask questions of members of that professional community of practice, even though I don't share primary connections with everyone on LinkedIn who is also a member of the group.

The strength of connections is different

As Clay Shirky also observes in his work *Here Comes Everybody*, social networks' secondary connections are weak. He writes, "The potential ties are too weak (any two users of Google are not likely to have much else in common)"([5], 102). In other words, even though I have a direct connection to Mary James on LinkedIn as Figure 2.2 shows and even though Mary and I share nine connections, the other 120 people who are connected to Mary are very likely people whom I don't know. What's more, other than the fact that they have some relationship to Mary, I don't know very much about them and can't really predict what one of those individuals may find interesting, what they value, how they're educated, and so on. Our secondary connections in the social network are weak.

In communities, however, the secondary connections are far stronger. Communities aren't just a collection of individuals; instead, members have made a commitment to achieve the shared passions and goals of the group. What's more, they agree to cooperate toward achieving the goals in particular ways, through a shared set of means. That's why communities tend to be much more structured and have much more overt organizational structures, rules, and rituals than social networks. And that is also the reason why the connections I share with other members of a community are stronger and more predictable than those in social networks.

You've probably experienced the strength of this kind of secondary connection when you go to professional conferences. For example, when I go to the Usability Professionals Association (UPA) conference and I meet someone for the first time, someone with whom I don't share a primary connection, I can still make a number of predictions about their values, background, and common practices. It's a pretty good bet that they wouldn't be in the UPA if they didn't have a commitment to making products and services more usable (i.e., the community's goals and values). It's also the case that most UPA members are committed to making products usable through empirical research (i.e., the community's background expectations for members). And since usability testing is one of the core means that members of the UPA share as the accepted practice for achieving the organization's goals, I can probably assume that they will know what I mean if I use the expression "protocol analysis" to strike up a conversation about some work I recently completed in my usability laboratory (i.e., the community's accepted practices).

Having this stronger secondary connection in a community means that it's easier for me to make primary contact with others in a community than it is for me to make primary contact with 1 of the 120 people in Mary's LinkedIn network.

Differences in the strength of relationships creates difference in activities

Because secondary relationships in online communities are stronger than social networks, it is possible to engage in more complex tasks and activities in communities than it is in social networks. Clay Shirky in *Here Comes Everybody* explains these differences as rungs in a ladder requiring more and more organizational complexity in order to support the activity required by the group. He lists three types of activities:

- sharing
- cooperation
- collective action

SHARING

Sharing requires the least amount of organizational complexity because it's the easiest activity in Shirky's ladder, which is also why it's ideal for social networks. Here's an example that should illustrate the point.

In 2009, the parents of seniors who were graduating from D.W. Daniel High School in South Carolina decided to have a party for the graduating class. One of the parents decided that it would be fun to provide a place where everyone who took photos at the event could upload and share their pictures. The complexity of the activity involved in sharing the photos in this social network is extremely low, and the process is simple—discover the activity, observe the activity, contribute to the activity. As Figure 2.3 illustrates, the sharing involved in viewing the images only requires that a student or parent go to the URL, which they learned about by text messages, Facebook updates, Twitter hashtags, or just plain old-fashioned e-mail messages. Once they learned the URL and visited the site, they can comment in the Guestbook or add a "Journal entry" to the Class of 2009 updates, and if they choose to subscribe to the RSS feed, they can get updates whenever new content is added to the site. Sharing pictures through uploading them isn't much more difficult. All that someone needs to do is to click on the "Add pictures" link, create a free account on Shutterfly.com, and then share their files with the group.

In this case, it quite literally took Wendy (the person who created the sharing site) about 15 minutes to create the space and then to e-mail a few friends she

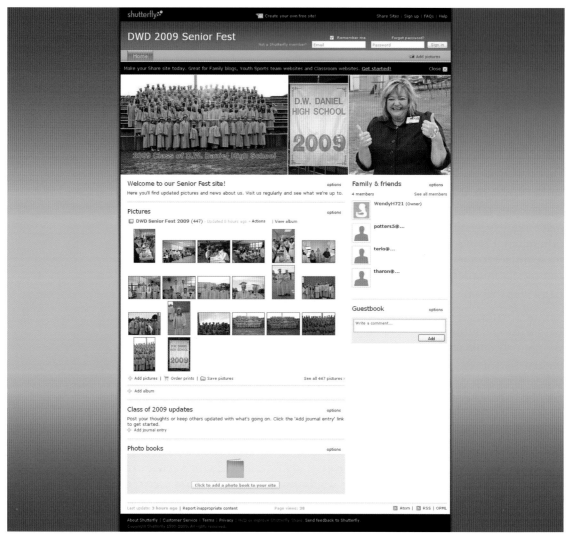

FIGURE 2.3
Sharing in a social network.

knew who had been at the event, inviting them to contribute as well. Hence, the organizational complexity required for sharing is minimal and really only required that Wendy contact a few of her primary connections in order to get the ball rolling, which makes sharing ideal for social networking.

COOPERATION

Activities involving sharing are simple, but an activity requiring *cooperation* takes more effort and demands more complexity. If exchanging photos taken during SeniorFest was an example of a sharing activity, then an example of coordination would be the organizational complexity required to pull off the 2009 SeniorFest in the first place.

Organizing the parents so that all of the resources needed for the SeniorFest party were obtained was what Shirky calls a "collaborative production." And rather than the 15 minutes needed to produce a sharing activity, it involved weeks of planning. First of all, it required that parents accept specific roles and responsibilities. There needed to be leaders in different areas of the event. Someone needed to be responsible for barbequing the hamburgers and hot dogs, and someone had to be sure the tents and tables were set up so people could eat in the shade. Someone had to work with the local fire department and convince them to bring their ladder truck to spray the students with water on a makeshift slip and slide. Someone had to volunteer to bring a dunking booth and then to find a group to set it up and operate it. Plates, napkins, music, and even a tethered hot air balloon ride needed people to take responsibility for them. In fact, so many people began volunteering to be responsible for pieces of the event that the group ended up needing someone to coordinate the leaders.

Beyond coordinating roles and responsibilities, however, another major aspect of the organizational complexity needed to pull together this event was establishing lines of communication and setting up protocols so that participants understood how they were supposed to behave. There was very little point in having the fire department show up or in passing out squirt guns to spray the graduates with water if none of the students knew that they were supposed to wear swimming attire at the event. Consequently, flyers, Web sites, announcements on the school's intercom, and e-mail blasts all had to be used in order to ensure that participants understood how they were supposed to behave when they showed up for the event (see Figure 2.4).

Communities are really good at establishing these lines of communication where social networks aren't because communities have much tighter secondary connections. We've already seen that members in communities share understandings of their goals, background expectations, and common practices, which members of social networks do not. Thus, it's easier to utilize communication channels that probably already exist in communities than it is to create and maintain new ones in social networks where lines of communication are almost entirely dependent on the primary connection between individuals.

COLLECTIVE ACTION

Pulling together activities requiring *collective action* is even more complex and even more difficult to organize than activities involving cooperation. With cooperation, different individuals or small teams work on their own toward a common goal. They don't sacrifice their identity or even really compromise much to achieve those goals. With collective action, however, we're dealing with large organizational structures, such as unions, government agencies, corporations, and professional organizations, which are setting policies or making binding agreements as part of their collective action.

DWD 2009 SENIOR FEST

A day of celebration for all 2009 Seniors

When: May 22, 2009
(immediately following Awards Day morning activities)
Where: DWD Baseball Outfield
(Rain location is DWD's gyms)

Lunch:

Hamburgers/Cheeseburgers
Hotdogs (with chili)
Chips
Sodas & water
Fruits & vegetables
Popcorn
Ice Pops
Ice Cream
Cookies
Brownies

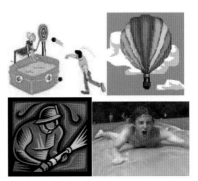

Activities:

Tents with tables and chairs
Music
Dunking Booth*
Slip'n'slide*
Fire Hose*
Volleyball & Badminton
Horseshoes
Tethered hot air balloon rides (*weather permitting*)
Pictures will be posted after the event at:
http://dwd2009seniorfest.shutterfly.com/

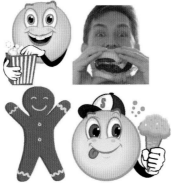

*Students wishing to participate in the water activities need to wear a dark, loose fitting t-shirt that is made from a heavier-weight cotton. No "see-through" shirts allowed. All students should also bring a change of clothes if they plan to re-enter the building. Bathroom facilities will be available.

FIGURE 2.4
Senior Fest flyer distributed to high school seniors through the school's existing communication channels.

An example of collective action can be seen in the Usability Professionals Association BoK (or "Body of Knowledge") project (Figure 2.5). Usability is a relatively young field; as a result, the standards for what it means to be a usability professional aren't entirely worked out. What sorts of educational experiences should usability professionals have? What ethical obligations do usability professionals need to meet? What best practices are essential to successful usability professionals? Although individual practitioners may have their own personal answers to these questions, the UPA as a whole is working them out, and BoK projects are an effort to solidify the position of the UPA on these important issues.

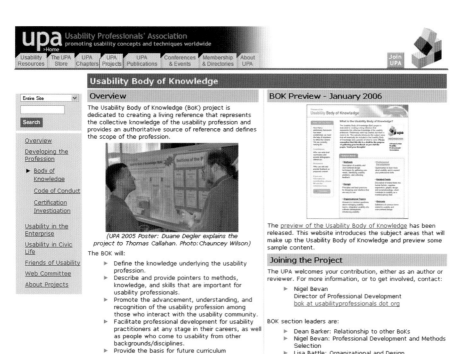

FIGURE 2.5
Usability Professionals'
Association Body of
Knowledge project.
© UPA, Reprinted from
the UPA website at
http://www.upassoc.org/
upa_projects/body_of_
knowledge/bok.html

What requires the organizational complexity here is that these issues are extraordinarily politicized and highly charged issues for many individual members of the UPA. The fight comes when someone who has been practicing in the field for, say, 20 years is told by an organization that she supports that she's ignorant of an entire area of research the organizers of the BoK project say is essential. The BoK project is supposed to define areas of knowledge considered requisite in order to be successful as a professional, yet here's this person calling herself a "professional" for 20 years who is a respected and successful practitioner. This creates a lot of angst between the collective need for action on the one hand and the individual's needs on the other.

Therefore, getting an organization like the UPA and all of its members to get behind collective action projects like a BoK takes considerable negotiation and organizational complexity. There have to be officers who run the discussions, people who contribute information, facilitators who negotiate agreements, and representation systems such as balloting or elections so that the members' views are taken into consideration. You can see how much more complex collective action is than cooperation when you consider that cooperation doesn't need a representative elected by members to speak on behalf of a whole organization the way collective action does.

However, the point here is that online communities can achieve the kind of complex organizational structures needed for both cooperation and collective action; social networks can't. A social network has an organizational structure focused around an individual user's one-to-one relationships, its secondary connections are generally weak, and its users can be members of many communities in the network at the same time. Social networks are good for sharing activities, but they are less effective at activities requiring cooperation and collective action. They can, however, make it easier for people to build communities able to support cooperation and collective action activities.

WHAT IS AN ONLINE COMMUNITY (COMPARED TO LISTS, DISCUSSION GROUPS, OR FORUMS)?

So far, by starting with established descriptions of social networks and comparing them to online communities, we've got fairly high-level definitions of what social networks are. We've also partially defined online communities by looking at how they're distinguished from social networks, but we really haven't given an established definition of online community from the field the way we did for social networks.

One of the best definitions of communities in the literature comes from Jenny Preece's book *Online Communities*. Preece's definition is as follows:

> An online community consists of
> - *People*, who interact socially as they strive to satisfy their own needs or perform special roles, such as leading or moderating.
> - A shared *purpose*, such as an interest, need, information exchange, or service that provides a reason for the community.
> - *Policies*, in the form of tacit assumptions, rituals, protocols, rules, and laws that guide people's interactions.
> - *Computer systems*, to support and mediate social interaction and facilitate a sense of togetherness.
>
> [4], 10

Preece's definition is much more successful than others because it doesn't rule out the possibility of online communities existing in other media. Preece doesn't limit online communities to the Web, as was the case with the definition of social networks. However, Preece's definition doesn't capture the concept of organizational complexities and the types of actions, such as sharing, cooperation, and cooperative action, which we've discussed already and which are possible in an online community.

Still, her definition does capture the major elements of community. Indeed, many of the elements that Preece articulates are elements of sustainable communities, which we will be focusing on in the RIBS heuristic. For example, the chapter on Remuneration discusses the role purpose plays in long-term communities, the chapter on Influence discusses policies and creating safe spaces in order to sustain communities, and the chapter on Belonging discusses how rituals and protocols are needed for communities that are built to last.

Because we'll be going into detail about these and other elements of community in subsequent chapters, there's no need to discuss them here. Instead, I'm going to focus on how the term "community" is often applied inappropriately to describe other groups commonly found in online environments: lists, discussion groups, and forums. I do not want to be interpreted as saying that e-mail lists, UseNet discussion groups, and Web-based forums cannot be communities. They can be. But oftentimes, they are called "communities" when they're not, and that's the issue addressed in the next section.

Online groups aren't automatically communities

All too often, people confuse the technology that is used to enable a community with the community itself. A community might use a Web-based "forum" or "bulletin board" as one of its communication channels, and if that is the primary or possibly the only communication channel used, then it's easy to understand why people might confuse the technology with the community itself. However, designers can't afford to make that mistake. Designers and architects of communities have to be able to distinguish between what it takes to build a "community" beyond e-mail lists, news groups, bulletin boards, and Web forums.

What is an e-mail distribution list or "listserve" list? As the name suggests, e-mail distribution lists depend on e-mail as the medium in which they function. And they are, quite literally, lists of e-mail addresses, usually with some "list header" at the top that controls how they function (Figure 2.6).

Although they're often called "listserve lists," they may not necessarily be running on a piece of software known as Listserv. The Listserv software was originally written by Eric Thomas back in the old BITNET days, and today it's run by a company known as L-Soft. However, e-mail distribution lists can actually run on other software packages such as LISTPROC, Lyris, major-domo, and Postman—just to name a few.

Basically, what Listserv and these other software packages do is receive an e-mail message that comes in from a "subscriber," a member of the group, and then check it to make sure that the message hasn't been distributed previously in order to prevent catastrophic e-mail loops from starting. If the list header has been configured to limit "postings" to members only, then it will check to make sure that the e-mail address on the "From:" line is authorized to send to the list and then distribute the message to all of the e-mail lists on the list. Different packages enable additional configuration possibilities. For example, the software might

- send the message to a moderator for approval before distributing it
- save the message to an archive
- make the archive available via the Web

```
*
* STAFF IN THE MATRF AND DDL
*
* SEND= PRIVATE
* SERVICE= LOCAL
* SUBSCRIPTION= CLOSED
* CONFIDENTIAL= YES
* REPLY-TO= LIST,RESPECT
* DEFAULT-OPTIONS= REPRO,NOACK
* VALIDATE= YES,CONFIRM
* REVIEW= OWNERS,POSTMASTER
* LOOPCHECK= NOSPAM
* OWNER= THARON@CLEMSON.EDU Tharon Howard
* ERRORS-TO= OWNERS,POSTMASTER
bricke@CLEMSON.EDU        Bryan Ricke
nsnell@CLEMSON.EDU        Nicole Snell
tharon@CLEMSON.EDU        Tharon Howard
ltellis@G.CLEMSON.EDU     Lara Tellis
*
* Total number of users subscribed to the list:    8
* Total number of local host users on the list:    4
*
```

FIGURE 2.6
Sample "list" with list header configuration.

- send out an acknowledgment message to let the list manager know the message has been distributed
- restrict the size of the messages that can be distributed
- limit the size and types of attachments that can be distributed
- limit the number of messages per day that can be distributed, etc.

But while it's terrific that distribution list software can do these things, it's what the software *cannot do* that prevents the word "list" from being used synonymously with "community." List configuration headers can't establish purpose. List headers don't describe the nature of the relationships that people can have between one another. List headers don't tell people what is the appropriate way to treat each other. List headers don't have traditions, histories, or rituals. These are just some of the things that communities have and do that lists cannot.

The same is true for GeekLog, phpBB, PostNuke, PlumTree, Jive, or other community collaboration tools available. A forum on a Web-based bulletin board or a "read news" group on USENET such as alt.flame is no different than an e-mail distribution list in this regard. Yahoo groups, Xing, Ning, and Google groups also fall into this category, and it's a mistake to automatically call these groups "communities." These groups might become communities, but as we shall see when we discuss RIBS in detail, it takes far, far more to provide a community experience to users than a simple communication technology can provide alone.

In sum, the situation is analogous to a manager calling together a group of people for the first time and calling that event a "team meeting." A "group" is a collection of individuals; it's not a "team." It's just as silly to assume that just because someone created a list, forum, bulletin board, distribution group, or a LinkedIn group that the person also created a "community." Creating a communication channel for the group may be a necessary condition of community, but it should *never* be considered or treated as a sufficient condition.

Community versus "adhocracy"

The last definition issue that needs to be discussed before we can launch into the RIBS heuristic and design sustainable online communities is the tendency to confuse virtual teams or what I call "adhocracies" with actual communities. An adhocracy exists when a group comes together in order to solve a problem or to address an issue, works on that problem or issue, and then eventually disbands.

For example, in 2009 President Obama and Congress produced an economic stimulus package intended to jumpstart the economy. The idea was to pump funds into education and infrastructure support that state governments could use to fund jobs and give citizens more purchasing power. In South Carolina, however, Republican Governor Mark Sanford refused to accept the $350 million dollars earmarked for the people of his state because he was told that the money had to be spent on education and infrastructure rather than paying down debt that the state government had accrued. Sanford went so far to make his point that, after the South Carolina state's legislature voted that he had to accept the Federal funds, he sued his own state government.

As one might expect, this issue attracted a lot of public attention, including at least one adhocracy on Facebook (Figure 2.7). Outraged by the perception that Sanford was attempting to further his national political ambitions at the expense of South Carolina jobs, Marilyn Hemingway from Greenville, South Carolina, started a Facebook group called "Impeach Mark Sanford."

The Impeach Mark Sanford adhocracy has many of the hallmarks of a full-blown community. It has people who are passionately using technologies to achieve shared goals. Furthermore, the members had also organized themselves so that there were clear "officers" providing leadership, direction, and policies enabling the group to develop the organizational complexity needed to cooperate. By June of 2009, the group had grown to over 4000 and had organized a "Save Our Jobs SC" rally on June 8, 2009, which was held in four different locations around the state.

Thus adhocracies can meet all of the criteria in Preece's definition of community. They can have *people* socializing, they always have a shared *purpose*, they

Although the Impeach Mark Sanford adhocracy originally became popular because of anger over federal stimulus funds, revelations that Sanford had participated in an extramarital affair with an Argentinean woman made the group's popularity take on national recognition.

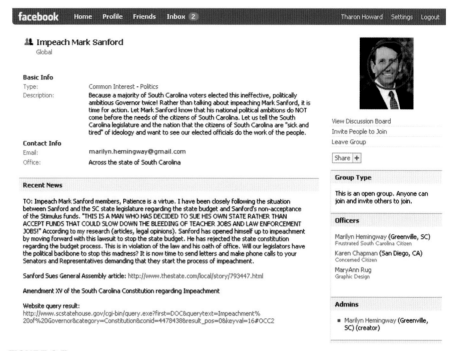

FIGURE 2.7
Sample adhocracy group on Facebook.

can have *policies* that guide their behaviors, and they use a common *computing* environment. Adhocracies can even achieve the same degree of organizational complexity that communities enable so that they can complete actions such as cooperation. They even differ from social networks in that their members share stronger secondary connections because of their dedication to a shared goal.

So why aren't adhocracies worthy of the sobriquet "communities?" Basically, they aren't built to last. Once the core issue around which an adhocracy was constructed is resolved, the adhocracy fades away. It doesn't really matter whether Mark Sanford is impeached—once it is clear that the Impeach Mark Sanford adhocracy has been successful or it has failed, the group will dissolve. The same situation can be obtained for educational classes, research teams, proposal writing committees, and other groups organized around the achievement of a well-defined, short-term objective. These groups are not communities because the game ends once the team wins or gives up.

CONCLUSION

Adhocracies are powerful, useful tools for getting things done. And because adhocracies share virtually all of the characteristics of online communities, many of the techniques discussed in the rest of this book will also work when attempting to build adhocracies aimed at achieving short-term goals. But this book is about how to build communities and social networks that last. So in subsequent chapters, we will discuss the RIBS heuristic and consider techniques for designing sustainable social networks and online communities.

WORKS CITED

[1] boyd dm, Ellison NB. Social network sites: Definition, history, and scholarship. J Comput-Mediated Commun 2007;13: article 11. http://jcmc.indiana.edu/vol13/issue1/boyd.ellison.html.

[2] Buss A, Strauss N. Online Communities Handbook: Building Your Business and Brand on the Web. Berkeley, CA: New Riders; 2009.

[3] Linden Z. Second Life residents logged nearly 400 million hours in 2008, growing 61% over 2007. Second Life Blogs 15 Jan 2009. 21 May 2009. https://blogs.secondlife.com/community/features/blog/2009/01/15.

[4] Preece J. Online Communities: Designing Usability, Supporting Sociability. New York: Wiley; 2000.

[5] Shirky C. Here Comes Everybody: The Power of Organizations without Organizations. New York: Penguin; 2008.

[6] Swartz J. Social-networking sites work to turn users into profits. USATODAY.com 12 May 2008. 13 May 2009. http://www.usatoday.com/tech/techinvestor/industry/2008–05–11-social-networking_N.htm.

CHAPTER 3

Why Invest in Social Networks and Online Communities?

WHAT ARE THESE SYSTEMS GOOD FOR?

SYNOPSIS

Chances are you're a busy professional, and maybe you manage a product development team for a large international corporation or perhaps you're an information product developer charged with providing user support for your company's products. Maybe you're a marketing specialist or a consultant and need to help your clients share information about their products and service. Regardless of your title, chances are you have been asked the same question: What are the benefits of using social networks and online communities? This chapter discusses 10 ways that an organization can benefit from building a social network or online community.

WHY BUILD SOCIAL NETWORKS AND COMMUNITIES?

At some point, you either have already or soon will be called upon to justify building your online community or social network. Fortunately, there are a lot of good reasons available, and they include:

- Enhancing and sustaining your "intellectual capital"
- Increasing creativity and cross-fertilization
- Improving decision-making processes with "epistemic communities"
- Preserving institutional knowledge
- Providing a higher quality interaction with your organization
- Improving retention and loyalty
- Reducing training and support costs
- Identifying customer needs and new product opportunities
- Reducing travel costs and addressing problems "just in time"
- Flattening organizational hierarchies

These are just a few of the potential benefits you or your company might obtain by investing in sustainable social networks and online communities. Because the ways these may work for you depend in large part on whether you're designing your systems for internal use by your employees or whether you intend your system to be used by the public and your customers, we need to discuss each in more detail.

Enhance and sustain intellectual capital

Communities are like "invisible colleges." For those privileged enough to participate in them, well-led and well-managed communities provide members with access to the same kind of state-of-the-art research and thinking that one expects to find in the best university departments. And there's real power there *IF* you're connected to the right kind of community.

The Significance chapter will expand on the concept of "invisible colleges."

For example, I supervise a usability testing facility at my institution and, just recently, we had a problem that we were able to solve because of connections to the right kind of community. One of my clients had collected verbal responses to open-ended questions from 20 different customer surveys she gave out over a 3-month period. Because data were qualitative rather than quantitative, analyzing and manually coding the mountains of text into actionable findings were going to take a tremendous amount of labor and would prove costly in hourly wages expended. What she needed was an automated software package that would code the text and categorize patterns in the data for her in order to keep from trashing months of work because the analysis costs were going to put her over budget.

Fortunately for my client, I'm a member of a closed, private community of usability testing and user experience design professionals. I posted a message to my colleagues in the community asking for help at 9:46 p.m. on a Thursday night. By 10:12 p.m., I had received two responses from colleagues with hands-on expertise using four different software packages that could do the job. Bottom line: by tapping into the extraordinary intellectual capital available in this professional community, we were not only able to save thousands of dollars in labor, but also saved the new products and services that will be produced because of the results of the surveys.

Chances are that your company or organization recruits new hires from certain kinds of colleges because they're known for producing high-quality people in particular areas. If you want a computer scientist, you might go to MIT. If you want an electrical engineer, you might go to Purdue. If you want a lawyer, you might go to Harvard. There are many reasons why certain schools are more successful at training people in particular areas, but having directed a nationally ranked graduate program, I can tell you that a lot of the reason programs are successful are *the people in the community* that make up that program. The colleagues and students you talk to on a daily basis and the ideas that you share when you're socializing over coffee have a profound impact on how you think about the world and the intellectual capital that you bring to your job. It's the ecology in which you're immersed that facilitates intellectual growth.

Online communities are no different, except the people who participate in those communities are obtaining access to conversations that no longer require geographical boundaries. I don't have to build my company in Silicon Valley in order to benefit from the conversations that are taking place in that ecology if I can access those same kinds of conversations in online environments. Consequently, if it's the case that intellectual capital in your organization is just as important to your success as financial capital, then investing in building *excellent* and *sustainable* online communities makes business sense.

It's worth the resources required to build a strong community rather than giving lip service to them and throwing up a space where, like Kevin Costner, you hope that they will come. Giving your people access to important conversations going on in their fields is just as important as sending your employees to professional conferences and other training opportunities. If it's that important, isn't it worth doing well?

Increase creativity and cross-fertilization

Networking involves reaching across communities. It requires that you and your employees become exposed to ideas from other disciplines, other business models, and other world views.

Even though it's a cliché to say "two heads are better than one," the adage is true. Post an entry on Wikipedia, and if it's wrong, the community will purge it of error. Indeed, there was a study published in the prestigious journal *Science* that showed that Wikipedia actually has roughly the same number of factual errors as single-authored entries in the *Encyclopedia Britannica* [1]. This is because in order for an entry to survive the judgment of a community, a higher degree of accuracy is necessary.

Like many authors, I value the opportunity to try out my new ideas with colleagues, and a well-maintained online community allows me to do this easily. The community purifies my thinking, and the multiplicity of perspectives sniffs out any errors or limitations in the idea. As shown in the Influence chapter, when a community has been built around providing its members with a *safe space* for these kinds of interactions, then they can help us see when we're in a blind spot or haven't given enough consideration to some aspect of the concept.

But communities and networks don't merely improve the rigorousness of ideas and force more creative thinking. Better yet, frequently someone will turn me on to a conversation that's taken place in an entirely different field of which I am completely unaware. And the theories and frameworks provided by that alternative perspective give me the explanatory power that I need in order for my idea to be successful. For example, as I was conducting the research for this book and studying communities, one of my colleagues in the Boys and Girls Clubs of America helped me see a connection between the work he was doing with urban street gangs and techniques that online communities can use to strengthen emotional ties between members. Bottom line: participating in online communities makes you more creative through cross-fertilization.

Improve decision-making processes by creating "epistemic communities"

The term "epistemic communities" is used in international relations and global trade negotiations, and basically it's just building on the same idea discussed in the previous section, i.e., the idea that different disciplines have different "epistemologies" or ways of validating knowledge. Each different professional community or academic discipline has its own definition of what it means to "know" something and its own standards for providing evidence upon which to make a decision.

A classic example of this clash of disciplines in the decisions-making process occurs when usability and marketing professionals consider whether it's appropriate to "up-sell" on an ecommerce Web site. Have you ever gone to a Web site to buy a computer, stereo, or other high-tech product, and just as you're about to check out, the system prevents you from making the purchase with a series of pop-up windows that won't let you out until you tell the site that you don't want to buy the extended warranty or add-ons for your new system? For a usability professional, the annoyance and inefficiency users experience through this attempt to increase the amount of the sale is sufficient evidence for making the decision not to include up-sell pop-ups on the Web site. Marketing professionals, however, have different standards for making decisions like this, and the difference between usability professionals' standards and marketing professionals' competing goals means that they will have a difficult time negotiating those differences and making a decision.

When countries send negotiating teams to meet to hash out an arms agreement or an environmental impact treaty, they send representatives from the same disciplinarian traditions to the meeting and allow those scientists and economists to talk to each other. They do this because, even though members of epistemic communities come from different countries and have different national interests, they share a common epistemological framework. They're able to come to decisions more effectively and with greater facility because they share a common set of procedures for arriving at decisions. Biologists from Chile speak the same disciplinary language as biologists from Germany or the United Kingdom. As a result, they don't have to argue over details like which species of animal in a rainforest ecosystem is an effective predictor of environmental impact. They're able to build consensus quickly and move on to other important issues.

> **TIP**
> To have an "epistemology" is to have a theory of what "knowledge" is, how it is produced, and how it is verified.

The value of operating like an epistemic community in your organization is probably obvious if you've ever been a member of the typical cross-functional

TUCHMAN'S STAGES OF TEAM DEVELOPMENT

Bruce Tuchman developed a theory of team development while working as a social psychologist for the Navy through a meta-analysis of 50 psychoanalytic research studies of small group dynamics [4]. Tuchman found that as teams develop, they go through four distinct phases.

1. Forming—members of the team begin to get to know each other and use rules of polite society to communicate
2. Storming—this is a necessary stage that all teams go through when differences in perspectives and proposed directions are offered and challenged (some groups never leave this phase)
3. Norming—the group ultimately agrees on a set of rules, procedures, and practices for making decisions
4. Performing—the team is able to make decisions and to function autonomously and without supervision

development team. People are often slammed together at the last minute, and they aren't always sure how or why they were picked to serve on the project. And when the team does begin meeting, the marketing person brings branding and look-n-feel issues to the table, the engineer thinks those ideas are silly and only cares about functionality, and the graphic designer doesn't care about brand as long as it's aesthetically pleasing. In order for your team to function, you have to go through what Bruce Tuchman called the Forming, Storming, Norming, and Performing stages of team development (see sidebar), and it often feels like the majority of teams spend most of their time storming.

The same thing happens when you build an electronic community in your department or on your project development team. Members still have to go through the storming and norming process, but the difference is that the online community doesn't have to repeat the process over and over. Because the member of the teams have been together for a long time online as part of the electronic community you built, they're able to function like epistemic communities on an international trade mission, and a similar phenomenon happens. Members are more quickly able to pass through the storming and norming phases and to develop shared understandings of how your team will arrive at new understandings of the problems your organization faces. They become an epistemic community that's much more facile and able to solve problems more effectively. They are able to build consensus more quickly about the most effective course.

Preserve institutional knowledge

Whenever a long-time employee leaves, everything that person knows about your organization's policies, procedures, practices, and rationale for understanding why decisions were made the way they were made walks out the door with them. The loss of this kind of institutional knowledge can be devastating in many industries.

For example, at my own institution, I direct the Multimedia Authoring Teaching and Research Facility (MATRF). The MATRF plays an important educational role at the university; however, one of its principal missions is to build and maintain all of the Web sites for the departments, centers, institutes, and programs in the College of Architecture, Arts, and Humanities. MATRF puts a public face on the college and creates rich media such as digital movies, slide shows, animations, podcasts, and interactive Flash movies. It takes a lot to impress potential graduate or undergraduate students whom you wish to recruit to your school these days, and MATRF provides the 10 departments in our college with the rich media they need to do so.

Getting the opportunity to work with rich media and cutting-edge digital publishing technologies is just flat out cool, but the toughest part of my job in MATRF is the fact that I lose every member of the MATRF staff each year. The MATRF is staffed by five first-year graduate students from our Master of Arts in Professional Communication program who, because of the work they are required to perform developing rich media for the college, are provided with an extraordinary opportunity to develop a highly marketable skill set. But this terrific educational opportunity for staff would also be a tremendous threat to the college if we didn't use online communities to protect and preserve the institutional knowledge each of these students develops as they work with various departments across the college.

We're able to sustain a 100% annual turnover rate because the knowledge the staff obtain is shared in MATRF's communities. The video of Dean Egan shown in Figure 3.1 and the XML-based slide show that plays next to it were both developed by Bryan Ricke, who worked for MATRF. Bryan has married and moved on in his career, but what he learned and the process he used to create these media products are available to me as his supervisor and to the next MATRF staff member in our online communities at MATRF_STAFF-L and on our podcasting site shown in Figure 3.2. Because screen video capture tools such as Camtasia, Captivate, Jing, and Freez Screen are so easy to use, Bryan and other MATRF staff are not only able to share detailed text messages about the projects they are developing, but they also share videos of how they produced the work.

Provide a quality interaction with your organization

How often do you feel like you're connected to a company when you read their advertisement in a magazine? Or when you get one of those corporate-wide memos that describe some new policy or procedure dictated by some disembodied voice from above, does it make you feel like you belong to the company? They might make you feel like you're "part of something bigger," but more often than not, you probably don't feel like you're part of the conversation.

Building an online user group for your product or providing an online community to support your employees goes far beyond the simple brand recognition that a 30-second television commercial or a banner ad on a Web site provides.

FIGURE 3.1
CAAH Web site with digital video and slide show in header block.

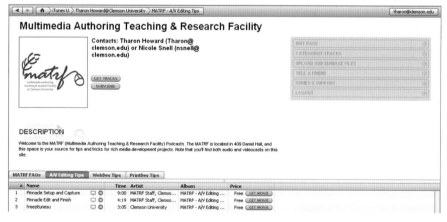

FIGURE 3.2
MATRF staff podcasting community.

When potential customers become involved in an online community you have an opportunity to do something that no advertisement can provide. You have an opportunity to provide a *relationship* with your user. Communities give your users and customers an opportunity to do more than simply buy from you.

Communities provide an opportunity for your customers to interact with you, to have a *conversation* with you. This is a fundamental change in the quality of the relationship that marketers and companies have with the public.

The same thing also is true for management and employee relationships with internal communities in very large organizations. The employee is no longer simply a cog in a machine being turned by unknown forces. Communities (or at least the kinds of communities designed around RIBS) allow employees to get to know managers and decision makers in much more personal and sympathetic ways. CEOs, project managers, and department managers who participate in online communities quell the gossip mongering and put a human face on decisions that are made by the organization.

Improve retention and grow loyalty

Communities and networks provide emotional support systems. For people inside an organization, an online community can function like a "virtual water cooler" and give people a place to regain their emotional equilibrium. This is also the case for external communities where your customers may go to blow off steam about a problem they're having with your product. Neither of these types of communities necessarily lead to the bad PR that, traditionally, the corporate communication director wants to try to avoid. Quite the opposite, in fact. These kinds of communities can be opportunities.

> For an excellent example of a company turning customer venting into a positive opportunity, see Jeff Jarvis's discussion of Dell's responses to angry bloggers [3]. In February 2007, Dell started IdeaStorm, an online space where Dell's customers could communicate directly with Dell and each other to vote on different product innovations. Through intelligent uses of social media described by Jarvis in *What Would Google Do?*, Dell completely changed the company's reputation from one where nearly half the postings in the blogosphere were negative, to one where bloggers were actually recommending Dell products.

We humans aren't solely rational, logically oriented beings. Your employees, users, and customers aren't like the Vulcans on *Star Trek*—all head and no heart. They're sensitive beings who often need emotional support in order to perform effectively. One of the places where I've seen this emotional need being met successfully is in the Breadloaf Rural Teacher Network (BLRTN). The BLRTN has been in existence since the 1980s and was begun by Dixie Goswami and Rocky Gooch as a way to offer isolated teachers in rural settings a means of connecting with other educational professionals around the country.

BLRTN has been a success for almost 25 years now. Much of that success is certainly due to the hard work and dedication of Rocky Gooch and Dixie Goswami, the network's director and designer. But it's also lasted because it meets the emotional needs of the K-12 teachers who use it. According to the

National Education Association, 50% of teachers leave their jobs within the first 5 years, and in 2007 the rate of teacher turnover was estimated to cost U.S. schools more than $7 billion each year [2]. Half of all teachers leave their jobs because the life of a secondary school teacher is tough. It's not unusual to have 120 students a day, all of whom are special and many of whom impose extremely difficult personal demands on your time. To be an effective teacher, you have to be up close and personal with your students, and doing so can be incredibly rewarding, but just as often it hurts. BLRTN provides a place where teachers can go and tell the stories they desperately need to release to other professionals who also have dirt under their fingernails and can lend an empathetic ear.

Online communities such as BLRTN provide a space where people can unburden themselves and make their grievances known. Among user groups when people are dissatisfied with a product, they're upset and angry. Online communities provide a vehicle for expressing that anger and dissatisfaction—but it also provides a space for addressing it. As any technical support person can tell you, often customers are upset because they simply don't understand why things work the way they do. Once someone explains to them the logic behind an interface and why the system behaves the way that it does, their anger melts away. What's more, when an employee or a customer expresses their frustration in an online community and that frustration is addressed by another customer or by a representative of the company, it shows a commitment to that individual that they appreciate and which they respond to in the form of product loyalty. They're not a nameless face in the crowd from whom you've taken money. They have a voice that you care about, which you've heard and responded to. That builds loyalty. People understand if you've made a mistake, and they'll forgive it, but they never forgive being ignored.

Reduce training and support costs

When your customers and employees help each other and provide answers to the questions they have, you don't have to pay someone to be available to answer all their questions. Well-managed user groups can reduce a company's support costs significantly. Macromedia and now Adobe have been tremendously successful at this. Adobe's online user forums provide a space where users can go, ask questions, and get answers from other users who are delighted to demonstrate their expertise with the product and to share their experiences. What's more, Adobe has taken the old bulletin board forums to the next level by providing new video support forums that utilize its Adobe Media Player platform. On Adobe TV, users can "tune in" to a product channel where other users have created video-based tutorials that illustrate solutions to common problems as well as innovative uses of Adobe's products (Figure 3.3).

Building online communities that enable these kinds of user-to-user and employee-to-employee support is one of the most compelling reasons for building online networks.

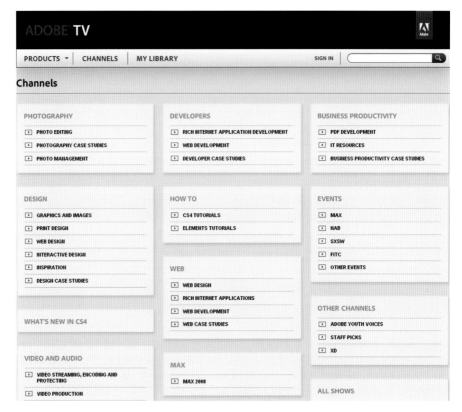

FIGURE 3.3
Adobe TV Photoshop channel. Adobe product screenshot(s) reprinted with permission from Adobe Systems Incorporated.

Show where needs exist for new products and services

Building user group communities allows you to collect feedback on how your products are being used by actual customers in actual settings that complete tasks that *they* think are important.

Normally, a company has to expend a tremendous amount of money on conducting research studies that enable them to discover what their customers' needs are. Putting together focus groups, sending research teams out on site visits, and conducting diary studies of users are all useful but they're also resource-intensive. Monitoring user discussion groups allows you to learn more about how your customers are actually using your product and how your product may or may not be addressing all their needs. In user support groups, users will frequently share work-arounds or even software patches that will extend the functionality of your product so that it's able to perform tasks and help users complete goals that you never anticipated.

Building online communities so that you can see these patches and work-arounds and can incorporate them into new product designs is an inexpensive way to increase market share as well as a way of building customer loyalty because you've demonstrated that you're listening and responding to the way customers are using your products.

Cut travel costs and address problems as they arise

Trainers and educators know that the best time to deliver training and educational materials is when the student is ready to learn. Training is most effective when someone has a problem or task that training enables them to complete "just in time." Online communities provide managers with the opportunity to deliver training, advice, materials, and lessons at any time. This can be a real advantage in a large corporate environment where new employees aren't able to assume their duties until they've received the proper training.

For example, a youth development professional who is just beginning to work for the Boys and Girls Clubs of America isn't able to assume their responsibilities and actually start working with kids until they've undergone the approved training regimen. Kids are just too important to leave in the hands of the untrained and uninitiated. The problem was that delivering that training without online communities was contingent on an actual member of the national headquarter's training staff meeting physically with the employee. That required the travel of either the youth development professional or the national staff member. It was costly and it took time to arrange. Often employees would have to wait weeks before they were able to attend the necessary training. By building online communities, however, the BGCA enabled the materials to be delivered "just in time."

Just-in-time intervention in the development process is also critical when you're managing a department. You've probably been a member of a project development team where the whole team ended up "sitting on their thumbs" because a problem developed that required additional resources or decisions from a manager who wasn't available to provide the support that the team needed to begin making progress again. However, when your department is connected, online, and functioning in a community environment, project managers can see what's happening on the team and are even often able to anticipate and respond to needs so that the team isn't stuck waiting for information and resources they need to proceed.

Flatten organizational hierarchies

Many organizations these days are moving toward flatter organizational structures, where managers are expected to interact with greater numbers of staff and where the staff members are expected to work together with less managerial intervention. Social networks and online communities can support these broad organizational goals, as the whole point of an online community is to disseminate information broadly across the community. This has significant implications for the way an organization works because it flattens out hierarchical structures.

Managers who are accustomed to traditional information distribution chains can often struggle with online environments because they tend not to provide privileged access to key pieces of information. To manage effectively in an online environment, these managers have to adapt to a flat organization. The advantage of this flatter organizational structure is that it leads to increased and shared responsibility across the community rather than locating all the responsibility in a single individual who can become a choke point.

To be successful, managers need to ensure that all of the employees in a unit have all of the information that they need in order to be successful in making decisions and choices about how best to approach business problems. The thinking here is that it doesn't matter where good ideas come from—if you empower all of your employees and all the members of a community with the same information and if members of a department also understand that they're expected to share all the information that they have with you—then the best solution will evolve. For example, on the manufacturing line at the BMW plant in Greenville, South Carolina, the saying goes that workers up and down the line actually produce communication, not just cars. The line manufactures information; cars are just a by-product of the communication process.

Rather than looking at process management in a hierarchical fashion or looking at project management in terms of faculties that handle different pieces of the problem, managers can use an online community's ability to flatten out and remove all differences, to empower everyone in the organization, and to create and maintain an "ecology" that will grow success. Management takes a macro view and is concerned with the whole department again rather than being forced to address micro problems that emerge from small groups or even individuals working on isolated projects.

In 2009, for example, my department experienced a serious budget cut where we lost $600,000 in permanent funding from a $3.2 million budget. Had we been operating in the old management model, the department head would have discussed this cut with a few trusted, senior members of the department whose offices were located on the same floor of the building as his. This "cabal" would weigh the options—or at least those options of which they were aware—and then the department head would announce to the department the decisions that had been made.

In the new approach and with the support of an online community, however, the department chair was able to go to the department, explain that the budget cut was coming, and solicit suggestions for ways to address the problem. In this particular case, because 96% of the budget involved personnel delivering course content, the only way we could absorb these kinds of cuts was to eliminate programs from the catalogue of course offerings. This was painful because there was no way to avoid eliminating some people's positions. But because it was done online and discussed openly in a safe environment where people were encouraged to share the information that they had and to help everyone understand the consequences of the various choices, a bad situation was made more tolerable. People came to understand the criteria by which decisions were made and could plan accordingly. They weren't terrified of an unknown process in which they had no input at all.

Even the people who ultimately lost their positions were able to find positions more quickly because they learned that they needed to act much more rapidly and felt that they were treated humanely because the decision to take their jobs wasn't made behind closed doors and they had the opportunity to make the case for the importance of what they did. Absolutely, they were disappointed; after all, they just lost their jobs! But the point is that they didn't leave the department mad and with a desire to never come back, to hurt the reputation of the department, and to warn other potential employees from ever working there.

As this illustrates, social networks and online communities can have tremendous positive effects in organizations that have made a commitment to flattening their organizational hierarchies because they enable information to be shared that leads to better morale, shared responsibility, and more creative solutions to problems.

CONCLUSION

This chapter discussed 10 different reasons your organization might be able to benefit from the development of social network and online communities. Whether or not all 10 of these make sense for your particular needs depends, as I indicated at the beginning of the chapter, on whether you're building your system for internal use by employees, for public use by customers, or possibly for use by an organization you support, such as a social group, church, or professional organization. Still, these are some of the most compelling reasons I've found in my experiences over the years for investing the time and resources required. There are probably other reasons you may also find for building your particular systems.

No matter what reasons you have for building social networks and online communities, however, you're almost certainly going to have to design your networks and communities effectively before you can expect success. We need to design them to thrive in order to enjoy success—and that is precisely what the RIBS heuristic, which we will begin discussing in the next chapter, is intended to help you do.

WORKS CITED

[1] Giles J. Internet encyclopaedias go head to head. Journal Science 2005; 438.7070:900(2). Expanded Academic ASAP. Gale. Clemson University. 25 Jan. 2009. http://find.galegroup.com/itx/start.do?prodId = EAIM.
[2] Hernandez N. Teacher turnover costs systems millions, study projects. Washingtonpost .com. 21 June 2007. 16 May 2009. http://www.washingtonpost.com/wp-dyn/content/article/2007/06/20/AR2007062002300.html.
[3] Jarvis J. What Would Google Do? New York: Collins Business; 2009.
[4] Tuchman B. Developmental sequence in small groups. BNET Jan 2001. 15 May 2009. http://findarticles.com/p/articles/mi_qa3954/is_200104/ai_n8943663/.

CHAPTER 4

Remuneration

CRAFTING MEANINGFUL SOCIAL EXPERIENCES

SYNOPSIS

What are people seeking from social experiences? Why do they return over and over to some communities and social networks and abandon others after only a few experiences? This chapter discusses *remuneration*, which, simply put, is the commonsense observation that individuals remain members of a social network when there is a clear benefit for doing so. People need to believe that they will obtain some positive return on the investment of their time and energy in order to be attracted to participation in an e-community. They need to believe that some value will come from joining a group. The key to long-term success is recognizing that the most important remuneration community and network managers have to offer is the *experience* of socially constructing meaning about topics and events your users want to understand.

Because remuneration is a concept that's often discussed, we begin by spending a fair amount of time debunking some of the myths and unproductive approaches to providing remuneration in a community. More specifically, the chapter begins by laying the groundwork for understanding remuneration in terms of user experience and the development of a positive situational context rather than traditional measures such as business models or technological models. Ultimately the chapter will take a deeper look at the social ways in which we, as human beings, attempt to scratch the itch of "cognitive dissonance" and the ways that we use social systems to make sense of the world around us. Looking at this construction of meaning is important because it will help designers better understand how to craft social user experiences that address these fundamental human needs.

The chapter ends with a list of specific techniques and examples of their actual use that designers can use to create social experiences that remunerate their users.

INTRODUCTION

Most people have an intuitive grasp of remuneration in terms of its importance to building an electronic community or a social network. After the dot-com crash of 2001, there are few who no longer realize that the "field of dreams" approach only works in movies, i.e., if you build it, they decidedly will *not* come. As Mitch Kapor once said back in the early 1990s, the Web is "a competition for eyeballs," so you need something special to attract those eyeballs to your community or network. Marketing professionals have beaten into us that we have to incentivize and attract users to a product by giving them something. In short, we have to remunerate them.

The "economy" here is pretty straightforward and commonsensical. Users of a community or social network have a limited amount of time–capital to invest in their online experiences. Plus, they have a lot of competition placing demands on that temporal capital. As designers of communities, therefore, our job is to figure out how to convince users that the time they spend on our site is the best investment of their limited resources. For most of us, the answer to this question is going to involve providing a richer, more satisfying user experience. We are essentially looking for ways to attract users to our online spaces by telling users that the time they invest in us will be rewarded or will purchase them some experience they are seeking. The analogy that I think works well here is that of going to a restaurant.

FIGURE 4.1
Grease fire entertainment during a birthday party.

If you think about it, you don't really go to a restaurant to fulfill your body's needs for sustenance. You could go to the grocery store, buy bread and peanut butter, and make yourself a sandwich if all you wanted to do is feed yourself, right? You're really after something more than just food when you go to an expensive restaurant for dinner. What, for example, is the attraction of Japanese steak houses and sitting around a hibachi grill with a bunch of other people—usually complete strangers—watching your food cooked in front of you and worrying if your hair is going to be singed by the obligatory grease fire that you know is coming (Figure 4.1)? Indeed, I asked my 18-year-old son about this recently when he chose to have the family go to a Japanese steak house in order to celebrate his birthday. Wouldn't you, I asked him, rather go to the local, family-owned steak house that serves a better quality 20-oz. angus Porterhouse for less money than the 5-oz. beef tips and six

FOCUS ON TECHNIQUE

Just as the environment of a restaurant creates a mood, using emoticons in postings can create a mood that encourages member participation. See the Techniques section at the end of the chapter for more discussion of this remuneration technique.

SHARING VS COMMERCIAL ECONOMIES

In his influential book, *Remix*, Lawrence Lessig makes a critical distinction between the two kinds of "economies" that exist online today. First is the "commercial" economy, which we typically think about when we think of "economies." Second is what Lessig calls the "sharing" economy, which we use in communities and social organizations. In the commercial economy, we exchange money for some goods or services. However, Lessig observes that "money in the sharing economy is not just inappropriate; it is poisonous" ([10], 119). In a sharing economy, it is perfectly reasonable for a girlfriend to demand that her boyfriend spend several hours of an evening with her, but as Lessig observes, "it would be very, very odd if your girlfriend, at the end of the date, offered [her boyfriend] $500 to spend the night" ([10], 119). This same dynamic operates in online communities, which it's why "remuneration" shouldn't be confused with the expectation that money is what members of communities are seeking when they participate in online communities or social networks.

small shrimp you're going to get at a hibachi grill? What's the attraction, I asked. Wouldn't you rather have a better steak?

Of course, answering a question like that takes far too much conscious effort on the part of an 18 year old, so I got the same, long-suffering, "you're-so-clueless-Dad" look that I get when I ask questions about what makes being a member of a World of Warcraft guild so compelling. Still, I think the answer is pretty obvious. It's not only about the food; you're also paying for the atmosphere, the service, and, most of all, it's about the entertainment provided by the chef. The remuneration is *the experience*.

REMUNERATION AS USER EXPERIENCE

Google's early success in the search engine wars is another pretty good example of this same kind of remuneration. Prior to Google's introduction in 1998, the search engine of choice for most users was Digital's AltaVista. Begun in 1995, AltaVista was one of the very first true search engines on the Web (Yahoo was begun in 1994 as a portal or guide to the Web rather than a true search engine). In January 1999, AltaVista was reaping the benefits of being one of the first search engines to market with the functionality that people wanted. However, as Figure 4.2 illustrates, AltaVista had begun to try to look more and more like its competitor Yahoo, and it began to suffer from what some might call "feature creep."

Although the impact for a 21st-century reader may not be so obvious, as the page in Figure 4.2 isn't nearly so cluttered and busy as many of today's Web sites have

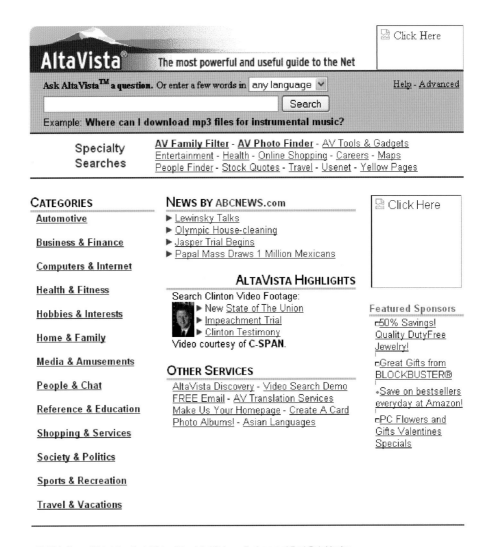

FIGURE 4.2
AltaVista on January 17, 1999 [1].

become, AltaVista's 1999 page provided the less computer literate and web-savvy users of the 1990s with an excessive range of "entry point options." As Lidwell, Holden, and Butler discuss in their book *Universal Principles of Design*, the concept of an entry point says that an interface should have a clear starting point for a user [11]. The visual design of the interface should make it clear to the user where to click in order to start using the software. However, in the "Categories" area alone, AltaVista's 1999 home page offered 13 different choices where users could begin their search! And in terms of layout, the choices available for users under "Specialty Searches" were even more daunting, particularly when compared to the absolute simplicity of Google's search inter-face from the same period (Figure 4.3).

Unlike AltaVista's page, which offered users the same kinds of choices one would expect from a Web guide such as Yahoo, Google's interface pro-vided users with a simple, obvious entry point. Users didn't have to read through long lists of nominal compounds and categories in order to make a decision about where to start searching or, as Steve Krug would say, the page didn't "make me think" and didn't expect users to ponder the choices available to them ([9], 11). Instead, users had time to enjoy a more aesthetic and fun expe-rience afforded them by the use of bright, car-

Search the web using Google

Google Search   I'm feeling lucky

More Google!

Copyright © 1999 Google Inc.

FIGURE 4.3
Google home page from April 22, 1999 [5].

toonish colors in the Google masthead, as well as the somewhat wry and cheeky "I'm feeling lucky" button. In short, Google captured an enormous share of the search engine market because it offered the kind of *user experience* people appre-ciated. Google's interface "remunerated" users because it was more fun to use than AltaVista's 1999 home page.

BING'S USER EXPERIENCE

It's interesting to note that, when Microsoft released Bing.com in 2009, its market-ing efforts focused almost entirely on distinguishing Bing from Google in terms of user experience. Microsoft initially marketed Bing as a "decision engine" and aired a series of television commercials that mocked "search engines" that provided users with a decision-making experience requiring them to filter out clutter and useless information. The implication is that, just as Google's experience gave users less information to pon-der than Altavista's, Bing will remunerate users with a more efficient and less time-con-suming decision-making experience than its competitors.

REMUNERATION DOES NOT EQUAL FUNCTIONALITY OR THE BUSINESS MODEL

Now at this point, my hard-core programming friends typically jump in and object that I haven't taken into consideration the superior search capabilities Google was using. "You're ignoring the functionality," they say. "It was the ele-gance of the code and the advanced search capabilities that made Google's late entry into the search engine game so remarkable," they say. And they certainly have a point. The functionality of Google's search is certainly a necessary condi-tion of providing users with positive experiences.

But my point here is that functionality is not a *sufficient condition* for remunera-tion. If you look at Figure 4.3 and Google's interface from a user's perspective, you don't see any code. Users don't see the elegance of the functionality. Users

GOOGLE'S PAGERANK

When it was introduced, Google used "PageRank" technology to provide its users with the highest ranked search engine results, and it's interesting that Google did this by taking advantage of a type of social vetting. Basically, Google's algorithms looked at which sites had the most referrals from other sites. Sites with the most links using a particular term would then be listed higher in Google's results page, with the idea being that the more frequently people linked a term to a site, the more likely it would be that search engine users would also think the site was important. Google's search engine thus rewarded sites that had the most social impact.

However, this observation about the social nature of Google's PageRank technology doesn't negate my point about users not caring about the functionality of the underlying code. Most Google users have never heard of "PageRank," and, in my experience, those who have think that it refers to page ranking in the search engine when, actually, it's a reference to Larry Page, the Google cofounder who created the algorithms. Users care *that* they have a positive search engine experience; they rarely care *how* that experience happens.

FOCUS ON TECHNIQUE

Although users can't see what's happening "under the covers," it's important that they understand exactly how they are going to remunerate their new community. In order to accomplish this, managers can employ a variety of techniques, including:

- Using a subscription application form that specifically asks how the member will remunerate the community.
- Encouraging members to become mentors who teach new members.

don't know what's happening "under the covers," and they usually don't want to know. When you're building a community or a social network and you're considering the remuneration that you're trying to provide users, the only thing that *they* know and the only thing that they understand as contributing directly to remuneration is their user experience.

I have the same issues for my colleagues in the business world who look at social networks or Web 2.0 applications such as Google and who want to argue that what made Google the success that it has become is Google's superior business model. Amy Shuen, for example, provides an outstanding overview in her book *Web 2.0: A Strategy Guide* of why Google is such a successful Web 2.0 social application. Shuen points to four different features of Google that made it successful.

1. Google used "PageRanking" to increase the "user relevance" of the search engine.
2. Google "increased traffic and usage with affiliate deals with AOL, Ask Jeeves, and others, using a different revenue split with affiliates than was normal at the time."

3. Google used a "performance-based pay-per-click" payment strategy called "AdWords" for its online marketing customers, which made it easy for those advertising customers to monitor the effectiveness of their advertising and to ensure that they were getting a good return on their investment.

4. Google used a system called "AdRanking," which "dynamically priced keywords and created pricing auctions for advertisers" so that advertisers had to bid on and pay more to Google for socially popular keyword searches.

Adapted from Shuen [24], 47

Of these four strategies that Shuen lays out so admirably, only the first one has any relevance for remunerating the actual user of Google's search engine. Users come back to and continue to use Google because the interface is clean, because it's easy to use, and because the results are useful to them (and only secondarily because the results are ranked according to the popularity and relevance of the hits to the search terms being used). However, once again, users don't know that "AdWords" and "AdRanking" are even functioning on Google's site. For them, these are not forms of remuneration, even though they raise money for Google. Yes, AdWords, AdRanking, AdSense, and other aspects of Google's business model are necessary for Google's success. Like functionality, having a successful business model for a community is a necessary condition for sustaining a community, but it's not a sufficient condition because it doesn't contribute to remuneration that users actually experience.

> **REMUNERATING USERS THROUGH ADVERTISING**
>
> Digg recently announced it's going allow customers to "digg" ads so that markets will receive discounts on the price they pay for the more popular advertisements. The more members of the Digg community rate an advertisement as useful and entertaining, the less Digg will charge for it. Conversely, if few members of Digg like the advertisement, then Digg will charge the full rate, thereby encouraging marketers to produce advertisements that are focused on meeting the needs of the Digg user community.

Community designers absolutely have to pay attention to the infrastructure issues necessary to keep a community going, but functionality and business models always need to be considered secondary causalities of the long-term success of a social network or community. Providing users with an experience that they clearly recognize as positive and beneficial to their interests and needs is the ball you have to watch if you want to avoid the same kinds of difficulties AltaVista had.

BE RESPONSIBLE FOR THE USER EXPERIENCE

I realize that it may sound like I'm being disputatious and overly picky here; however, I want to press this distinction that I'm making between functionality and business models on the one hand and user experience on the other because in the day-to-day give and take of actually building and maintaining social networks and online communities, the primacy of the user experience gets lost. When you're at work, the software programmers will be pressuring you to help them understand how the Web application you need is supposed to work so they can start building it, which forces you to focus on functionality and makes it easy to lose sight of the community members' experience. Similarly, when you're talking to investors and they're pressing you to explain your business model so that you can maintain the infrastructure and resources necessary to keep the community going, again, it's easy to lose track of the importance of the user experience. The functionality and the business side of things are easy problems to address because there's always somebody there pressing you to pay attention to these issues.

When people come to me with ideas about how they want to start an online community and make the next Facebook, they almost always have a clear idea of the topic around which they intend to build their community or network and how it's supposed to function. Whether it's a place for soccer fans to get together such as Nike's Joga.com or a community to help parents of children with autism, when potential clients describe to me the communities or social networks that they want to build, they rarely have trouble describing the functionality and the business model they wish to use. Indeed, although they may not know the term, they usually use the "freemium" business model, which is behind most popular social networking sites and online communities and which takes advantage of the nearly $100 billion spent on advertising in 2007.

THE FREEMIUM MODEL OF REMUNERATION

"Freemium" is the term venture capitalist Fred Wilson attributes to Jarid Lukin of Alacra in response to a prompt on Wilson's blog asking for a term that could describe the business model for how popular social networks function [28].

A combination of the terms "free" + "premium," the term basically describes the practice of giving away some services on a site for "free" and then charging subscribers for additional, "premium" services or, as Fred Wilson explained it, "Give your service away for free, possibly ad supported but maybe not, acquire a lot of customers very efficiently through word of mouth, referral networks, organic search marketing, etc, then offer premium priced value added services or an enhanced version of your service to your customer base" [29].

LinkedIn is a classic example of the freemium model. Anyone can create a LinkedIn profile without cost; it's free. But if you want to have additional services, such as the ability to send messages to others on the system or to track how your profile is being used by others, then you must pay a monthly subscription fee for these "premium" services. People often tell me that they're going to provide a space for people who suffer from diabetes to come together to talk about different treatment options, that anybody would be able to use the site for free, and that HMOs and doctors can advertise their services on the site and that they'll provide premium services such as the ability to search their database and archives on the site for an additional fee or a paid subscription.

All of which is great, but what they can't tell me is this—*what's the user experience that's generating the free eyeballs in the first place?* What many community architects and social networking engineers overlook is the difference between the AltaVista interface and the Google interface. It's the customer experience— or really the community member's experience—that is used in order to make a decision about whether the site or participation in the community adequately remunerates them for the time that they invest there. Consequently, the concept of remuneration is important because what it's trying to say is that the functionality of a site and the business model behind the community are only necessary conditions of sustainability and long-term success. They are not, however, *sufficient* conditions. For that, you need to consider what Jenny Preece calls "sociability"—creating opportunities for people to connect (in meaningful ways) with other people.

Preece states, "Sociability is concerned with planning and developing social policies which are understandable and acceptable to members, to support the community's purpose" ([20], 26).

SCRATCHING THE SOCIABILITY ITCH

When it comes to remuneration, as a designer your first job is to encourage social experiences in online communities and your networks. It might be useful to consider Facebook and the experiences that have made it reach 150 million users worldwide by January 2009 [32]. According to Forrester researcher Jeremiah Owyang in January 2008, Facebook experienced a growth rate of 250,000 new registrations per day throughout 2007. More importantly, however, Owyang found that "more than half of active users return daily" to the site and that "people spend an average of 20 minutes on the site daily" [18]. So what is it that drives Facebook users back to the site so frequently? What is it about Facebook and the user experience it provides that compel people to continue to use the site so frequently?

In an interview with Laura Locke from *Time* on July 2007, Zuckerberg describes Facebook's commitment to remuneration this way:

> Our whole theory is that people have real connections in the world. People communicate most naturally and effectively with their friends and the people around them. What we figured is that if we could model what those connections were, [we could] provide that information to a set of applications through which people want to share information, photos or videos or events. But that only works if those relationships are real. That's a really big difference between Facebook and a lot of other sites [12].

Facebook's extraordinary success is, in other words, its ability to tap into people's fundamental need to communicate with other people. It allows them to keep in contact with friends and family and others in their social circle. And the critical point that has to be made here is that it's providing users that social experience, that human connectedness, which has to be kept uppermost in mind when you're designing an online user experience for social networks. Indeed, later in his interview with *Time*, Zuckerberg goes on to say:

> I think there's confusion around what the point of social networks is. A lot of different companies characterized as social networks have different goals—some serve the function of business networking, some are media portals. What we're trying to do is just make it really efficient for people to communicate, get information and share information. We always try to emphasize the utility component [12].

FOCUS ON TECHNIQUE

There are many ways managers can encourage participation, including:
- seeding the discussion
- using stars on messages to show member participation
- ranking the value of users messages
- removing users' fear factor by providing examples of how to participate
- sending out reminders or "tickle messages" about upcoming events or recent activities
- creating regular events for users

What Zuckerberg appears to be saying here is that Facebook's success can be attributed to the company's priorities, i.e., making their users' desire to connect to each other an easy and pleasurable experience. Although he's using the language of functionality to express it, he suggests that Facebook's success can be attributed to remunerating the users' need to communicate above all other considerations.

SOCIAL BONDING WITH WILSON

In the popular movie *Cast Away* starring Tom Hanks, much of the storyline deals with how we humans understand time and the world through social relationships. In the movie, Hanks is so desperate for social connections that he befriends a volleyball that appears to have a face on it and talks to "Wilson" in order to have a social experience of some kind—any kind. Taken at face value (no pun intended), the idea that a grown man would emotionally bond with the image of a face on a volleyball stretches the bounds of credulity. But the fact that it works in the movie and, as far as I know, has never been challenged in any country where the movie was shown is a testimony to how powerful our drive for sociability is.

PUTTING "BUSINESS BEFORE PLEASURE"

If Facebook's success can be used to illustrate the importance of prioritizing remuneration over business models and functionality, then the failure to use this same set of priorities should also be revealing. Although they're not technically social networks or online communities, another way that we can see the importance of this aspect of remuneration is by comparing Wikipedia's strategy with its direct competitor, Knol by Google.

In Wikipedia, entries about different subjects are created by the public and aren't attributed to any particular individual. The collective society corrects any factual or stylistic errors in the entry rather than a single editor or moderator. It's the "wisdom of the crowd" that keeps Wikipedia's information both dynamic and accurate. This has been an incredibly successful strategy, which has produced well over two and a half million entries and made Wikipedia larger than *Encyclopedia Britannica* and nearly as accurate, according to a study published in the journal *Nature* in December 2005 [4]. Wikipedia has tapped into people's social connections. In contrast, Google's Knol system is based on stories by individual authors. An individual author posts a "knoll," which is one unit of "knowledge," and that "knol" is attributed to that individual writer. The accuracy of the information is dependent on the *ethos* of the individual author, not on shared, communal knowledge.

It appears that Google's idea here is to take advantage of the same kind of business model that has worked fairly successfully for them on Blogger.com where bloggers can use "AdSense" to share profits from the blog. On both Blogger .com and Knol, the authors of the entries can receive a cut of the profits Google receives when readers click on the advertising links displayed on the page—thus, a successful Knol entry that drives a lot of eyeballs to Google's online advertising is financially rewarding for the author.

It remains to be seen whether Google's Knol approach will become successful, as it's a fairly new system and is still in beta. However, so far in early 2009, the reception has been hostile to lukewarm at best. It appears that Google has made a serious error by putting its business model, i.e., AdSense, ahead of community and social connectivity. As Farhad Manjoo has pointed out, "Knol diminishes community involvement" and, as a result, it doesn't allow members of the community to correct errors in the Knol entries. Second, Knol "rewards authors with advertising lucre, creating a huge incentive for people to post as much content as possible." As a result, users of Knol who are searching for definitive answers to questions are remunerated with a plethora of articles on the same topic, frequently copied from other online sources and "fraught with factual and grammatical errors" because they haven't been subjected to review by any communal group [13].

The reason I use the Knol example is because Google usually gets it right.

WAVE

Google's Wave is an example of Google getting their priorities right and designing for user experience first. With Wave, Google asked how they could redesign the user experience of e-mail, blogging, and instant messaging using networking tools that weren't available 40 years ago when e-mail was invented.

My point here is that even Google is susceptible to falling into the business-model-before-user-experience trap. With Knol, Google, ironically, is making the same type of mistake that AltaVista made back in 1999 that allowed Google to capture market share in the search engine market. They put the business model ahead of the user experience in order to keep pace with a competitor. By confusing priorities and allowing their users' experience with the product to be degraded, it seems likely that Knol will fail to compete successfully with Wikipedia.

WHAT *IS* REMUNERATION?

So far, other than talking about creating a positive user experience, I've talked more about what remuneration is not than what it is. So many people have an intuitive grasp of remuneration and the concept seems so commonsensical that it's ripe for abuse. Its simplest formulation basically says that individuals will not become members of a social network unless there is a clear benefit for doing so. People need to believe that they will obtain some positive return on the investment of their time and energy in order to be attracted to participation in an e-community. They need to believe that some value will come from joining a group.

FOCUS ON TECHNIQUE

Part of the users' remuneration is the experience of communication in your community, not by looking at archived postings or content from your community posted on other sites. Therefore, managers can give as much value as possible to users' participation by employing the following techniques:

- Don't archive your postings.
- Discourage attempts to send conversations to other blogs, Web sites, and discussion groups.
- Ban redistribution to servers and cross postings.

Many make a serious mistake because they think that the remuneration needs to be financial; in fact, we've already seen this kind of remuneration at work in Google's Knol where they use AdSense to pay knol and bloggers. However,

THE ROOTS OF "COMMUNITY"

As observed in my earlier book, *A Rhetoric of Electronic Communities*, this idea of remuneration is embedded in the very etymology of the word "community" [8]. The word "community" can be broken down into

Com + munity

"*Com*" is, of course, the Latin prefix for "with" or "together." There's some debate about whether the "munity" suffix comes from "*munis*," which is Etruscan for "obligation," or from the Latin "*munus*," which means to "bestow a gift" or "duty." Either way, the term "community" can be taken to mean that members are bound together with an obligation to repay a duty. It's also interesting and enlightening to note that the etymological opposite of "community" would be "immunity," or "not obligated to bestow a duty."

"Remuneration," of course, has its roots in the same suffix as "community." Both share "munus" at their core and, consequently, both convey a sense of obligation to give back, to repaying, and to give duty to others. Dictionary.com defines "remunerate" as: "1. To pay, recompense, or reward for work, trouble, etc. 2. To yield a recompense for (work, services, etc.)" [22].

often the most successful communities and social networks don't provide any clear financial incentives for participants. Instead, they satisfy some basic, psychological, or emotional need. Certainly, massively multiple online role playing games (or MMORPGs) such as World of Warcraft or America's Army would fit into this category as these remunerate participants through entertainment (just to name one of the most obvious benefits). Another good example of this can also be seen in Facebook's partnership with CNN, which allowed Facebook users to chat in real time as they watched the presidential inauguration of Barack Obama.

The numbers for this social networking event were groundbreaking. According to Randi Zuckerberg's Facebook blog immediately after the event, "there were over 2 million status updates posted" to Facebook during the event. Facebook members were posting an average of 4000 updates per minute like those shown in Figure 4.4, and during President Obama's address, this number jumped to 8500 updates per minute [33].

FIGURE 4.4
Comments from Facebook friends watching the Obama inauguration on CNN.com.

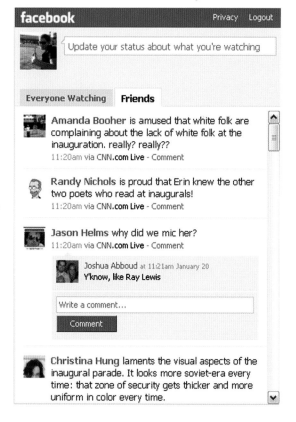

Why? There have been experiments with combining video streams and live chats in the past; what was it that made this event nearly double the previous record for Web traffic? According to the *Los Angeles Times*, a YouTube Live concert held the previous record at 700,000 concurrent streams, but CNN.com was able to serve 1.3 million concurrent streams and a total of 18.8 million online users [21]. What made this event different? What was so compelling about watching the inauguration while sharing comments with friends? Why not simply watch the CNN feed alone?

Part of the answer lies in the way we human beings make meaning. Consider the following comment that was posted by Christina Tynan-Wood on the ReadWriteWeb blog site the day after the event where she reflects on her experience:

> It was a very cool experience. I wanted to go to DC but couldn't manage it. But I never would have known what that person next to me was thinking. But using this allowed me to not only watch with my own friends but see what the crowd was thinking, too. Outstanding [26].

Tynan-Wood's comment here is revealing because it is a clear, unpretentious expression of the social constructionist epistemology needed in order to understand how remuneration is operating. We humans have a deep-seated, primal need to be part of a social experience because that's how we make events meaningful. How we interpret the world around us and make sense of events, such as the inauguration of the first African-American president, is a function of the communities we inhabit. Meaning, for us, isn't found in the event itself; it isn't "self-evident." There is no act of pure, unmediated perception through which we know the truth. Meaning is neither immediately obvious nor intuitive; it emerges out of a social system of differential relationships.

DIFFERENTIAL RELATIONSHIPS

The way I explain "differential relationships" to my students is this: Take a quarter, hold it up, and ask "What does this mean?" Typically, students will say it means that it's 25 cents or ¼ of a dollar, which is indeed what it means. But the point is that it doesn't "mean" by itself; it only has meaning because it *differs* from a dollar or from cents. The fact that it is made of silver doesn't mean by itself because the value of silver is also relative to the cost of gold, just like the meaning of a quarter is relative to a dollar. So what makes a quarter intelligible is its place in a system of differential relationships.

That's why we want to watch an event such as the Obama inauguration with other people because even in our very language we make meaning from differences that exist between ourselves and others, between this group and that group. Between Republican and Democrat, conservative and liberal. As humans, we have to have a system to put it in and having other people around us makes this possible. Not having people around us leads to madness. That's why being banished is a punishment. Being "excommunicated" (or literally to be cut off from language) is to be cast adrift in a sea of meaninglessness, to have no value, no purpose, and no means of understanding the world around you. Thus, the remuneration that comes from the social networking is the ability to understand events through differences through social construction.

How we think about, feel about, and place value upon a singular event such as Obama's inauguration is a result of a complex negotiation among the different voices we hear in our respective communities. Each posting on the CNN feed through Facebook Connect makes a competing knowledge claim on us. When my conservative, Republican father-in-law who is sitting in Shanghai where he owns a consulting business makes a comment during Obama's speech, all of the ideological baggage of his relationship with me is brought to bear on how he wants me to see and to interpret the event. Similarly, when one of my academic colleagues from the art department makes a comment drawing parallels between the visual spectacle of secret service guards in the inaugural parade and soviet-era military parades, that also shapes the meaning we attach to the event.

The remuneration participants obtain from this event is extraordinarily satisfying to us as human beings because it helps eliminate cognitive dissonance within each of us. As the famous social psychologist Leon Festinger observed in 1957, human beings suffer both emotionally and intellectually when we experience cognitive dissonance [3]. As humans, we seek to bring order to cognitive dissonance so that we can locate and accept our place in the world. Through the communing inherent in communication, we are able to make sense of the event. Order is socially constructed out of chaos, and the maddening itch of cognitive dissonance is scratched.

Scratching the itch of cognitive dissonance is intensely satisfying on a basic, fundamental level. Hence, scratching that itch is the remuneration designers must seek to provide in order to build sustainable social networks and communities. Bottom line: figure out what users in your community want and need to understand (such as the social significance of a political election and other news events) and then create an environment so they can socially construct that understanding.

TIP
The key to long-term success is remembering that the most important remuneration you have to offer is the *experience*.

The key to long-term success is remembering that the most important remuneration you have to offer is the *experience* of socially constructing meaning about topics and events your users want to understand.

TECHNIQUES

So what are some of the ways that you can help ensure that users of your social network or community help remunerate the group? Remuneration not only addresses the obvious question of what individuals get out of a community, it also requires that community architects consider what the individuals give back to the community so that communication will occur. It's probably not possible to provide an exhaustive list, as the number of possibilities is only limited by human imagination. Nevertheless, the following techniques or strategies have been successful for communities I've built or which I've observed.

CHECKLIST OF TECHNIQUES

1. Make the text editor fun; add emoticons
2. Use a subscription application form
3. Mentors teach
4. Seed the discussion
5. Use stars to show membership contribution levels
6. Rank the value of members' messages
7. Remove the fear factor by providing examples of how to participate
8. Create a safe environment by sending out "tickle" messages
9. Create a regular event
10. Don't automatically archive
11. Discourage attempts to send conversations to other blogs, Web sites, or discussion groups
12. Ban redistribution servers and cross-postings

1. MAKE THE TEXT EDITOR FUN; ADD EMOTICONS

If you want to encourage users to add content to your site and participate, it's important that you make that experience fun, even when you're working with a professional community. For example, from 2001 to 2006 I worked on a project where we were building a social networking suite of tools for the Boys and Girls Clubs of America (BGCA) in order to improve the retention rate of adult youth development professionals who work in the clubs. The idea was to help the individuals who worked in the clubs connect with other youth development specialists in order to increase their sense of professionalism. As a result, we tried to build a professional-looking site around the metaphor of a "conference center," as our initial task analyses with users told us that it was at their professional conferences that BGCA employees felt the most like part of a professional movement (see Figure 4.5).

Ironically, however, one of the things that we found tremendously successful in terms of encouraging people to post messages to the communities on the site was through the use of emoticons that we allowed them to choose in the text editor. This may sound like a trivial thing, but at the time (we were working in 2001–2002), accessing Web sites to check for messages from friends and colleagues wasn't the norm it has become in these post-MySpace and Facebook days. Indeed, most of the BGCA youth development professionals with whom we were working didn't access the Internet at all as part of their professional practices, as they were busy working with the kids all day. Many didn't even have access to the Internet at home, and the clubs only had dial-up modems. Encouraging them to use an online social network to create communities of practice as part of their regular work routine was something of a challenge for us. Working with the kids already put lots of demands on their time, and asking them to login and post messages just made an already short day shorter. We needed to find ways to motivate the BGCA staff to participate regularly.

Welcome to The Virtual Conference Center   Wednesday, January 21 2009 @ 05:26 PM EST

Lobby | Discussion Rooms | Chat | Exhibit Hall | Theatre | FAQ's | Contact Us | Search

Today's Thought

Few things in the world are more powerful than a positive push; a smile; a word of optimism and hope.--Richard M. De Vos

Conference Services

User Directory
Online Skill Development
Technical Support
FAQs

Announcements

The VCC is scheduled to be discontinued on June 30, 2006.

Featured Projects:

N.A.T.I.V.E.
Cost of Part-Time Staff Turnover vs. Retention Within Boys & Girls Clubs
E-Mentoring in the Movement: A Pilot Program for Staff Retention
Associate Board Resource Guide

Policies

Disclaimer
Privacy Policy
Netiquette

Who's Online

Guest Users: 1

Admin Check In

Admin Login

Welcome to the VCC!

What is the VCC (Virtual Conference Center)?

Welcome to the Virtual Conference Center! The VCC is an electronic community designed for you, a B&GC leader. Through the VCC, you can connect with other B&GC leaders nationwide. It's like attending a national conference all year long, at your convenience!

What services does the VCC offer?

When you attend the national conference, you have convenient access to various services. This is also true here at the VCC.

Meet with colleagues to complete projects at your convenience!

View research and other projects completed by your colleagues

View conference presentations and videos from BGCA National Programs.

Seek advice from Clemson University's Professors and Researchers.

Discussion Rooms

At the BGCA national conference, you have the opportunity to participate in discussion sessions with your colleagues. The VCC Discussion Rooms are similar to conference meeting rooms. Each discussion room is an electronic bulletin board, where you can post questions or share information with your colleagues. The feature of the VCC Discussion Rooms is that this tool does not require "real-time" interaction. You can post messages anytime, making this tool very flexible to your schedule. Through the Discussion Rooms, you have the potential of reaching 35,000 Boys & Girls Club professionals, which make the Rooms an excellent place for you to begin sharing resources and ideas with others in the Movement.

Chat

The Chat tool is a "real-time" meeting place. Like face-to-face meetings, the chat tool allows you to talk with your colleagues and get an immediate response to your questions and ideas. Many community members have found this tool useful for conducting meetings without the cost of long-distance conference calls or travel to distant sites. But many people use it just for sharing ideas and opinions with friends.

Exhibit Hall

The Exhibit Hall will provide you with presentations and reports from other leaders in the Movement. In the same way that you would go to the National Conference to learn about new ideas for recruiting, staff retention, or resource development for your organization, you can go to the Exhibit Hall to find reports on projects happening around the country. Many of these reports were designed and completed as part of the **Advanced Leadership Certificate Program (ALCP)** at Clemson University.

Theatre

The VCC's Theatre provides you with conference presentations and videos for you to view at your convenience. Visit the Theatre to view streaming content of the ALCP group project presentations and other important videos.

Lobby

Just like in a real conference hotel, if you get lost and need help finding your way around, return to the Lobby.

This project is funded by the Office of Justice Programs.

Powered By: GeekLog v1.3.11 Created this page in 0.31 seconds Copyright © 2009 The Virtual Conference Center
All trademarks and copyrights on this page are owned by their respective owners.

FIGURE 4.5
The BGCA Virtual Conference Center Lobby/Landing page [27].

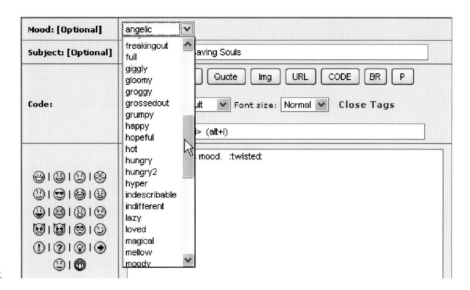

FIGURE 4.6
Mood menu choices in open source text editor.

The site was designed in Geeklog (an open source community management tool), and the PHP-based text editor Geeklog uses for members of the community to compose and post their messages already came with a few emoticons built into the module (see Figure 4.6).

The idea was that when people posted a message to the site, they could choose an emoticon that gave other users on the site a sense of how they were feeling as they were writing their messages. For example, if they were happy, they might choose the "rockin'" emoticon, or if they were upset, they might choose the "angry" emoticon. These "moods" would show up next to the text of messages they posted along with the number of stars indicating their level of contributions to the community, how many messages they had posted to the system that month, and how long they had been a member of the community (see Figure 4.7).

FIGURE 4.7
Angry mood and rockin' mood with contribution stars.

As we were programming the site, just for fun, we threw in a "pokey-stick" animated emoticon. The animated pokey-stick emoticon basically showed two "smileys" opposing each other, and one of the "smileys" had a tree branch, or stick, which he was using to poke at the other emoticon in the animation. We wanted to give people a way to indicate that they wanted to argue about a topic in order to help prevent flame wars destroying the trust that we had built up in the community (see Figure 4.8).

Our BGCA users went crazy over all the different "smileys." What we found was people, particularly new users to the site, were encouraged to post more messages just so they could find ways to use the different emoticons. We kept getting recommendations for different emoticons that our users asked us to add to the library, different emotional states, different kinds of animations—all with increasingly humorous names. Our users would vie with one another to become the first to be able to use, for example, the "crossing swords" emoticon when we added it to the library. So even though we were initially afraid the emoticons were demeaning, members of the network really took them seriously, driving up participation on the site.

FIGURE 4.8
Pokey-stick and crossing sword-animated GIFs.

2. USE A SUBSCRIPTION APPLICATION FORM

One of the major decisions that community designers and social network designers need to make is whether to have open subscriptions to their system or invitation-only subscriptions. Whether the site is by invitation only or open, I still recommend that community managers require that users complete a subscription application form. Further, I also recommend to new community managers that their subscription application form have questions that let users know that they are expected to give back to the community and that lurking in the community isn't something that's encouraged.

In the most mature and perhaps most successful electronic community I maintain, for example, every member of the community is required to have completed a subscription application form that is reviewed by the list owner and members of the group's advisory council. The subscription application form asks potential subscribers to indicate why they want to be a member of the community, which isn't unusual for sites that use subscription application forms. However, this question is immediately followed by the following question:

> 5. One of the differences between a public email "list" and a private "community" is that members of a community are expected to give back to and to support a community. Please explain how you expect to support and contribute to the community.

It is hoped that the purpose of this question is obvious. The advisory council and I hope to make new users understand from the very beginning that they aren't just joining a forum, but are entering into a community where part of the remuneration is their ability to add content and to respond to other members of the community. We want users to understand that taking content from the community without giving anything back is a problem. Using presupposition triggers in the questions you ask before someone ever even starts participating in a community helps signal to them the expectation that they will actively contribute and remunerate others in the community—even if that remuneration merely involves reading other members' postings regularly.

Many people regard "lurkers" as a pejorative term. I use it here because it has become commonplace in the field. However, Chapter 5 discusses different types of members and draws a distinction between "spectators" and "inactives." Spectators (a group many lump into those they call lurkers) make a positive contribution to a community, whereas "inactives" do not contribute positively.

3. MENTORS TEACH

One of the problems with becoming an active member of any discourse community is learning the ropes. In a typical discussion group community, it's generally accepted that only 10% of the membership is going to be "active" at any given time. Although Nonnecke and Preece did a study in 2000 of 109 different "discussion lists" that showed that the number of lurkers in a group could vary depending on factors such as the number of members and traffic level in the group [15], it's still generally accepted that, as a rule of thumb, 90% of a group are likely to be lurkers. Jakob Nielsen's *Alertbox* states that

> User participation often more or less follows a **90-9-1 rule**:
> - **90%** of users are **lurkers** (i.e., read or observe, but don't contribute).
> - **9%** of users contribute **from time to time**, but other priorities dominate their time.
> - **1%** of users participate a lot and **account for most contributions**: it can seem as if they don't have lives because they often post just minutes after whatever event they're commenting on occurs.
>
> **Nielsen [14]**

Because lurkers are, by definition, not talking, it's difficult to collect much information about why lurkers lurk, and even when data are collected on them, the reasons for lurking can be quite varied. In a 2003 follow-up study to their earlier work, Nonnecke and Preece conducted in-depth interviews with 10 lurkers representing 47 different groups and found that they gave 117 different reasons for lurking ([16], 115). Still, Nonnecke and Preece found that at least 50% of the participants in the study indicated the following reasons for lurking:

> - they wished to preserve their anonymity in order to ensure privacy and safety
> - there were work-related constraints preventing them from posting
> - the volume of messages was too low or high
> - the quality of messages was poor
> - they were shy about posting
> - they had limitations on their time
>
> **Nonnecke and Preece [16], 116**

In informal surveys that I've conducted with many of the online communities that I maintain, I've also contacted members directly who don't post regularly and asked them why they don't participate. One of the most common answers I get, especially from new members, is that they're too intimidated to post, even when they feel like they have something to contribute to a discussion. They are keenly aware that frequently it's not what you say, but how you say it, which can lead to flame wars or which can damage people's reputation and a community, so they're reluctant to post.

One way to help users overcome this fear is to build a cadre of experienced community members who are willing to serve as electronic mentors for new members. The mentors work with a new user and send "whispers" (i.e., private messages sent directly to the new community member). In their whispers, mentors are trained to interact with new users by:

- asking them how they're doing
- filling them in on the back story that might be informing an ongoing conversation
- giving them information about the people participating in a conversation
- providing information so that new members become familiar more quickly with the personalities and dynamics in the group

Mentors give new users someone to talk to in the community to help break the ice and learn the appropriate methods for participation.

When a new member is accepted into a community, he or she can be assigned a mentor. It's important to train your mentors in order to make sure they understand their responsibilities. For example, provide an e-mail message that mentors can send to their mentees once they've been admitted into the community. This message (which I ask my mentors to personalize) basically tells the mentees that the mentor will be sending them messages and keeping in touch for the next 30 days. It explains that the mentor's role is to help provide a context for current discussions happening in the community in order to help the new members get acclimated more quickly and it encourages them to ask the mentor questions about the community.

Mentors are then expected to send at least one message per week (i.e., three more messages after the initial welcome message). Typically, these messages involve a simple exchange of personal information about things such as where people went to school, how they became interested in the field, what sorts of job responsibilities they have, and so on. The mentors will also share information about how the community got started, significant moments in the history of the group, and sometimes stories about some of its leaders and more colorful personalities.

By building common ground, the mentors help new members develop a sense of other people in the community. There are no physical bodies to see in e-mail discussion groups, and even though some Web-based forums allow photos of the posters, the people reading the posts still lack bodies. This "lack of the body" in cyberspace frightens many people. Mentoring helps overcome this by giving new members a sense of the audience they are addressing when they post and by removing that particular barrier to contributing to the community.

> The chapter on Belonging discusses the importance of storytelling and how "stories of origin" shape members' sense of belonging and purpose.

4. SEED THE DISCUSSION

There are large numbers of social networks and online communities on the Net today that are ghost towns. There was an initial impulse to create a community, it seemed like a good idea at the time, it got started, people joined, conversations were begun, but the communities eventually lost their exigency and stopped talking. This is particularly a concern for companies such as Adobe or Novell, which are trying to use electronic communities and social networking strategies in order reduce the amount of content that their information product developers need to create in order to support their information products. Adobe needs to create conversations about how to create animated gifs in Photoshop for Web sites, for example, in order to keep people subscribed and interested in the sites. To do this, Adobe and Novell pay people to participate and "seed" the discussions with conversations that are appropriate to the group.

By posting a question, encouraging an activity, reporting on a new book, or making a contentious point, these staff members plant the seeds for future conversations and keep the community active. They remind people that they have a commitment to a community. Although you want to avoid a flame war, nothing encourages activity and participation from the membership nearly so well as a good, substantive controversy. Many community managers and social network administrators are so afraid of getting flame wars started that they make their sites' policies far too "PC" and virtually discourage all kinds of conflict. While people are certainly disgusted by flaming and hooliganism, they are nonetheless fascinated by conflict. A good argument has incredible entertainment value, even if you're not particularly interested in the controversy at hand. It's a lot of fun to sit on the sidelines and watch "the game" or, better yet, you might find yourself getting drawn into the game and contributing.

When you're trying to "seed" a community with messages, look for these kinds of controversies and ask thought-provoking questions. And it's probably worth your time as the manager of a community to work with the people who are seeding discussions on how to introduce controversial topics without starting acrimonious debates. For example, if you're trying to get a community of user experience designers talking, you could post something like

```
Does anyone else think that Microsoft's ribbon menu on
Office 12 sucks?
```

This is almost certainly going to provoke a response in the community, but the term "sucks" here is clearly inflammatory, and the propensity for "Microsoft bashing" among interface designers is so clichéd these days that the comment is really only likely to start a flame war rather than the substantive debate you were hopefully seeking. A better approach might be something like

```
I was working on the problem of how to lay out lots of
controls for users without giving up too much screen
real estate recently. I began rereading Jensen Harris'
"Office User Interface Blog" at http://blogs.msdn.
com/jensenh/archive/2005/09/14/467126.aspx, where he
talks about why Microsoft felt they had to develop the
ribbon interface for Office 12 [6]. How do members of
this community feel about the ribbon as a potential
solution to this problem?
```

Both of these questions are thought-provoking and both were controversial at the time, but the difference between them and the conversations they were likely to stimulate is obvious.

5. USE STARS ON MESSAGES TO SHOW MEMBERSHIP CONTRIBUTION LEVELS

Many social networks, such as Facebook, MySpace, LinkedIn, and so on, require that members create user profiles and then other members can use these profiles to obtain information about individuals in the network. When we built the network for the Boys and Girls Club of America, we also provided the ability for people to create user profiles. However, we added a competitive dimension that really drove up use of the network.

The technique was very simple: allow people to earn stars for the amount of participation that they exhibited in the network. The more messages you posted, the more complete your membership profile. The more responses that you gave to other people's messages and the more views that you had of other people's postings, the more stars you earned as a user. For some members of the community, earning stars was analogous to advancing to the next level in a video game.

LinkedIn uses a similar strategy by giving users a percentage of completeness of their profile and giving them feedback on what they need to do to raise the percentage of completeness (Figure 4.9).

Other communities give advanced features or permissions to members who have established themselves as deserving of higher rank in the community. For example, in some MOO communities the ability to program new spaces is something that a community manager can control. In the PoohMOO community I built, for

FIGURE 4.9
Profile completeness prompts from LinkedIn.

example, new members of the community could experience rooms, or spaces, that were available in the MOO, but they couldn't create their own rooms or customize their own spaces until they had gone through a series of training activities and undertaken a prescribed series of "adventures" (see also Howard Rheingold's description of the space colony MOO in *The Virtual Community*, [23]).

Once they had achieved this level, then they were given permission to create their own personal space that they could describe and evolve. After they had been a member of the community for a sufficiently long period of time, they would be entrusted with a programming bit that enabled them not only to create and customize their own personal space, but also develop public spaces that other members in the PoohMOO could then enjoy. One of our members, for example, built a nine-hole golf course that anyone on the system could play once they had personally introduced themselves to his online character and received an access bit in exchange. These badges of rank and increased access privileges motivated many members of the community to participate more and kept them returning to the site.

6. RANK THE VALUE OF MEMBERS' MESSAGES

This is a fairly common technique that is used on sites such as Epinions.com and Amazon.com. Basically, it allows users to read a posting by another member of the forum and to assign a score to the value of the contribution. The scores of individual members can then be averaged over time and equations can be developed that allow those members of the community who have a high number of postings that have received a high rank to float to the top. On Boxesandarrows .com, for example, contributors earn "reputation points" (see Figure 4.10).

Just as in a WoW guild where members of the guild compete to see who does the most damage to the bosses, these reputation point rankings allow people to see who makes the most effective contribution to the site (Figure 4.11).

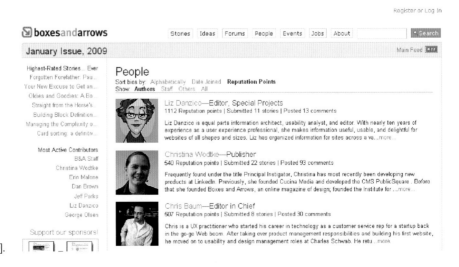

FIGURE 4.10
Reputation points on people page in Boxesandarrows.com [19].

FIGURE 4.11
Damage done during raids in WoW guild [31].

This has two positive effects in terms of remuneration for the community. First, it gives members something to shoot for (as in a video game) and it has a certain entertainment value that many people enjoy. Second, reputation and effectiveness scoring has the effect of shutting down and discouraging inappropriate postings and ineffectual messaging techniques. It discourages people from participating in flame wars, name calling, and *ad hominem* attacks, which are going to lead to lower average scores over time.

DISINCENTIVES TO FLAMING

It's important to note, however, that if you use this technique and yet fail to average the scores over time and give members of the community feedback on whose messages have been consistently ranked higher than other members of the community, you're not going to enjoy the positive effects that ranking messages can generate. There's no disincentive to participating in a flame war or to getting a low ranking score if those scores aren't being averaged over time.

The technique of ranking is particularly useful on sites where people share audiovisual content, such as videos, music, or images. Video blogs or vlogs in particular are becoming increasingly popular as a means of providing users with social media interactions. However, because it's difficult to scan or preview a video in order to decide if the content is something you want to watch, giving users the ability to rank the content's usefulness is a valuable addition to a social media site.

7. REMOVE THE FEAR FACTOR BY PROVIDING EXAMPLES OF HOW TO PARTICIPATE

As indicated previously, users often fail to post messages or provide content because they're afraid of looking foolish to other members of a community or network. They don't know the audience well enough to feel like they can construct their message in a way that will be well received. And there's probably good reason for that feeling. In September 2008, for example, *CIO Magazine* reported on a survey of 31,000 employers from CareerBuilder.com that found that one in five employers use social networks in the hiring process; what's really scary is that one-third of them reported rejecting a candidate because of information they found [7].

Because people don't want to damage their reputation or their professional status in the community, they won't post unless they're fairly sure that their contribution will be received as a contribution and will not open up them up to critique. A simple, yet surprisingly often overlooked, technique for addressing this is to simply provide members of a community or social network with examples of the kinds of behaviors that you want to encourage. Typically mentoring can achieve this goal, but usually mentoring activities only last for 30 days, whereas having a Web site with examples that illustrate how to participate can be accessed 24/7.

On one of the closed, professional communities I maintain, members of the community's advisory council and I created the following guidance on how members can ask questions in ways that are more likely to get responses from other members of the community.

There is an extensive discussion about how to set up and administer "advisory councils" in the Techniques section of the Influence chapter.

This particular community (which I'll call UserTopoi to protect its closed, private nature) is populated by busy working professionals who also have a very low tolerance for doing somebody else's job for them. They tend not to respond to questions that they perceive as lazy, novice, or unhelpful to the community at large. Consequently, when people ask a question and fail to show that they've done their "due diligence" and, at least, a little bit of research on the topic, UserTopoi members will frequently ignore or fail to respond to the question. They don't want to be made to feel like "free consultants." Figure 4.12 attempts to illustrate for members how they can ask questions productively and participate in the site in a way that will help them earn the respect of other members of the community and contribute in productive ways.

Catherine Weeks' sample message is reproduced in this book with her permission.

How to write posts on UserTopoi that get responses

When UserTopoi members see a new post, they usually decide from the subject line whether they want to look at it at all, in the first few sentences whether they want to read it further, and, after a bit more reading, whether they want to respond to it. It's important, therefore, to get the meat of your message right up front. Consider the following tips when you craft your post.

1) Conferences, RFPs, and other announcements require permission before posting. See Special Policy #4 at http://usertopoi_policies.html.

2) Keep the subject line brief, but make sure it states your purpose for posting the message. For example:

   - Position opening: Director of Usability, Earmuff, ND.
   - Anecdotal evidence wanted on links embedded in text
   - Evaluating usability of low-traffic, long-visit-time Web sites.

3) In the first few sentences, make sure you relate your purpose to something with which readers can identify, and tell them what you'd like them to do.

4) Give readers a clear reason for responding, including a "what's in it for me" message. You may offer to:

   - summarize and post the responses
   - post the results of a survey
   - explain how addressing the issue will help other practitioners and the field
   - take action based on the responses you get, and tell them of the outcome.

5) Keep the message brief. If you need to refer to supplementary information, do so with a hyperlink.

6) Be sure to define any specialized terms with which readers may be unfamiliar.

7) Follow up. If you promise feedback or results, deliver on the promise in a timely manner.

Here's a sample of a post that follows many of these tips:

```
Subject: Misleading trial data

Has anyone had any experience with performing usability research on
users of a software trial that yielded misleading data about how
real users use the system?

My concern is that we had some software trials that we performed
Usability studies on. The studies done up to this point were
Interviews with users of the software. The software product is not
in use beyond these trials at this point, but we need to start
making recommendations back to the team for the next version to stay
ahead of the competition. While I intend to perform usability tests
and site visits as the product is released regardless, some
```

FIGURE 4.12
Sample Web page illustrating how members can participate.

```
knowledge about if this is a common occurrence could help me
prioritize our plans.

Thanks in advance for any input!

Catherine Weeks | User Experience Engineer

SeaChange International, Inc.
```

Note: The Advisory Council wishes to thank Catherine Weeks for giving us her permission to use the sample message above. See http://usertopoi_policies.htm for more information on the limitations of how UserTopoi messages may be used.

FIGURE 4.12—CONT'D

8. CREATE A SAFE ENVIRONMENT BY SENDING OUT "TICKLE" MESSAGES

Like most community managers over the years, I learned a long time ago that it's a really bad idea to punish the entire community or social network for the misbehavior of a few hooligans or a "troll." As a result, I make it a rule on all the communities that I maintain and administer not to send out system-wide e-mail messages, blasts, or "administrivia" spam when I am dealing with policy issues. Indeed, one of the complaints about MySpace is the number of administrivia and "nag" messages that it sends out.

DON'T FEED TROLLS

"Troll" is an extremely negative term used to describe people who are deliberately dis-putatious and disruptive either to call attention to themselves or to derail a conver-sation about a subject they don't want discussed. The common expression "DNFTT" means "do not feed the trolls" and is another way of saying that it's a bad idea to pun-ish an entire group by addressing a troll publicly.

SuperNews! - Social Networking Wars

FIGURE 4.13
Viral video lampooning social networks for nagging users.

There is a famous viral video from http://current.com/Supernews about this called "SuperNews! Social Networking Wars" in which a MySpace character attacks a young man sitting on a couch for not visiting the site often enough and for cheating on him with Facebook, Second Life, Friendster, and other social networks (Figure 4.13 [25]). The popularity of the video is a testimony to how closely users identified with its scathing critique of the ways social networks and communities can quickly annoy their members with administrivia and nags.

Unfortunately, however, if you don't have a strong, visible presence as an administrator in the community and if members are not aware that policies and netiquette practices are being vigorously enforced, they don't get the sense that you're providing a safe space for collaboration. The way I address this is to send out a formulaic message once every 60 days that describes:

1. Any disciplinary actions that have been taken in the community
2. Any new policy changes that have been made
3. Responses to any questions that members may have asked regarding policies
4. Reminders about policies that haven't been discussed and may have been forgotten by long-time members

Of course, these messages don't use anyone's names, are anonymous, and I make every effort to make sure that nobody in the community is embarrassed by the messages. Part of the reason I wait 60 days is to make sure that enough time has passed that members don't feel like I'm singling someone out or deliberately calling attention to a thread or conversation that might embarrass some individual or group. Figure 4.14 is an example of a message I send to members of my communities' advisory councils. How to use advisory councils in your community is discussed in more detail in the Influence chapter, so for now I'll just explain that the individuals on the advisory council help the community manager set and enforce policies. In the case of the message shown in Figure 4.14, I use Unix's CRONTAB to automatically e-mail the message six times per year.

By sending these out regularly, it reminds users that they are in the community, that the community is being policed, and that a safe space is being provided for them so that they can carry on conversations without fear of being attacked or abused. Again, it helps reduce any potential impediments to their remunerating the community by contributing to the conversation. However, by keeping the posting frequency low, the "nag" factor is kept to a minimum.

9. CREATE A REGULAR EVENT

One of the problems with keeping a social network or community active is that there often times aren't regular events to encourage participation. I need to exercise regularly in order to lose weight. However, as anyone who has ever tried to lose weight can tell you, if you don't have a regular schedule and a regular time built into your schedule for exercising, you're almost certainly not going to achieve your goals. If you only exercise when you feel like it, chances are you're never going to do it. The same thing obtains to participating in communities. If you don't have regularly scheduled times when you check the social network for news or participate in the conversation, then activity is going to fall off. Once again, this is an incredibly simple thing you can do but extraordinarily important to long-term success. WoW guilds are an excellent example of this. One of my sons is an officer in a guild and is responsible for scheduling regular raids for its members. Every Tuesday, Thursday, and Saturday night at 8:30 p.m. Eastern

```
Dear Advisory Council Members:

This is an "automagically" generated message intended to serve as a
"tickle file" to remind us that it's time to think about sending out an
administrivia message to our subscribers.

Is there a "netiquette" or policy issue that we need to remind members
to consider?  If so, would one of the Council members volunteer to send
a message to the community about it?

Below is an example of the type of message we might send that may be
used as a "canned" form.

"Virtually" Yours,

Tharon

-----<cut here>-----
Advisory Council Update

The [listname] Advisory Council works with the listowner to help decide
questions of list policy and enforce the list rules. Periodically, we
publish a message to keep list members informed about the recent
activities of the Advisory Council and how issues have been handled.

 -- The Council recently . . .

 -- Council members took action on . . .

 -- etc.

If you have information which you feel would be of interest to the
[listname] community but would like to make sure it is appropriate,
please feel free to contact the Advisory Council. Address your message
to THARON@CLEMSON.EDU.  Your message will be forwarded to the Council
members, the issue will be discussed, and a representative of the
Council will respond in a few days.

[listname] Advisory Council
-----<cut here>-----
```

FIGURE 4.14
Sample tickle message.

Time his guild has a regular raid (see Figure 4.15). Additionally, they'll schedule special events, but the core group meets regularly.

On many of the Listserv communities and forums that I maintain we also have regular events. For example, in one user interface design private community I maintain, every Friday one of our members hosts a "Friday Thought for the Day," which is intended to encourage people to have a conversation about some important issue going on in the field while they're relaxing over the weekend.

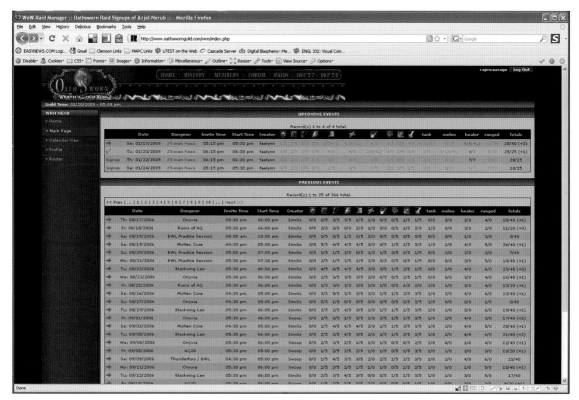

FIGURE 4.15
Meeting schedule for a WOW guild [30].

In another group I maintain, Fridays are "Fun Day." During all the other days of the week in this particular community, jokes are discouraged because of the mis-understandings and flaming behaviors they can occasion. Members are serious and sober and have important conversations about professional subjects, but on Fridays, they vie with each other to see who can make the most puns or tell the funniest anecdotes from their professional experiences.

These kind of regular events are critical because they encourage users to partici-pate in a community. They help members remunerate the community by mak-ing the community a regular part of their lives rather than a happy accident.

10. DON'T AUTOMATICALLY ARCHIVE

Knowledge isn't static. That old saw that encourages people to "collect pearls of wisdom" is false because, unlike pearls, knowledge changes. Knowledge is a process; it's something that is made, and consequently, communities and social networks aren't about and shouldn't be about collecting facts. That's the busi-ness of libraries and databases. If someone wants to find a collection of all the known facts that exist on Subject A or if they want to go "data mining," then they shouldn't be looking for it in communities and social networks. As I've said several times now, the key to providing long-term remuneration for users is providing them with *the experience* of creating meaning together.

I don't mean to suggest here that you shouldn't ask questions in a community and that a community isn't a great place to go to get information about a topic. In fact, that's probably one of the most important things that social networks and online communities do. Sharing information and crowd sourcing are major reasons that people participate in communities. What I am arguing, however, is that community managers and social networking administrators should not maintain keyword searchable, public archives if they want to ensure the long-term health of their communities.

Yes, I understand that maintaining an archive does allow the elders in a community to tell newbies to check archives to the same old questions that tend to be repeated over and over again in a community. But my point is that convenience comes at a cost that is too steep. In the communities that I maintain, newbies do ask the same questions and topics do reemerge, but conversations about them aren't always the same and the community doesn't address them in the same way each time. Each time the discussion comes up, new voices contribute to the conversation. New facts get added. New spins are put on old topics. In fact, people address the topics in more creative ways *because* they've seen them before and *because* they're trying to make the conversations more interesting and engaging. In short, the knowledge changes even though the questions remain the same.

Publicly accessible archives can also have a chilling effect on creativity in a community because of users' concerns about how their messages might be used in the future. We will discuss users' need to control how messages are used in more detail in the chapter on Influence, but the point to be made here is that members of a community are less likely to take risks and to post potentially controversial approaches to a topic if they have to be concerned that their messages might be entombed in a publicly accessible archive where they can always be resurrected at some future date and out of context in an embarrassing fashion.

In terms of remuneration, however, the more important point is that archives don't contribute anything to the long-term health of the community. Public archives are only good for the people who want to get in, get their answers, and get out without giving anything back to the community. Public archives are like banks that you set up as targets for knowledge thieves. Archives are static. They're not dynamic. They don't grow. And they don't give back. Archives precipitate what experienced community managers call "scraping." Scrapers are automated data mining tools that steal from a community. As Patrick O'Keefe in his book *Managing Online Forums* notes:

> You need to be able to protect your content and take down those that steal from your site. Besides the obvious matter of principle, part of what is appealing about the community is the unique voices within it. You

Private archives maintained by individuals are a different issue. As shown in the next chapter, one membership type known as "collectors" use this archiving behavior as their primary means of contributing to a community so that private archives can be encouraged.

don't want to build up your community only to allow someone to steal your posts. If I were a member of a community where this happened and I knew that the people behind it were doing what they could to pursue the scraper, I would think more highly of them than if they just allowed it to happen openly and didn't attempt to do anything [17].

If you want to encourage members of your community to remunerate the community by contributing, then allow them to ask the same questions and allow the community to undergo the process of knowledge making. Don't reify conversations. Don't silence the community by bottling it up in an archive. Let your members talk.

There are, of course, exceptions to every rule, and there are reasons why it might make sense to have a public archive. For example, imagine you're the manager of a project team and your team is responsible for end-user support of, say, a software product. Let's say you're running a wiki-type system for the members of your team to develop and modify manuals, tutorials, and tips that they provide to customers who need help with the company's software. There might be legal or institutional reasons why the users of your wiki would need an archive that allowed them to go back and to research how different versions of the help files evolved.

However, while there may be exceptions, the rule should be that public archives need to be avoided because of the harm they do to the long-term success of a network or community. All too often community managers set up archives automatically just because they can, but the rule should be the other way around. Don't automatically archive; only do so in extreme circumstances where the failure to archive has consequences that outweigh the benefits of letting members talk.

11. DISCOURAGE ATTEMPTS TO SEND CONVERSATIONS TO OTHER BLOGS, WEB SITES, OR DISCUSSION GROUPS

As I hope the discussion on archives made clear, the coin of the realm when you're talking about social networks and communities is *communication*. People join social networks and communities in order to communicate with other people. That's their payback. That's their remuneration. When somebody comes in to a community and tries to redirect a conversation to their blog site or to another community, leaders of the community need to intervene and make clear that the discussion needs to stay in the community where it began and shouldn't be redirected elsewhere.

Typically what's happening here is you're dealing with a consultant who's maintaining a blog site in order to gain name recognition for their organization and they're attempting to "leverage" the unique voices and power of your community in order to capture eyeballs for their blog. Your community members are going to immediately recognize this as little more than an attempt at spamming and, if you don't act, those members of the community who have already contributed to the thread will feel that you failed to protect their interests and their ability to earn the "remuneration" they were seeking when they posted their messages in the first place. They will be unhappy that the discussion and feedback they were hoping to receive was stolen from them and redirected to another space where they may or may not have access. As a community manager, you need to create policies that treat these content thieves in the same way that you would treat a scraper or a copyright thief in order to protect your community and to ensure that the members who post there are remunerated by others in the community and don't have the conversations stolen out from under them.

12. BAN REDISTRIBUTION SERVERS AND CROSS-POSTINGS

Redistribution servers can come in a number of forms. Frequently, however, the way that I have to deal with them is when a department manager at a company will set up an "alias," NNTP feed, or Monarc-style archiver for a shared e-mail account and then subscribe to one of my communities as though he or she were an individual subscriber/community member. Typically what will then happen is that messages from this corporate account will be fed to an rn Usenet group at the site or redistributed to all of the members in a department. But the technologies used to redistribute the community's messages aren't important. The problem with these redistribution servers is that members of the department who are receiving the messages on the other side of the server have probably never read the community policies of the group or never agreed to use the messages from the community in ways that members of the community have a right to expect that they be used and they're treating messages in exactly the same way as scrapers and content thieves treat the messages.

Many software users groups, such as the Adobe User Group Managers community, for example, require that its members enter into nondisclosure agreements as a condition of membership. Many internal communities in corporate settings also have intellectual property restrictions on their members.

Even if these individuals did want to participate in the community, because they're sitting behind a redistribution server and their personal e-mail addresses haven't been authorized to post to the community, these individuals are unable to give back to and remunerate the community even though they might have a desire to do so. You need to create policies that state only individuals can join the social network or community in order to ensure that they know that they're supposed to give back to the community and that they have the ability to communicate in the community.

In addition to prohibiting redistribution servers, you should also discourage cross-posting. Cross-posting is when an individual sends a message or posts to multiple communities simultaneously. The problem here is the same as the problem with sending conversations to other blogs. Many people belong to multiple communities at the same time and, chances are, the cross-posted message would be of interest to those communities that have multiple members. For example, a message might be cross-posted to the Society for Technical

Communication's Usability and User-Experience (UUX) group and to the Interaction Design Association (IxDA) e-mail list simultaneously, as the UUX group deals with usability and user experience design, whereas IxDA deals with information design and user experiences. Both groups share a number of members in common so it's not clear to them whether they should respond to a cross-posted message on the STC's UUX or the IxDA group. Worse yet, if conversations do begin in both groups, there's temptation to forward messages from one community to another that, once again, steals content from those members of the group who don't happen to belong to both lists. It also has the effect of violating the message usage policies and potential intellectual property agreements the groups might have claimed as a condition of membership.

Having policies against redistribution servers and cross-postings is important again because it protects the remuneration expectations of your community members. It helps them enjoy the payback they deserve for answering questions and keeps content that they "earned" by starting a thread or conversation from being directed to some other location that they can't obtain.

CONCLUSION

This chapter demonstrated why remunerating your users, whether you're building a social networking Web site or building an online community, should be your highest priority. Using historical examples from Yahoo, Altavista, Google, and more recent examples such as Knol and Wikipedia, I've tried to show that you'll experience a greater return on investment and will more likely make a profit from your system if you keep your eyes on the remuneration ball and subordinate functionality or short-term profit. However, I have also argued that you can't have successful social networks without functionality and innovative business models. These are necessary conditions of success, but remuneration is the only sufficient condition. They will enhance remuneration, but they won't replace it.

I also showed—using Leon Festinger's concept of cognitive dissonance and the example of watching Obama's inauguration on Facebook Connect and CNN Live—how the remuneration that people get at its fundamental level is scratching the primal itch of cognitive dissonance. It's for that reason that Facebook has been so extraordinarily successful. As its creator, Zuckerberg said, Facebook's top priority is "just make it really efficient for people to communicate, get information and share information" [12]. Finally, we looked at several strategies for encouraging remuneration in social networks and online communities that you, as a community architect, designer, or manager, can use to help your site. However, these strategies are really just attempts to prime the pump of creativity. These are by no means exhaustive and now that you're familiar with remuneration and how it functions, I hope you'll be able to use these as jumping off points for creative and innovative techniques in your own systems. How can you, like a Japanese steakhouse chef, provide the kind of remuneration in experience that your users are seeking?

As you're constructing your social network and online community, it's important that you create the kind of opportunities that CNN and Facebook jointly provided Tynan-Wood. This is the sort of user experience that leads to long-term success because it scratches that will to knowledge itch all human beings have, and it does it in the most comfortable way that we typically make sense of the world around us, i.e., through social construction.

WORKS CITED

[1] AltaVista Home. AltaVista Home. 17 Jan 1999. 25 Jan 2009. http://web.archive.org/web/19990125093146/www.altavista.com/.

[2] CNN.com live with Facebook. CNN.com Live with Facebook. 20 Jan 2009. 20 Jan 2009. http://www.cnn.com/video/fb/facebook.html?stream-stream1.

[3] Festinger L. A Theory of Cognitive Dissonance. Stanford UP; 1957.

[4] Giles J. Internet encyclopaedias go head to head. *Nature* 2005; 438.7070:900(2). Expanded Academic ASAP. Gale. Clemson University. 25 Jan 2009. http://find.galegroup.com/itx/start.do?prodId=EAIM.

[5] Google Homepage. Google Beta. 22 Apr 1999. Google, Inc. 25 Jan 2009. http://web.archive.org/web/19990422191353/http://google.com/.

[6] Harris J. Enter the ribbon. Web log post. An Office User Interface Blog 14 Sept 2005. 23 Jan 2009. http://blogs.msdn.com/jensenh/archive/2005/09/14/467126.aspx.

[7] Havenstein H. Beware job seekers: Facebook, myspace could harm your job search. CIO 8 Sept 2008. 21 Jan 2009. http://www.cio.com/article/449094/.Beware_Job_Seekers_Facebook_MySpace_Could_Harm_Your_Job_Search.

[8] Howard TW. A Rhetoric of Electronic Communities. Grand Rapids: Ablex Corporation; 1997.

[9] Krug S. Don't Make Me Think!: A Common Sense Approach to Web Usability. New Riders: Grand Rapids; 2005.

[10] Lessig L. Remix: Making Art and Commerce Thrive in the Hybrid Economy. New York: Penguin; 2008.

[11] Lidwell W, Butler J, Holden K. Universal Principles of Design: A Cross Disciplinary Reference. Rockport 2003.

[12] Locke L. The future of Facebook. Time 17 July 2007. 24 Jan 2009. http://www.time.com/time/business/article/0,8599,1644040,00.html.

[13] Manjoo F. Chuck Knol: Why Google's online encyclopedia will never be as good as Wikipedia. Slate 22 Sept 2008. 24 Jan 2009. http://slate.com/id/2200401.

[14] Nielsen J. Participation inequality: Encouraging more users to contribute. Alertbox 9 Oct 2006. 15 Jan 2009. http://www.useit.com/alertbox/participation_inequality.html.

[15] Nonnecke B, Preece J. Lurker demographics: Counting the silent. In: Proceedings of CHI 2000. The Hague: ACM; 2000.

[16] Nonnecke B, Preece J. Silent participants: Getting to know lurkers better. In: Lueg C, Fisher D, editors. From Usenet to CoWebs: Interacting with Social Information Spaces. Springer, 2003.

[17] O'Keefe P. Managing Online Forums. American Management Association; 2008.

[18] Owyang J. Social network stats: Facebook, myspace, reunion (Jan, 2008). Web log post. Web Strategy by Jeremiah 9 Jan 2008. 25 Jan 2009. http://www.web-strategist.com/blog/2008/01/09/social-network-stats-facebook-myspace-reunion-jan-2008/.

[19] People. Boxes and Arrows: The design behind the design. 25 Jan 2009 http://www.boxesandarrows.com/people?order=reputation.

[20] Preece J. Online Communities: Designing Usability, Supporting Sociability. Wiley; 2000.

[21] Record Web crowd flocks to CNN and Facebook's live inaugural stream. Los Angeles Times. 20 Jan 2009. http://latimesblogs.latimes.com/technology/2009/01/cnn-live-inagur.html. Accessed 1/24/09.

[22] remunerate. Dictionary.com Unabridged (v 1.1). Random House, Inc. 24 Jan 2009. Dictionary.com http://dictionary.reference.com/browse/remunerate.

[23] Rheingold H. The Virtual Community: Homesteading on the Electronic Frontier. New York: MIT P; 2000.

[24] Shuen A. Web 2.0: A Strategy Guide. O'Reilly; 2008.

[25] SuperNews! Social Networking Wars. Video blog post. Current 22 Apr 2008. 18 Jan. 2009. http://current.com/items/88913552/social_networking_wars.htm.

[26] Tynan-Wood C. Comment. Weblog comment. In: Perez S. editor. ReadWriteWeb. 20 Jan 2009. 24 Jan 2009. http://www.readwriteweb.com/archives/facebook_and_cnn_the_power_of_the_social_web_revealed.php.

[27] Virtual Conference Center Lobby. Virtual Conference Center. BGCA & Clemson University. 21 Jan 2009. 21 Jan 2009. http://glacier.clemson.edu/vcc2/.

[28] Wilson F. Free is a great way to make money. Web log post. A VC: Musings of a VC in NYC 25 Feb 2008. 25 Jan 2009. http://www.avc.com/a_vc/2008/02/free-is-a-great.html.

[29] Wilson F. My favorite business model. Web log post. A VC: Musings of a VC in NYC 23 March 2006. 12 Jan 2009. http://www.avc.com/a_vc/2006/03/my_favorite_bus.html.

[30] WoW Raid Manager: Oathsworn Raid Signups. OathSworn Guild. 17 Jan 2009. 17 Jan 2009 http://www.oathswornguild.com/wrm/index.php.

[31] WOW Web Stats for Oathsworn. WOW Web Stats. 17 Jan 2009. 17 Jan 2009. http://wowwebstats_com_2glcobdtaps45.

[32] Zuckerberg M. A great start to 2009. The Facebook Blog 7 Jan 2009. 12 Jan 2009. http://blog.facebook.com/.

[33] Zuckerberg R. Just the beginning. The Facebook Blog 24 Jan 2009. 24 Jan 2009. http://blog.facebook.com/blog.php?blog_id=company&m=1&y=2009.

CHAPTER 5
Influence

DIFFERENCES IN MEMBERS' SOCIAL EXPERIENCE NEEDS

SYNOPSIS

How do you help your individual members feel they are in control or have influence over their environment and yet still achieve a balance between meeting the needs of an individual on one hand and protecting the goals of the community on the other? This chapter addresses the art of designing influence or helping members gain a feeling of control in the environment.

First, the concept of "meaningful play" is introduced in order to better understand the need for balance between structural boundaries on the one hand and individual responsibility on the other. Like the "play" of a guitar string, if there's too much tension, you break the string (your members feel stifled by the community policies). If the string gets too loose, it can't vibrate and create a tone (your members don't know how to contribute productively). If you give too much individual responsibility, then it lacks the tension necessary for productive meaning. Too much social tension and too little individual responsibility stifle creativity and steal motivation from the individual. You need balance to create "play."

Next, the chapter introduces three of the major approaches to understanding who are members of social networks and communities:

1. Li and Bernoff's social technographic ladder
2. Kim's process five-stage membership life cycle
3. Wenger's five learning trajectories

The chapter explains how each of these membership models operates, but more importantly, it uses each of these models to examine the particular *influence needs* of each membership type in order to help designers understand what kinds of policies and community management strategies will have productive impact on the different members of their communities and networks.

The second half of the chapter provides specific techniques supported with actual examples that other designers and community managers can use that can serve as models and patterns for own networks.

INTRODUCTION

Of the four RIBS elements, remuneration is probably the best understood; however, if I had to pick the element that contributed most to the long-term success and overall health of a virtual community, I believe "influence" is the factor that would get my vote. When members feel the pull of influence on them in a community and once they feel they have "buy in" from a community, they'll often stay in that community and continue contributing to it even when it's no longer clear to them how they are being remunerated. And yet despite its power, how community architects and designers can create influence for members in a community rarely gets attention in discussions of what makes for a successful community.

THE IMPORTANCE OF INFLUENCE

We all want to shape our environment; we seek to control our environment so that they make us feel comfortable and safe. That's what humans do. According to evolutionary biologists, we humans like savannahs and plains—environments with the occasional tree. So we clear the brush and undergrowth around our houses so that we have yards that we then have to go out and mow regularly because that's the kind of environment we want. We influence the world around us and shape it to our liking. When we can't influence and change the environment, we leave and we find new environments that we can influence and change.

> ### INFLUENCE
> can be said to exist in a community when its members believe that they can control or at least shape the policies, procedures, topics, and standards of evidence used to persuade others in an online community or social network.

In the social realm, history is full of examples of communities where the people weren't able to control and influence their environment and so its members migrated. The Puritans left England for the colonies in order to create their version of utopia. Similarly, the Mormons in the United States migrated west to avoid persecution and thereby have influence. The modern Jewish state of Israel was created to give the Jews a homeland that they could control, and of course, Palestinians are still fighting to recover the influence they feel they lost. And lest these examples suggest that the desire for influence is always about religion, there are also examples of the need to have economic influence. Two examples of this are the Irish migrations to the Americas during the potato famine and Oklahoma families moving from the dust bowl-plagued Midwest to California to give their families a chance to control their own economic destinies. As humans, the need for influence seems primal, even in a social network or online community. As surely as Protestants left the Catholic Church in order to have a voice in the community, members of on online community in a social network will have the same need for influence.

THE CONSEQUENCE OF DISALLOWING INFLUENCE

So far, I've only provided examples of "big picture" influence needs; however, influence needs occur primarily at the personal, individual level. You've probably experienced this in your work life. I know I certainly have, and sometimes painfully as the following story will illustrate.

ANDREA'S INFLUENCE NEEDS

Years ago, I obtained a position as the director of a multimedia authoring studio where I had a team of six highly motivated, hard-charging graduate student staff members. The goal of this organization was to work with local businesses, industries, and university clients developing information products such as interactive tutorials, online help systems, digital training videos, and Web sites. These products would meet our clients' professional development needs, while providing the graduate students with an opportunity to apply what they were learning about multimedia design to real-world challenges. The studio was and continues to be a real success, but in the early days, it suffered some bumps because of my inexperience as a supervisor, particularly with one staff member whom I'll call Andrea.

Unfortunately, when we were first starting up the studio, we didn't have many clients or projects for the staff because our advertising hadn't taken effect. I needed to keep Andrea busy, and I wanted to give her the opportunity to learn development tools such as Adobe Premiere, InDesign, Macromedia Dreamweaver, Director, and other packages she would need to build a solid portfolio. Since we had training and advertising needs of our own in the studio, I began assigning Andrea projects that helped us internally. For example, I asked her to create a tutorial that would help new staff members learn to build Web sites. I asked her to design a new brochure advertising our services. I also asked her to develop a manual on policies and procedures for new staff. I met with her, explained what I wanted, and gave her documents and other resources I thought she needed as content for these products. I spelled out for her exactly what content to cover so that she could focus entirely on learning multimedia technologies and design.

I was stunned when Andrea informed me that she was quitting. I thought I had met her remuneration needs. From my perspective, she was getting paid a stipend for her time and she was getting the opportunity to learn skills that would help her obtain a job later—and Andrea acknowledged that although this was true—she was quitting because, as her supervisor, I hadn't paid sufficient attention to her influence needs. By "micromanaging her," she felt I had stolen her ability to impact the studio.

As a supervisor, I should have created an environment where Andrea could see how she could have an influence inside a set of boundaries, and I should have focused on creating a safe space for her to have that influence. I should have described the problems that needed to be addressed (i.e., set the boundaries by detailing why we needed to train the new staff on our working procedures). Then I should have invested my time in creating systems that would allow Andrea to locate the content and resources she needed to be successful in solving the problems for herself. I should have sought a better balance between Andrea's need for structure and direction on the one hand and ability to manage and control her own space on the other.

As the designers of social networks or virtual community managers, your role is essentially the same as was mine with Andrea. You need to understand the influence needs of your members first. Then you need to find a balance between keeping your members on task and performing inside reasonable boundaries, while still giving them the ability to play with and to control the space inside those boundaries.

PLAY

Poststructuralists have a useful term for describing this space of influence within the boundaries you will need to set for your network and communities. They call it the space of "play," and they intend for it to connote two different meanings. First, the "play" of influence in a community is analogous to the "play" in a guitar string. As the string travels back and forth across space, it outlines the boundaries of the space. It can only travel so far before it reaches the limits of flexibility and then it must stop and return. In this sense, "play" describes boundaries beyond which members of your community or network should not go.

POSTSTRUCTURALISM

is a school of thought that critiques the structuralist's view that there are universal truths or deep "structures" in the nature that are foundations of meaning. Poststructuralists believe that meaningful thought, insight, or intelligibility emerges from the interplay of contingent factors in social systems rather than self-evident "facts" found in nature.

PLAY

is the space designers create in their communities and networks by setting boundaries which guide an individual member's creativity so that other members of the social system enjoy and appreciate it.

Second, it also means "play" in the sense of creative freedom and joy. For just as a guitar string makes a beautiful sound as it vibrates across the play available to it, members of your network and community must perceive themselves to be able to have play in the space you provide. Of course, different types of people experience that sense of creative, joyful play in different ways. Some individuals, such as Andrea in the example given earlier, are able to play in open space where they find joy in broad, open-ended challenges that they need to solve. Others, however, are intimidated and frightened by open space of this sort. They need to see the organization and structure provided by a boundary. Their joy comes from finding creative ways to "stay inside the lines" and still achieve their goals. Of course, because there are still other ways to experience this sense of play, we need to begin to consider what kinds of members occupy social networks and communities.

TYPES OF MEMBERS AND NEED FOR INFLUENCE

Common sense tells us that virtually all human beings need some degree of influence in a community in order to remain in it. It's also the case that some members of the community are going to need more influence than others. This is a problem for community designers because when you're considering how to enable your users' influence in your community or network, you're almost immediately going to be confronted with the problem of making trade-offs. Different members are going to want to take the community in opposing directions, while other members won't have a preference on the direction of the community. As a result, you're going to need some means of differentiating between types of members and their influence needs. Currently, there are three popular classification systems available.

1. Li and Bernoff's social technographics ladder
2. Kim's five-stage membership life cycle
3. Wenger's five learning trajectories

FOCUS ON TECHNIQUE

Managers can employ several techniques in order to help them understand the amount of influence their users want and need. These include:

- Include in your application why they want to join.
- Have exit surveys for members who leave.
- Run periodic surveys asking what changes members would like to see made.

The social technographics ladder

Forrester Research analysts Charlene Li and Josh Bernoff, in their [4] book *Groundswell* [5], provide a ranking system for community members that they call the "social technographics ladder." According to Li and Bernoff's classification system, types of members can be categorized by the degree of participation that different groups can have in a social network. The more involvement a type has in a social network or community, the higher the "ladder rung" that group occupies on the social technographics ladder ([4], 43). There are six rungs on the ladder:

- Creators
- Critics
- Collectors
- Joiners
- Spectators
- Inactives

CREATORS

Creators occupy the uppermost rung on the ladder. These are the members who create the primary, initial content for a community or network. Depending on the type of delivery system and medium the community uses, Creators "write blog entries," "create Web pages," "upload video clips," record podcasts, "upload music files," publish newsgroup stories, and create new threads in e-mail groups ([4], 42–43). These are the members who make the most obvious contributions to your community, and Li and Bernoff argue that to be considered a member of the Creator rung, an individual needs to engage in one of the behaviors just given at least once a month. The name "Creator" is a little misleading because, while the term certainly conveys the sense these folks generate new content for the group, it doesn't really connote the regularity and repetition needed to be considered a Creator in the way, for example, that a term "active contributor" might suggest regular participation.

Interestingly, Li and Bernoff argue that a much higher percentage of Creators exist in communities than other researchers recognize. As discussed in the Remuneration chapter, Jakob Nielsen, for example, developed the "90–9–1 rule" because his research showed that, "in most online communities, 90% of users are lurkers who never contribute, 9% of users contribute a little, and 1% of users account for almost all the action" [5]. Conversely, Li and Bernoff cite a Forrester's 2007 survey of over 10,000 users that showed that, "in the United States, Creators represent 18% of the online adult population" ([4], 43).

The 90-9-1 rule—"In most online communities, 90% of users are lurkers who never contribute, 9% of users contribute a little, and 1% of users account for almost all the action" [5].

The influence needs of Creators

In terms of considering what you, as a designer, need to do to meet their influence needs, Creators' needs are probably pretty obvious. Creators want to shape and persuade the minds of other members. They want their "creations" to be read critically, yet fairly. Consequently, Creators will often want to have input into a network or community's policies regarding personal attacks, flaming, and what constitutes valid forms of evidence in persuasive arguments. But most of all they need to know they're being read and having some impact—even if that impact is negative. Creators can stand to be told that they're wrong; in fact, many believe that criticism is a form of respect. What they can't stand is no feedback at all.

FOCUS ON TECHNIQUE

Network and community managers can help members see their influence by showing the number of times a message has been viewed. See Technique #3 at the end of this chapter.

CRITICS

On the second rung of the social technographics ladder are *Critics*. Critics contribute to the community by adding content, but it's not as original as that of Creators. Whereas Creators will create a blog entry, Critics will comment on the entry and respond to it. And because commenting on someone else's ideas requires less energy and effort than creating the original content, the Critic rung is below the Creator rung on the social technographics ladder. Critics react to e-mail messages posted to listerv lists, they edit the information a Creator published on a wiki, and they "post ratings/reviews of products and services" ([4], 43). According to Li and Bertoff, 25% of U.S. adults online are Critics in some community. It's also interesting to note that the Critic and Creator categories aren't necessarily mutually exclusive, as Creators can also engage in the same behaviors as Critics do (which partially explains why Li and Bertoff's research reports participation numbers are so much higher than other researchers'). Still, their division between Creators and Critics is useful because it provides means of distinguishing between the simple "contributor" categories found in most systems.

The influence needs of Critics

The influence needs of Critics are very much aligned with that of Creators. They need to know that their comments on blogs are at least being viewed and they need to see if the number of stars that they assigned to a video posting or a product review aligns with other members of the community. Critics are consensus builders, in that regard, and they need feedback to help determine how the values in the network or community are lining up. In terms of influence on policies and governance, Critics are like Creators, and they will often want to have input into a network or community's policies regarding personal attacks, flaming, and what constitutes valid forms of evidence in persuasive arguments.

> **FOCUS ON TECHNIQUE**
>
> Managers can encourage participation by giving Elders opportunities to help lead the community. See Technique #12.

COLLECTORS

On the third rung of the ladder are *Collectors*. Collectors are an interesting group in the social technographics system because they serve a role beyond the simple archiver that their name suggests. According to Li and Bernoff, Collectors add value to and thus influence social networks and communities because they tend to sort the content created by Creators and Critics into ranked categories. In effect, they are a bit like the librarians of a community who, through their use of social bookmarking services such as Digg or del.icio.us, impose order on the chaotic and often inchoate content generated by the Creators and Critics.

WEB LINK

Digg
www.digg.com
del.icio.us
delicious.com

The influence needs of Collectors

Collectors need to know that they're collecting behaviors that are valued by the community; for example, they need to have questions sent to them asking if they have information in their archive that will help the community. They also need to see that the categories and terms that they are using to organize the information correlate in some way with that of other Collectors in the community. An excellent example of this feedback loop can be found on del .icio.us. When someone creates a bookmark on del.icio.us, they're prompted with tags that others have used previously to bookmark that site, which helps the Collectors see that they're contributing to the value add of others for the community. Collectors need occasionally to hear that their social bookmarks, archives, or collecting behaviors are valued by the community. For example, my wife is the team manager for the football team. As such, she constantly sends out e-mail messages to all of the parents on the high school football team providing information about uniforms or t-shirts or schedules, etc. But one of the things that she does is to bookmark directions to opponents' fields and their win–loss records. It means a great deal to her to hear from other parents that the collection of information that she provides has value for them, even though she didn't actually create it. She still takes pride in knowing that her "collection" impacted the community team parents, that there's consistent value being placed on information and there's comfort in knowing that those values are shared.

JOINERS

On the fourth rung are the *Joiners*. Frequently dismissed as mere lurkers and noncontributors in most other classification systems, Li and Bernoff's system recognizes that Joiners play a role in communities and have influence simply by virtue of the profiles that they choose to complete. For example, on networks such as LinkedIn and Facebook, a Joiner's profile can still provide a useful point of information that other members can use to help develop a sense of who they are addressing when they compose a message for the community.

The influence needs of Joiners

Joiners need to see that other people have viewed their profile information. They also want to know how their own information relates statistically to the community at large. They need to see that there are "X" number of people in the community and know that they've been counted. They need to see that their mere presence had influence. The needs of Joiners are analogous to people in a survey. When I respond, for example, to a salary survey from the Society for Technical Communication, I expect to receive a copy of the survey results so that I can verify that my numbers were counted and to see how I relate to others in the organization.

SPECTATORS

Spectators occupy the fifth rung of the ladder. This group benefits from and "consumes what the rest produce" ([4], 45). These are the folks who read the blogs, download and watch the videos or podcasts, read the forum postings, and so on. To their credit, Li and Bernoff once again avoid the commonplace view that Spectators are a drain on your network or community because they expend no energy on it. Instead, they observe that "since being a Spectator requires so much less effort than the other activities in the groundswell, it's no surprise that this is the largest group, with 48% of online adult Americans" ([4], 45). Like Nonnecke and Preece in their [6] study "Silent Participants [8]," the Spectator category does not occupy the bottom rung of the "ladder" because consumption is still a form of participation requiring some effort. The act of reading is, for example, still a kind of influence in a community as it implies appreciation for the content generated by the Creators and Critics. Without the energy expended by Spectators, the motivation to create content is lost. Through affirmation provided by the act of consumption, Spectators paradoxically become producers, and community managers who dismiss them as mere "lurkers" imperil their communities by ignoring their influence.

The influence needs of Spectators

Even though they don't need to be singled out in the same ways that Creators and Critics expect to receive name recognition for their contributions, Spectators do need to see that Creators and Critics think about and value the time that Spectators invest reading their blogs and postings or watching their videos. Spectators need to be recognized by Creators and Critics in order to be valued as members of the community. If Spectators feel neglected or ignored, then they may leave a community or network and stop supporting it through their consumption of the content that the Creators and Critics generate. The kind of recognition that Creators and Critics give Spectators occurs fairly frequently, but its value is often overlooked. Often you'll see messages posted in a forum that will refer to the Spectators. For example, a Creator might post a message that begins, "As many in this group already know …" or "I'm sure that many of us will agree …" or some other reference addressed to members who are Spectators in the community. These kinds of messages recognize the fact that Spectators are in an important and influential position to disagree with whatever assertions the Creator is making. This recognition of the influence of Spectators is extremely important for long-term community building.

INACTIVES

Finally, on the bottom rung of the social technographics ladder are the *Inactives*. Because Inactives expend no energy on behalf of the social network and don't participate, they appear on the lowest rung. Inactives don't read posts, don't connect via RSS feeds, and don't collect or organize information. Their influence is, thus, minimal at best. They can't even be considered lurkers because they aren't consuming and reading the community's content.

The influence needs of Inactives

The influence needs of Inactives aren't being met, which may be the reason that they have become inactive. While I don't want to suggest that inactivity in a community is always caused by the failure to have influence in a community, it certainly can be. Creators who fail to see that they're having influence will stop creating messages, just as Critics will stop commenting and Collectors will stop logging in and creating bookmarks. Spectators who don't feel they're appreciated by the Creators will abandon the effort required to read. Thus, rather than saying that Inactives have no influence needs because they're inactive, it's probably more accurate to say that Inactives may have all of the influence needs of the previous five membership types. Recognizing this and taking into consideration the unique influence needs of each membership type on the social technographics ladders (see Table 5.1 for a summary) can help you, as a designer or administrator, find ways to meet your members' influence needs so they don't become Inactives in the first place.

The membership life cycle model

The second model of membership types you can use to consider your members' influence needs is Kim's membership life cycle model. Amy Jo Kim is a visionary social architect whose company, Shufflebrain, has been breaking

Table 5-1	Social Technographics Ladder Member Types, Characteristics, and Influence Needs	
Member Type	**Characteristics**	**Influence Needs**
Creators	■ Create the primary, initial content for a community or network ■ Want to shape and persuade the minds of other members	■ Need to know they're being read and have some impact
Critics	■ Critics will comment on the entry Creators post ■ Consensus builders	■ Need feedback that helps them determine how values in the network or community are lining up
Collectors	■ Add value to social networks and communities because they sort the content created by Creators and Critics into ordered and ranked categories	■ Need to have questions sent to them asking if they have information in their archive that will help the community ■ Need to hear that their social bookmarks, archives, or collecting behaviors are valued by the community
Joiners	■ Have influence simply by virtue of the profiles that they choose to fill out and complete	■ Need to see that other people have viewed their profile information ■ Need to see that their mere presence had influence
Spectators	■ This group benefits from and "consumes what the rest produce" ([4], 45) ■ Implies appreciation for the content generated by the Creators and Critics	■ Need to see that Creators and Critics appreciate the time that they invest reading their blogs or postings or watching their videos
Inactives	■ Expend no energy on behalf of the social network and don't participate	■ Have all of the influence needs of the previous five membership types, but these needs aren't being met

new ground using smart games to create social architectures for clients such as eBay, Yahoo!, and Electronic Arts. In her classic book, *Community Building on the Web*, Kim uses a life cycle metaphor to generate her classification of membership types. Kim describes five "successive stages of community involvement" and illustrates how each stage correlates with a different membership type.

1. **Visitors**: people without a persistent identity in the community.
2. **Novices**: new members who need to learn the ropes and be introduced into community life.
3. **Regulars**: established members that [sic] are comfortably participating in community life.
4. **Leaders**: volunteers, contractors, and staff that [sic] keep the community running
5. **Elders**: long-time Regulars and Leaders who share their knowledge and pass along the culture [2], 118

VISITORS

The *Visitor* stage, as Kim points out, is often a surprisingly overlooked stage when thinking about membership and particularly when thinking about how members can have influence on communities. I'm constantly surprised by the number of social nets, especially online communities, that fail to provide Visitors with an adequate means of interacting with the community. When I talk to community leaders, they will invariably tell me that they really want to recruit new members to their site. However, they only use one recruiting mechanism. They allow Visitors to view a select number of messages on their site. They're so focused on meeting the needs of their core membership (which isn't a bad thing) that they overlook and marginalize Visitors' needs. Visitors need to perceive that they can have influence. They don't need to see their influence confirmed, but they need to see what user experience designers call "affordances," or opportunities for interaction. In other words, Visitors need to see that there are opportunities or mechanisms available for them to influence and have an impact on the community. You can see a really good example of this by looking at the early efforts of Twitter.

When I first learned about Twitter, one of my former graduate students, Brian Verhoeven, who was working as a new media editor for a Washington-based online newspaper, sent me an e-mail telling me about social networking tools that he used routinely to keep in touch with colleagues and friends. Brian and I had worked together to build a social network for a not-for-profit organization, so he knew that I was interested in these tools and he wanted me to use Twitter so that he and I could stay in touch. He told me that he and his colleagues used the site to send each other short questions and answers about projects they were working on at the time. As a result, in early 2006, I went to the Twitter.com site and saw a screen very much like the screen shown in Figure 5.1.

FOCUS ON TECHNIQUE

Network managers can help their members personalize their community space (as the Twitter posts do in Figure 5.1) by requiring profiles and allowing avatars. See Techniques #8 and #9 in the Techniques section of the chapter.

From my perspective as a new Visitor, I confess that I was baffled by this page. I could see that people were posting public messages and that there were ways to visually represent myself and, conversely, to recognize a friend like Brian, but there was nothing on the site that suggested to me that I could learn more about how Twitter functioned, that I could learn more about how the notion of "followers" worked, or that I could learn how to become a member of the community and have influence in it. Basically, from a Visitor's perspective it looked to me like Twitter was really nothing more than a puerile means of indulging in self-aggrandizement. The only motivation I saw for participating in this was to stroke your exhibitionist tendencies. As a Visitor, the only way that I saw that I could have influence in the community, if there even was a community, would be to make sarcastic or outrageous comments that would either inflame or amuse the audience of the site, an audience who was completely hidden from me except for the few messages I saw on the page at the time. As a result, I thanked Brian for telling me about Twitter and told him that I looked at the site briefly but I would have to come back to it and investigate it in more detail when I had more time. In short, I dissed it because the designers of the site hadn't provided me with an opportunity to see how I could have a positive influence on people that I cared about.

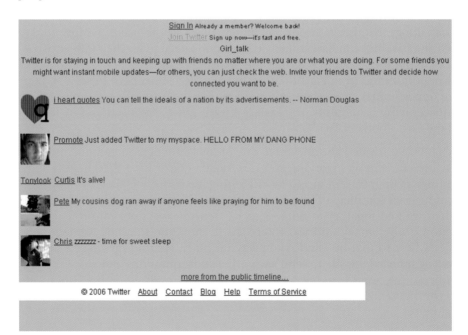

FIGURE 5.1
Twitter from a Visitor's perspective in October 2006.

However, as Figure 5.2 illustrates, evidently I hit Twitter at just the wrong time because its designers did eventually recognize the needs of Visitors like me and, possibly through usability testing of the site, realized that it wasn't going to grow into the phenomenon it has become today without providing some affordances for Visitors, some way for Visitors to understand how they might contribute to the community. As shown in Figure 5.2, the center of the screen is occupied by a Flash slideshow that illustrates the three steps that a Visitor would go through in order to become a new member of Twitter. More importantly, it helps Visitors understand what I didn't understand when I first saw the site, which is that Twitter allows you to have "followers" and to create your own network of social contacts.

FIGURE 5.2
Twitter from a Visitor's perspective in December 2006.

FOCUS ON TECHNIQUES

Another way managers can show new members how they can have influence is to create a visitor's center, which gives all the initial information a Visitor, and potential new members, needs about the community. See Technique #10.

NOVICE

The second phase of Kim's membership life cycle is the *Novice* phase and, as the name clearly suggests, this phase is where new members go through the process of learning the "secret handshakes," policies, rituals, and normal practices of the community or network. How long someone remains a Novice depends dramatically on the type of social network or community and the speed of its distribution channels. In the past, when I've become a member of a closed, private listserv-based discussion group of industry professionals, I've found that it can take several months before I pass through the Novice phase. The complexity of the values in a professional discourse community takes time for me to learn and absorb. Include the fact that e-mail conversations surrounding a particular thread typically can take 3, 4, or 5 days before they evolve means that I, as a Novice, have to spend a considerable amount of time in the community before I'm exposed to a sufficient number of conversations to have developed a sense of the discursive practices of that community. A system like Facebook, however, doesn't take nearly as long for the Novice to begin to develop a sense of how the society works. When I first became a member of Facebook, it took a few hours and log-ins to learn about applications, how to become a fan, and how to post on other people's walls, but the feedback loops are so fast and the exposure to different conversations is much more immersive on a network like Facebook that the Novice phase is considerably shorter.

The influence needs of Novices

In terms of meeting their influence needs, Novices are much more sensitive to the need for confirmation than other groups. Because they're just becoming members of a society, they need confirmation much more quickly that their messages have been read and they need to see responses and comments or they're very likely to drop out.

NOVICES' NEED FOR IMMEDIATE FEEDBACK

I recently had a person join one of the e-mail-based usability communities that I maintain, and he stayed in the group for a couple of weeks and got a feel for how it worked, went through the normal rituals of learning how people interacted with each other, what the topics were, how new conversations got started, and was encouraged to participate. So he posted a message at 10:26 a.m. on a Monday. By 11:15 a.m. that same Monday he had contacted me, as the listowner of the community, asking if his message had been posted and redistributed. If it had, he wanted to know why nobody had responded yet and how he should have written the message so that people in the group would take it seriously. Of course, because so little time had passed since he sent his e-mail to the group, it was likely that many of the messages were still sitting in the mail queue waiting to be distributed around the Internet. Few members of the community had even received the message, particularly people who receive their messages in a digested form. So I responded to him and explained that it wasn't unusual for an e-mail message to take at least 24 hours before it filtered out to everyone in the community and that oftentimes it could take 6 to 8 hours even after that before people found time to respond. Fortunately, a member of the advisory council who had been trained to respond when new members posted so that new members would get quick feedback did respond to the message. Furthermore, she did so in a way so that it generated an excellent thread that the entire community enjoyed. But the point is, again, that Novices really need that immediate feedback. They need to feel like they're having an influence on others or they'll abandon the group.

FOCUS ON TECHNIQUE

Setting up an advisory council whose members fill a variety of community needs, such as responding to new members' posts, can make your community much stronger. See Technique #1.

MEMBERSHIP

Membership is, of course, that phase when you are part of a community; you understand how it functions; and you engage in learning new patterns, new trends, and new practices as they emerge, but you have a sufficient history with the community such that these new practices and procedures don't typically cause you a great deal of distress. As a Member, you clearly understand your role in the community and you understand how to influence the community and take it in directions that you wish for it to go. You know how to suggest new policies to the leadership or how to have an impact on the community's governance.

The influence needs of Members

In terms of seeing their influence needs in a community, Members are like Creators, Critics, and Spectators in the social technographics ladder system. They need to see that their messages are being read or, when they're reading other people's messages, they need to see that there's an appreciation of that effort that they invest in keeping up with the messages. Members are also most likely to be concerned about policies in the community and the governance of the community. They're more likely to want to have influence over the policies and practices that other Members follow and they also need to see that those policies are being policed actively by the leadership.

LEADERSHIP

The fourth stage of Kim's life cycle is *Leadership*. The idea here is that once a member has become established, made a commitment to the community, and understands its practices, they are then able to assume a leadership role in the community. However, it's probably the case that not everyone in a community goes through this phase. Critics of Kim's model might argue that there are certainly established members of communities who can serve as role models for the community and who can "lead by example" without actually assuming the title of "Leader." Nevertheless, the leadership role is clearly a critical role to the success of a community, and Kim identifies seven possible leadership roles that can be assigned, depending on the type of community that's operating.

- **Support Providers** answer questions and help members solve problems they're having with the system
- **Hosts** keep the key community activities (games, conversations, shopping, etc.) running smoothly
- **Greeters** welcome newcomers, show them around, and teach them the ropes
- **Cops** remove disruptive members and/or inappropriate content
- **Event Coordinators** plan, coordinate, and run one-time and regular events
- **Teachers** train community leaders, offer classes, or provide tutoring
- **Merchants** run shops, provide services, and fuel the community economy

[2], 145

The influence needs of Leaders

In terms of seeing that their influence needs are being met, Leaders have perhaps the most at stake. Leaders are more concerned about the governance, policies, and day-to-day practices that go on in the network and community. Oftentimes they're less interested in receiving feedback on whether their content contributions are having an impact and they're more interested in seeing that they're having an influence on generating content from others. It's critical that Leaders always feel like their voices are being listened to in terms of the policies that are being set and the governance of the community. The quickest way to lose Leaders in the community is to make them feel like their voice isn't being heard and that they're being ignored. You can disagree with them, but you can't ignore them.

ELDERS

The final stage that Kim identifies in her life cycle model is that of the *Elder*. Elders are long-term members of a community who are essentially keepers of the community's stories, culture, and rituals, which—as shown in the next chapter on Belonging—is critical to community success. They've been members for a long time and have exerted tremendous influence on and earned the respect of the members. Elders have influenced and shaped the community in clearly recognizable ways, and their influence and contributions are honored by the majority of the established membership.

The influence needs of Elders

Elders' influence needs are somewhat different than any of the other five types. Like Leaders, Elders are often less concerned about whether their content contributions are being read. They don't need the immediate feedback that Novices do; however, they do need to have their long-time contributions recognized. They need to have their relationship with the community recognized. They are offended easily when the stories for which they have become famous, and the name recognition associated with them, are infringed upon by others. They also need to be reassured that the emotional bonds that exist in a community are operating with them. There's very little new content for them, as they've done and seen it all already. Consequently, what's important for Elders are the relationships they have with other members in the community. Hence, they need to see messages such as "as Bob has pointed out many times before" or "I'm sure everyone is thinking of Sally's famous mantra here." Messages or blogs that make references such as these are important to Elders because, first of all, the use of their first names in this way is a kind of epidictic demonstration of the Elder's familiar relationship with the group. Everyone knows Bob by his first name in this context, even though there may be several "Bobs" in the group. The form of address, in other words, is almost a celebration of the special relationship Bob has with others. Second, these messages presuppose the members' recognition of Bob or Sally's contributions to the community. A Novice in the group may not know Sally's actual mantra, but there won't be any question in the Novice's mind about who owns it or about Sally's role in the group.

Summary

Kim's five-phase life cycle model is useful because it provides a temporal diachronic view of the membership that offers a different perspective on membership than that of Li and Bernoff. Where Li and Bernoff's model helps us understand how a group like their Spectators can actually have influence in a community, Kim's model helps us understand how Visitors and Elders can influence communities. Novices, Members, and Leaders are obvious within a community and it's relatively easy to find ways of meeting their needs for influence. Visitors and Elders, however, are easier to overlook and yet equally valuable and also deserving of our attention.

The five trajectories of learners

Li and Bernoff organized their taxonomy of membership around degrees of participation. Kim organized her model around the membership life cycle. The third membership model we look at is organized around the sense of identity that a member feels based on his or her "trajectory" through a discourse community. This model is based on Etienne Wenger's "five trajectories of learners' identities," which were articulated in his 1998 book *Communities of Practice.* However, in order to understand what Wenger means by "trajectories" and how they differ from Kim's life cycle stages, it is useful to go back even further to Lave and Wenger's [3] book *Situated Learning: Legitimate Peripheral Participation.*

In *Situated Learning*, Lave and Wenger argue that learning is most effective in what they call situated learning within communities of practice. As I also argued in the previous chapter, Lave and Wenger reject the view of knowledge as a collection of static and memorizable facts. They write:

> Conventional explanations view learning as a process by which a learner internalizes knowledge, whether "discovered," "transmitted" from others, or "experienced in interaction" with others. This focus on internalization [...] establishes a sharp dichotomy between inside and outside, suggests that knowledge is largely cerebral, and takes the individual as the nonproblematic unit of analysis. Furthermore, learning as internalization is too easily construed as an unproblematic process of absorbing the given, as a matter of transmission and assimilation.
>
> **[3], 47**

In other words, learners, i.e., novices, don't acquire the professional skills of a community of practice by accumulating a collection of reified facts about the profession. Instead, they are socialized into a community through apprenticeship. Lave and Wenger thus examined the apprenticeships of midwives in Yucatec, tailors in Vai and Gola, quartermasters in the U.S. Navy, meat cutters in trade schools, and nondrinking alcoholics into Alcoholics Anonymous. Through their examination, they sought to better understand how novice tailors, for example, learned to be professional tailors through the novices' observations of and interactions with practicing professionals and master tailors in that community of practice. By examining the key members in those apprenticeship communities, Lave and Wenger saw three sets of relationships emerge, which they described as follows:

> In situations where learning-in-practice takes the form of apprenticeship, succeeding generations of participants give rise to what in its simplest form is a triadic set of relations: The community of practice encompasses apprentices, young masters with apprentices, and masters some of whose apprentices have themselves become masters. But there are other inflection points as well, where journeyfolk, not yet masters, are relative old-timers with respect to newcomers.
>
> **[3], 56**

In his 1998 work, *Communities of Practice*, Wenger builds on these earlier observations about relationships between learners and other members in a community of practice, and takes on the question of how learners develop an identity in a community, i.e., when do college chemistry students stop thinking about themselves as students and start thinking about themselves as chemists? Also, how are peoples' senses of identity changed as they move from one communal space into another?

FOCUS ON TECHNIQUE

In order for members to develop an identity in a community they must first feel safe in that community. Managers can use a variety of techniques, including:

- Publish and enforce safety policies. (Technique #14)
- Have a "report-a-problem" on every page of the site. (Technique #4)
- Respond to every concern and explain policy decisions, but keep "administrivia" out of the community discussion. (Technique #2)

In order to answer these questions, Wenger posits that there are five different trajectories that individuals can take. Trajectories basically describe the individual's position relative to the community and how they relate in time to the community. This relationship becomes the membership category and role, which they then play in the community. Wenger explains the five trajectories as follows:

- **Peripheral trajectories.** By choice or by necessity, some trajectories never lead to full participation. However, they may well provide a kind of access to a community and its practice that becomes significant enough to contribute to one's identity.
- **Inbound trajectories.** Newcomers are joining the community with the prospect of becoming full participants in its practice. Their identities are invested in their future participation, even though their present participation may be peripheral.
- **Insider trajectories.** The formation of an identity does not end with full membership. The evolution of the practice continues—new events, new demands, new inventions, and new generations all create occasions for renegotiating one's identity.
- **Boundary trajectories.** Some trajectories find their value in spanning boundaries and linking communities of practice. Sustaining an identity across boundaries is one of the most delicate challenges of this kind of brokering work […].
- **Outbound trajectories.** Some trajectories lead out of a community, as when children grow up. What matters then is how a form of participation enables what comes next.

[8], 154–155

While Wenger's five trajectories are certainly similar to Kim's life cycle model in that they both recognize a diachronic and temporal dimension in types of membership, some major differences need to be preserved.

TRAJECTORIES
describe the individual's position relative to the community over time. A trajectory maps their temporal relationship to the community's boundaries.

If we wish to use these three models to explore the wider and richer view of membership types that may exist in networks and communities, it would be a mistake to attempt to map Wenger's five trajectories onto the five stages of Kim's model. However, many people do attempt to smash the two systems together, as evidenced in the way that the authors of the Wikipedia entry for "Virtual Communities" attempt. Because Wikipedia gives us a snapshot of a socially constructed understanding of a topic (at least for topics that have been on Wikipedia long enough to have been thoroughly vetted by a number of readers), it is a very useful means of capturing the way groups typically interpret information.

LEARNING TRAJECTORY—ONLINE COMMUNITY PARTICIPATION

Example—YouTube

Peripheral (Lurker)—Observing the community and viewing content. Does not add to the community content or discussion. *The user occasionally goes onto YouTube.com to check out a video that someone has directed them to.*

Inbound (Novice)—Just beginning to engage the community. Starts to provide content. Tentatively interacts in a few discussions. The user comments on other user's videos. Potentially posts a video of their own.

Insider (Regular)—Consistently adds to the community discussion and content. Interacts with other users. Regularly posts videos. *Either videos they have found or made themselves. Makes a concerted effort to comment and rate other user's videos.*

Boundary (Leader)—Recognized as a veteran participant. Connects with regulars to make higher concepts ideas. Community grants their opinion greater consideration. *The user has become recognized as a contributor to watch. Possibly their videos are podcasts commenting on the state of YouTube and its community. The user would not consider watching another user's videos without commenting on them. Will often correct a user in behavior the community considers inappropriate. Will reference other user's videos in their comments as a way to cross link content.*

Outbound (Elder)—Leaves the community for a variety of reasons. Interests have changed. Community has moved in a direction that doesn't agree with. Lack of time. *User got a new job that takes up too much time to maintain a constant presence in the community.*

Virtual community, *Wikipedia*, 18 Jan. 2009 [7]

This entry makes the obvious connection between Wenger's Inbound trajectory and Kim's Novice, and it certainly seems reasonable to connect Wenger's "Insider" trajectory with Regulars in the community, or those Kim called "members." Wenger's use of "newcomers" to describe individuals whose identity within the group is defined by their inbound trajectory certainly lends itself to this connection. Consequently, it's reasonable to assume that the influence needs of Kim's Novices and Members are the same as those of the inbound and insider trajectories.

FOCUS ON TECHNIQUE

While it's important for all members of the community to interact, there are benefits for managers to provide opportunities for Novices to interact with each other. See Technique #11.

However, the connections break down rapidly after these two observations have been made. To suggest that Kim's view of Elders is that they are "outbound" and that *all* Elders are in the process of leaving the community does violence to both Kim's and Wenger's constructs here. Kim argued, as have I, that you need to preserve your Elders in a community. Because they play a critical role of preserving and transmitting the institutional knowledge about the community in Kim's system, it's probably unproductive and dismissive to think of your Elders as on their way out of your community or network. Furthermore, Wenger's "outbound" trajectory isn't his effort to exclude members who are leaving. Instead, it's

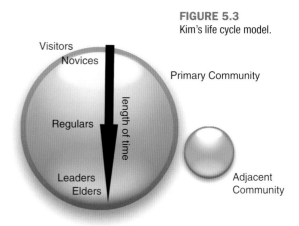

FIGURE 5.3
Kim's life cycle model.

an opportunity to extend the "play" in a community's or network's boundaries. As Wenger says, the influence needs for members who fall into this category, "What matters then is how a form of participation enables what comes next" ([8], 155). What outbound members are seeking, in other words, is a means of playing with the boundaries of the community or network so that they can continue to have relationships with others inside the community.

As a comparison of Figures 5.3 and 5.4 illustrates, there's a similar problem with connecting Kim's "Leaders" with Wenger's "boundary" trajectory. Insiders and Regular members can also be Leaders. For example, in several communities I maintain, Regular members can volunteer to be mentors and greeters, thereby playing a leadership role in the community by helping peripherals and Visitors see how they can have influence in the community and by helping Novices learn how to play with the community's procedures and practices. Wenger's boundary category isn't merely about being a leader or even a "veteran." Instead, boundary members actually occupy a space in multiple communities; they cross boundaries. They bring the insights and perspectives of one community to bear on another community that they also inhabit because they maintain an identity in both. Someone who is, for example, an insider in the graphic designer community of practice but who is a novice in the user experience and interface design community would be an example of this. Although she might be a novice among user experience designers, she could still speak from her knowledge of graphic design and have influence on a conversation among interface designers. It's her identity across the boundaries of both of these communities

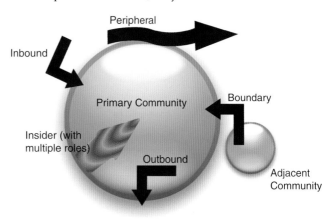

FIGURE 5.4
Wenger's trajectories.

that enables her influence. She might, for example, help interface designers understand how the concept of the "rule of thirds" from graphic design could be applied to interfaces in order to enhance users' experiences. If, however, as a community or network designer, you create policies that are so restrictive and lack sufficient play in them so that she couldn't introduce a concept such as the rule of thirds into the conversation, then Wenger's concept of a boundary trajectory membership type would help you, as a designer, understand and explain how you failed to meet her influence needs.

In summary, Wenger's five trajectories, Kim's life cycle model, and Li and Bernoff's social technographics ladder are all useful ways of raising your consciousness about the different types of members that you're going to have in your social network and your communities.

Each helps you better recognize the need for influence that different member types have so that you can then consider how to create boundaries for your sites that both have and enable play in your users' influence.

TECHNIQUES

So what are some of the ways that you can help ensure that your social network or community meets the influence needs of different members of your group? It's not possible to provide an exhaustive list since new techniques are emerging all the time and since the ways that your members can have influence will vary tremendously depending on the type of distribution media, policies, organizational structure, and purpose your network has. Nevertheless, the following techniques or strategies have been successful for communities I've built or which I've observed.

CHECKLIST OF TECHNIQUES
1. Set up an advisory council
2. Respond to every concern without "administrivia"
3. Show the number of times that a message has been viewed
4. Have a "report-a-problem" on every page of the site
5. Include in your application why they want to join
6. Have exit surveys
7. Run periodic surveys
8. Allow avatars
9. Require profiles
10. Create a visitor's center
11. Put novices with novices
12. Give Elders opportunities
13. Demand respect
14. Publish and enforce safety policies

1. SET UP AN ADVISORY COUNCIL

Creating an advisory council, an executive board, a leadership council, or a board of governors—whatever you call it—has been, in my experience, one of the most useful things that I've done in the networks and communities I maintain to help members feel like they have influence. Over time, I've learned that advisory councils or boards are worth every second of time you invest in them. Today, if I'm starting a large community that is going to have more than 60–70 people, I would rarely consider not using an advisory council.

But it wasn't always that way. Back in the late 1980s when listserv lists were the most popular means of communicating, the model for governing or managing a community was to have a single "listowner." The problem that I experienced as the sole "listowner" for several communities back in the 1980s was that I had too much power. I mean I had too much power in a couple of different ways. First, whenever I would step into the middle of a flame war, take someone to task for being excessively sarcastic in their e-mails, or "cyberexecute" someone for spamming the community—whenever I took some kind of administrative action as the sole listowner—I would invariably get criticized for my unilateral and independent actions. Although I always tried to act in what I thought was in the best interest of the whole community and tried to make clear to my community members that I was not letting personal friendships or bias influence the policy decisions I was forced to make as the listowner, it didn't matter. My motives as the listowner were almost always attacked.

Thus, when I say I had too much power, part of what I mean is that there was a danger that the community would become fragmented and Balkanized around any perceived favoritism on the part of a sole listowner. It's not in the best interest of a long-term, sustainable network for members of the network to feel like the only way they can have influence in the community is by addressing the particular and contingent and possibly petty needs of a single individual. If members feel that they have to kowtow to the needs of a single character in order to have influence in the community, it's unlikely that they're not going to run afoul of that individual at some point. Consider, for example, the criticism that Apple endured as a result of Steve Jobs' management style. Jobs wields so much influence over the design of Apple's products that the company's stock dropped when it was announced that he was suffering from a chronic illness, and despite Apple's success, Jobs has been widely criticized for demanding personal control of all design decisions.

It's also the case that enduring this kind of criticism from the membership is really hard on the manager because of the kind of attacks that you suffer. You need and may even have a pretty thick skin, but eventually a sole listowner, forum manager, or network system administrator is going to get worn down and abandon the cause. Eventually they're going to get tired of the snotty, unfair, spleen-venting remarks that cast aspersions on their parentage and character, and even though community managers are ultimately the glue that holds the community together, they're going to quit. Obviously, when that happens, it's not in the best interests of a long-term, sustained community or network.

But when I say that the sole listowner, forum manager, or sysadmin has too much power, I also mean that I needed help to keep from making stupid mistakes. Back in the 1980s I made a number of mistakes in the management of groups that I was maintaining as a sole listowner because I lacked the alternative perspectives that are sometimes necessary in order to interpret an event accurately. Messages that I might read as an overly defensive unreasonable argument could turn out to have an entirely different meaning when put in some other context. Frequently, for example, I found that independent industry consultants in communities I maintained read messages in a radically different way than did academic members of a community. Similarly, I found tremendous differences between international cultures in communities I maintained. Forms of address that I found insulting from my perspective turned out to be the "norm" for certain European audiences. I needed, as a result, the advice of Elders and Leaders in the communities I was maintaining.

Feeding and caring for your council

I began setting up what I called advisory councils for communities I maintained back in the early 1990s, and over the years, we have developed a series of practices and policies that have made these councils very successful for me. One of the first things that I would recommend when setting up a leadership council, advisory council, executive board, or whatever you decide to call it is that members of the council be *representative of different constituencies* in the network or community. Representation of key stake holders in the community is important if members of your community are going to feel like they have influence over policy decisions.

It's also critical that *members of the board or council select each other* for membership. Hand-picked members by a sole listowner, network administrator, or forum manager do little to mitigate against accusations of favoritism and personal bias. It's also the case that, at least in my experience with board members, the council will fall apart if the members can't work with each other and don't share a personal connection somehow. They understand those relationships far better than I ever could and I've learned the hard way that if somebody has a reservation about another potential board member, even if it's only one person's reservation, it's better to leave the nominee off the council.

Before members are invited, they have to agree, in advance, that all the *deliberations that go on in the group are kept in the strictest confidence*. No one will share information, even about topics the council is discussing, without the approval of the rest of the council. No one can speak on behalf of the council or even about the council without the approval of the council. This policy has been critical to the success of the councils and boards that I have maintained because it's the only way you can ensure that you're protecting your board members. No one is going to want to sit and participate in a group that everyone knows will be charged with talking about the inappropriate or potentially inappropriate behaviors of other colleagues in a professional community unless they can do so without fear of retribution. You need to protect your council members from the potential for professional abuse. Council members need to know that they're not going to lose potential customers, clients, or other professional opportunities because of their service. Thus, keeping the messages and deliberations of the council in strict confidence protects council members from anyone being able to identify a particular individual as having criticized them personally. And requiring that *the council always speak with one voice* creates a sense of consensus and prevents any individual member of the council from being singled out for potentially punitive treatment.

In order for the council to function effectively, the *listowner or network administrator needs to serve as the facilitator/leader* for all the discussions. The facilitator needs to:

- set the agenda
- call questions when it's time for a vote
- make very clear to the members what is the point of adjudication in conversations
- set some sort of time frame for deliberation

I've tried to run councils where all the members trade off roles so that the facilitator or chair will rotate. Other times I've tried to run councils where there was no chair role and the person who introduces an issue or topic for discussion manages and facilitates the discussion. Unfortunately, those systems don't tend to work as effectively as having someone whom everyone recognizes as the "administrator" lead the discussion. Although I personally like the idea that "we're all leaders" in a group, and I thought that sharing the facilitator role would also ensure that participants share influence, this approach hasn't worked as effectively for my councils as I'd like. Somehow, when it's your "job" to lead the discussion, it depersonalizes discussion and drains a lot of the drama out. Participants realize that they're not arguing with a person and, instead, they're addressing an action or a potential action. On the flip side, when council members operate as facilitators of the discussion rather than as an *ex officio* administrator, then they can't have an unbiased voice because *their role on the council is to have an opinion* and to express and defend that opinion. Council members are supposed to "have a dog in every hunt" and they're there in order to give their individual perspective and to represent a particular point of view. Consequently, it's difficult for the other members and the members leading the discussion not to feel this inherent conflict of interest and to be compromised by it.

Another important point is that everyone on the council is clear about how consensus is achieved. This may sound silly, yet I've found that there are some startlingly different understandings of what the term "consensus" actually means. At academic department meetings, I've had the chair of my department inform us that "consensus forms in the mind of the chair." Other people believe that consensus requires a majority vote, and I've even had some members of my councils tell me that consensus required unanimous agreement.

Because of this confusion over what consensus actually entails, the standard of consensus used on my advisory councils and boards is that I will state for the group what appears to be the majority view after listening to the conversation and the different points of view and then I explicitly request that the members correct any misunderstanding that I may have developed over the course of the conversation. Usually after a day or two of having given people an opportunity to respond to the statement of consensus, whatever position has been articulated becomes the decision of the council. There is disagreement, and certainly individual members can disagree with the council's view, so the standard is not unanimous consent. However, we all agree to abide by the council's majority decision.

2. RESPOND TO EVERY CONCERN WITHOUT "ADMINISTRIVIA"

This is more difficult to do on a listserv list or in a live chat channel than it is on a Web-based community or social network. But the idea here is that it's important to let your members know why the advisory council or board made the decision that it did on some policy. Chances are that members in the community had differing views and they need to see some evidence that those views were taken into consideration, even if they weren't adopted. If you don't do this, as the community manager, and you allow your members to feel that their input was dismissed and ignored, you run a serious risk of losing those members.

On Web-based communities, it's fairly easy to document these kinds of decisions by creating a new forum topic or a special Web page where the council maintains a blog explaining the issue and how it was resolved. In the listserv communities that I maintain, providing this kind of feedback is a little more difficult. Oftentimes the kinds of decisions and policies that the council has to address really don't influence the entire community at the time. For example, you may be dealing with a single individual who posted a message that was borderline spam. It might have been, for example, brochureware pretending to be an actual contribution to the community's conversation. If in an e-mail community the council posts a message explaining its decisions in response to every issue of this type, there are at least two consequences. First, the people involved in the issue may feel humiliated and victimized. Not only will they leave, but other members who perceive they are being humiliated and victimized will also leave. Second, the amount of traffic will disrupt the "flow" of the community experience. Members of the community will become annoyed with what they perceive as a high signal-to-noise ratio and they'll leave. The technique that I often use to get around this problem is to post an e-mail message to the community every other month summarizing the decisions that the council or board has made. You can see an example of this in Figure 5.5.

The advantage to this process is that the names are anonymous and you can refer to situations long enough after they have occurred so that no one feels that they're being unfairly singled out, and yet, at the same time, the community is made aware that policies are being enforced and they have input into the decisions that are being made.

```
[Community name] Advisory Council Update

The Advisory Council works with the listowner to help
decide questions of list policy and enforce the list
rules. Periodically, we publish a message to keep list
members informed about the recent activities of the
Advisory Council and how issues have been handled.

-- The Council recently answered questions about
   [insert member questions answered by the Council]

-- Council members revisited [insert policies the
   Council discussed and what revision was or was not
   taken]

-- Council members took action on [insert information
   about policies which had to be enforced during the
   period]

If you have information which you feel would be of
interest to the community but would like to make sure
it is appropriate, please feel free to contact the
Advisory Council. Address your message to [insert
address].  Your message will be forwarded to the
Council members, the issue will be discussed, and a
representative of the Council will respond in a few
days.

On behalf of the Advisory Council,

[insert Council Member's name]
```

FIGURE 5.5
Standardized council report form.

3. SHOW THE NUMBER OF TIMES THAT A MESSAGE HAS BEEN VIEWED

As we saw when we discussed the Creators and Critics category, membership types with Li and Bernoff's system, these types of individuals derive satisfaction from knowing how many times their messages have been viewed. I have a colleague, for example, who wanted to start raising African cichlids, a type of tropical fish that is notoriously touchy about the pH balance of the water and the types of mineral salts necessary to keep the fish healthy and happy. He began researching the different types of filtration systems and tank set-up options needed to maintain these types of fish and posted the information that

Give visual feedback—the Remuneration chapter described giving stars or visual feedback on the frequency of postings a member makes and how useful members found them. Slashdot, for example, uses "karma points" to give visual feedback on the usefulness of postings.

he found through his research to an online tropical fish community. Because this online community provides the number of views of the postings and also categorizes them by popularity, my colleague was able to see that his messages were the most viewed messages in the history of that community—a fact that is so important to him that he never neglects to mention it when he comes over to my house and sees my own collection of cichlids. He takes justifiable pride in the influence he has had helping others in this hobbyist community.

Figure 5.6 illustrates how we used this same technique in the form of a "Most Popular Post Page" for the Boys and Girls Clubs of America's (BGCA) Virtual Conference Center site. One of the interesting observations that can be made about this particular site is the ways that members of the BGCA used these page view counts to convince their managers that they were having a positive influence in their professional organization. We learned, anecdotally, that originators of the "three ways to recognize your staff" thread were citing the fact that the thread had over 22,000 people views as evidence of their influence and the value they had added to the organization. They wanted their supervisors to recognize their influence during their annual evaluations and used the statistics as leverage.

FIGURE 5.6
Sample of most popular post page.

4. HAVE A "REPORT-A-PROBLEM" ON EVERY PAGE OF THE SITE

WEB LINK

Slashdot
www.slashdot.com

In the listserv communities that I run, I've already mentioned how I send out regular summaries of the activities of the advisory board or councils of those communities. Consequently, members of these communities are made aware of the fact that they have an opportunity to influence the administration and governance of the community by providing feedback to the council. In Web-based communities, however, this goal is a little more difficult to achieve because they use a hypertextual pull technology that makes it more difficult to know what users are actually looking at. You need to find alternative methods of encouraging users to see how they can have influence in the policy making of the community. One simple technique for doing this, however, is to put a "report-a-problem" link on every page of the site. Figure 5.7 not only shows how you can use the "contact" information in the navigation space on the left side of the screen to allow users

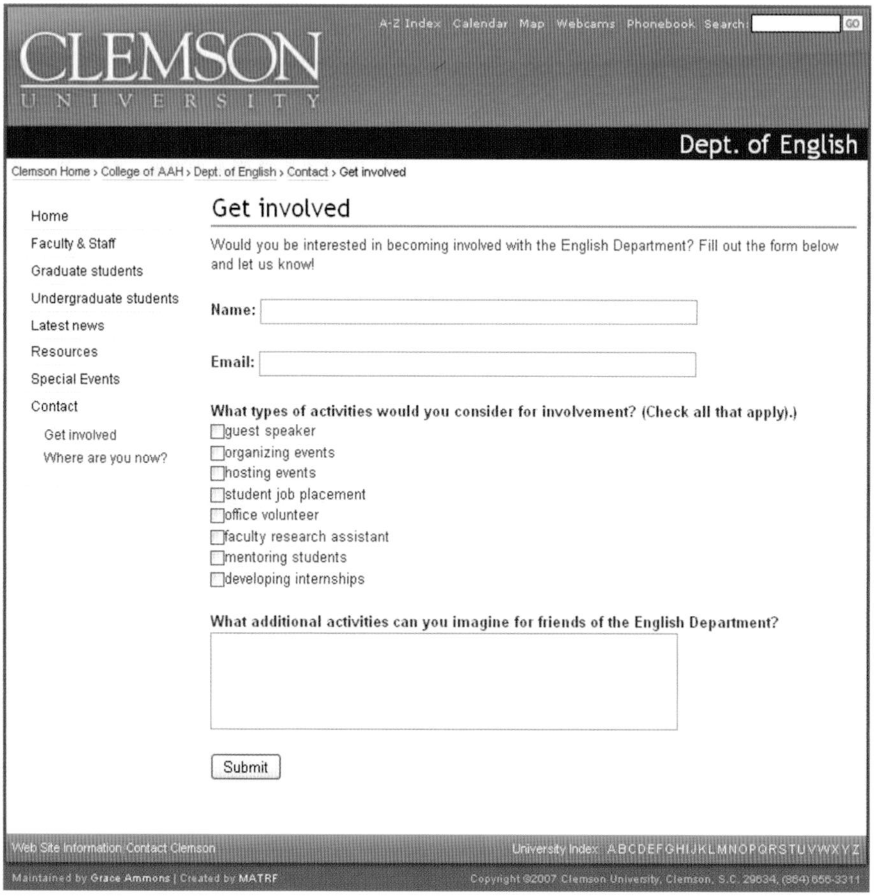

FIGURE 5.7
Sample report a problem/get involved page.

to report problems, it also shows how you can guide users in even more productive ways to have influence and to get involved in a community than simply reporting a problem.

Obviously, you need to make sure you give some thought to what kind of problem is likely to be reported on the particular page. If the pages are on your online forum pages, the kinds of problems that users might be reporting there are problems with other members' postings. For example, they might be reporting a problem with a copyright violation or a flame in someone else's posting. Thus, you might want the report to go directly to your moderator and advisory board. However, on administrative pages such as pages for changing a user profile on a site and updating a password, the problems users might be reporting are of a functionality or usability nature. In those cases, the problem obviously needs to go to your system administrator and programming team.

5. INCLUDE IN YOUR APPLICATION WHY THEY WANT TO JOIN

I'll discuss the membership application process in more detail in the next chapter on Belonging, but it's important to note here when we're talking about influence that the subscription application needs to ask potential members what kind of influence they want to have in the community. As we saw previously when I was discussing the Visitor membership type and the problems encountered with early versions of Twitter, it's important that potential new members of a community develop an understanding of what kinds of influence they can have.

Having an explicit question on your community membership application form serves three purposes. First, it helps you, as a community manager, understand the types of members and the influence needs of those members who are applying to your community. It's a terrific source of information about the kinds of experiences that you encourage in your community. Second, it requires Visitors to actually give conscious thought to the kinds of influence they want to have. Surprisingly, many people apply for membership in a community without first having given thought to how they might have influence in it. They come in, just to see if they can get in, poke around to see what's going on, and leave possibly after having damaged the system, but certainly without having contributed. Having this question on the application discourages this kind of behavior in people who aren't likely to be committed to the community on the one hand and encourages and gets more commitment from those members who are likely to want to stay and be part of the community on the other because it helps them realize that they do have a role to play in the community. The third positive benefit to having this question on your application is that it encourages more participation from new members because it helps them to understand that they're expected to have influence in the community and are encouraged to participate.

6. HAVE EXIT SURVEYS

Sometimes you can't always know what influence needs your network might not be meeting even though you do your best. In such situations, you need to collect data to help better understand why members might be leaving your community. In the listserv lists that I maintain I receive an e-mail message from the server indicating whenever someone has unsubscribed from the community. I have a canned e-mail message that either myself or a member of my advisory council sends essentially asking why the individual has left the community; we use this data to help us better understand if we're not providing sufficient opportunities for members to have influence (Figure 5.8).

As you might expect, sometimes people leave a community because they're changing a job and the remuneration they are seeking is no longer relevant for them. Most of the time, I've discovered that people are simply changing their e-mail addresses and are unsubscribing so they can resubscribe with their new address. But they tell me that being contacted in this way really encourages them to stay in the community because it helps them feel that they have value and influence and that their voices are important. Occasionally, individuals will say they're leaving the community because they are fed up with a particular topic, with another member's behavior, or with some other policy-related issue. Because they were angry, they didn't take the time to let the advisory council know about their feelings and, in a sort of knee-jerk reaction, decided to just quit. Contacting them with an exit survey enabled us to discover that the problem exists and, in a few cases, we've been able to encourage those people to come back to the community and to help us craft new policies and practices that

```
Dear [insert name],

The members of the Advisory Council and the Listowner
work actively "behind the scenes" to make
participation in our community as positive as we can
for the membership.  We noticed, however, that you
recently discontinued your membership.

In order to help us understand your needs and
potentially those of other members like you, we were
hoping that you might take a few moments to give us
some feedback regarding your decision to leave our
community.  Do you have suggestions for actions we
might take on behalf of the community which would make
for a more positive and effective experience?

On behalf of the Advisory Council,

[Council Member Name]
```

FIGURE 5.8
Sample exit interview message.

help them see that they had influence in the community and to share that information with others in the community, thereby strengthening the whole.

7. RUN PERIODIC SURVEYS

Just as surveying individuals who are leaving your community provides you with useful information about the influence needs of your membership, surveying members of the community before they leave allows you to take proactive measures to ensure that they will stay. Asking questions about the policies, governance, and opportunities to shape the direction of the community allows you to collect information that can lead to innovative new practices and policies.

Figure 5.9 is an example of a message that the members of one of my councils and I created and distributed to help us address policy changes we were considering. (Note that I've changed the names here to protect the closed, private nature of this community.)

```
Dear TEXComm Members:

The TEXComm Advisory Council members have had some discussion
recently about the nature of our community.  We'd like to know
your views about it, and in particular your views on these
issues:

1. TEXComm is intended for "practicing professionals."  Should
we tighten the criteria we use for accepting new members and
make it more difficult to be a member of TEXComm?  Should we
exclude people new to professional communication, people
changing careers, graduate students, and others? Or should we
continue with our present policy of accepting such people?

2. Should we as a community enforce and encourage
participation (and if so, how?) Or should we continue with our
present policy that it's not an issue if some members don't
post much -- if at all?

3. TEXComm was formed to be "safe," "closed," "private," and
"exclusive."

We have assumed that the safety of TEXCOMM is jeopardized when
people talk about TEXComm in places where anyone can pick up
the URL (e.g. through their blogs or portal sites.) Should we
continue our present policy, or should we consider that brief
factual references to our website are not harmful?

Please post your views and reactions on the TEXComm list, or
send them to me directly if you'd rather they were kept in
confidence.

On behalf of the Advisory Council,
```

FIGURE 5.9
Sample survey of
members.

But while the value of data you can collect from such surveys is obvious, what is less obvious is the value of simply asking the question. Indeed, if your experiences are anything like mine, it's likely when you send out your survey that you may only get a response rate of 20 to 30% of your membership (depending on the type of network and community, of course). However, you shouldn't be discouraged by this low response rate. Simply asking the membership these questions encourages them to see that their influence is there and is valued by the community leadership. Naturally, you can overdo this and if you send out too many surveys, you'll simply annoy your users. I try to survey my Web-based communities every 6 months and my listserv communities once a year in order to collect whatever useful data I can about their needs, but, more importantly, to remind them once again that they have the opportunity to have a say in the organization, direction, and governance of their community.

8. ALLOW AVATARS

One of the ways that members of Web-based communities assess influence is not through the "name recognition," which you see in listserv communities, but instead is through avatar recognition. In Second Life (SL) or World of Warcraft (WoW) communities, the dress or "gear" a character wears is a way of recognizing the role and influence that an individual has in the SL community or WoW guild. For example, Figure 5.10 illustrates just how many options WoW players have when they "gear up" their avatars. In this screen, the character is a Level 80

FIGURE 5.10
Sample of a World of Warcraft character's extremely wide range of "gear" options.

Death Knight Gnome named "Trydent." Trydent's choice of gear appears in all of the small square boxes that appear on both the right and the left sides of the screen. Hovering over a piece of gear brings up a dialog box shown in the center of the screen that explains the consequences of wearing that particular item, e.g., it might improve your character's stamina, ability to heal others in your guild, or the amount of damage done to enemies.

In WoW communities, earning the right to obtain and wear an item is usually determined by the members of the guild, as the equipment or gear is earned by participating in community "raids" where members attack a target collectively and collaboratively. As a result, wearing particularly valuable gear is a testimony to a member's influence in a community.

In Second Life communities, members also wear clothing, jewelry, or other objects to make themselves appear more recognizable to others. This practice is known among SL members as "showing off your bling" and is an effort to obtain influence in a community. Somewhat ironically, however, individuals are often asked to remove their "bling" at large gatherings, as wearing too much on their character can actually degrade the performance of the system and make it laggy for people without high bandwidth connections (Figure 5.11).

Two-dimensional communities also use photographs of themselves to achieve the same kind of effect. Putting a picture on your Facebook or Twitter profile is an important part of the visual recognition other members of the network need

FIGURE 5.11
Example of a group meeting in Second Life.

in order to see a user's influence. On both Twitter and Facebook, for example, people will scan the "walls" and look for a particular avatar and are more likely to read certain messages and tweets because they recognize the avatar. Because people realize that others in the network or community are engaged in this scanning and visual recognition behavior, they invest lots of time developing avatars or pictures that are visually striking so they're more likely to capture the interest of other users, thereby earning them more influence.

Consequently, it's important that members don't feel that they're being victimized by interface and prohibited from having the kinds of influence that they seek or that they see others in the network having. For example, in one social network I built, the system administrators were able (because of their special access on the system) to control their avatars in ways that other users on the system were unable to do. This inequity created a good bit of anger among the membership who felt like they had earned the right to control the look of their avatars because of their involvement in the community and the activeness of their participation.

9. REQUIRE PROFILES

In Web-based communities, as most people know, profiles are where members of the networks control the type of personal information about themselves, contact information, password information, and skins or themes used to display content on the site. Profiles are a standard part of virtually every Web-based community management system, and the functionality for profiles installs by default on packages such as Geeklog, Postnuke, Druple, Plum Tree, Jive, and Fuse Talk. What surprises me, however, are the number of online communities using these packages that don't require their users to complete any of the information in a profile beyond the user id and a password necessary for the log-in.

This failure to require profile information is, in my opinion, an error on the part of the community managers and system administrators because it weakens the influence needs of members of the community. The dynamic that happens here is that when people post a message to a forum or a blog site, the readers of those messages often want to assess the credibility of the person posting the message. Today's Web-savvy users learned not to take information on the Internet at face value, and we've learned to vet the information first. Of course, one way that information gets vetted by users is to look at the profiles of the people posting to the blogs, commenting on the blogs, or posting in a forum. Not requiring that information from members of your network or community thus creates a usability problem for your members (Figure 5.12).

From an influence perspective, however, this oversight weakens the community because it allows people to participate in the community without enabling them to build their influence and name recognition. In other words, because they don't have a profile, a posting by a member is vulnerable to being ignored and rejected and thus having no influence on the direction a conversation may take

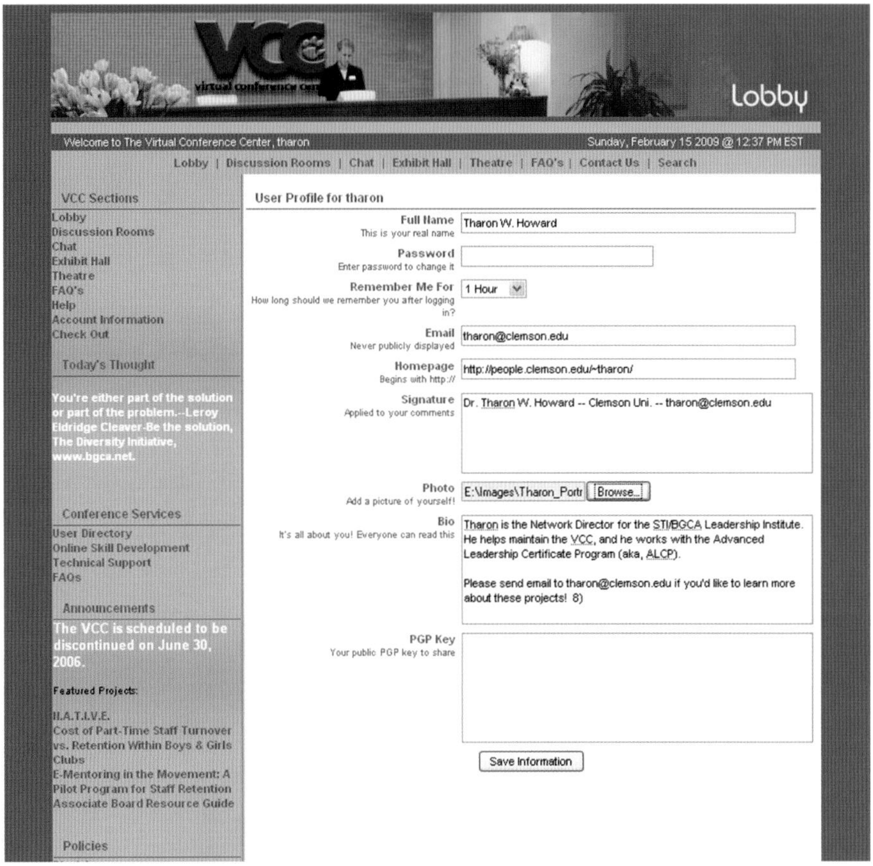

FIGURE 5.12
Sample profile from a GeekLog server.

because the other members of the community cannot assess the author's credibility. Allowing users to have an empty profile leaves them vulnerable to this kind of dismissal, particularly by "technorati" who use an empty profile as evidence of an author's "newbie-ness." Consequently, while I enable users in my communities to control their privacy levels so that they can limit access to information such as their e-mail addresses, telephone numbers, and snail mail, I do require that they put information in their profiles about their occupation, education level, and experience, as well as hobbies and interests. In other words, I require that users provide information that other users are examining in order to assess the credibility of the posting.

One problem that you need to address, however, if you are going to require profile information as I'm recommending is how to guide your "newbies" and Visitors through the decision-making process about what type of information they need to provide. In other words, you need to help them understand that other users are going to be looking at their profiles in order to make these credibility decisions about them. Because they're new to the community and they're not necessarily sure what types of information members of the community are going to find more credible and more useful, you need to find ways to give them examples of profiles that they can emulate. In other words, don't victimize your "newbies" by the profile requirements.

10. CREATE A VISITOR'S CENTER

Visitors to your site have influence needs as we've already seen through the discussion of Kim's five-stage life cycle model. Consequently, like Kim, I recommend that you create a visitor center Web site ([2], 120–128). The metaphor that I like to use in thinking about what kinds of information to put in the visitor's center is that of a national park. When you go to a national park that you've never visited previously, you probably don't know what attractions are available, the location of attractions in the park, what kind of wildlife to look for, or even where the boundaries of the park exist. You don't know what opportunities for interaction, education, and entertainment exist. You go to the visitor's center in order to get maps and to talk to one of the rangers (i.e., a leader in the community) and to say what you're interested in doing and to get some guidance, maps, and information. Communities and social networks are no different, and creating a visitor's center, particularly one that has greeters and opportunities for interaction with actual members of the community, is important because it decreases the likelihood that a visitor to your network will have a negative experience or, worse, no experience and abandons the community as a result. A visitor's center also decreases the likelihood that visitors will disrupt your community because they engage in inappropriate behaviors out of ignorance and increases the likelihood that they will have a positive experience because they'll have a better understanding of what they should look for and what they should do.

11. PUT NOVICES WITH NOVICES

In well-established communities that have Elders, Leaders, and long-time members, it can be really difficult for Novices to see that they're going to have an effect when they participate in the community. There's a danger in such communities that they and their contributions are likely to be dismissed as "newbies." In fact, I was recently involved in a conversation among leaders of Adobe's online user groups in which several of the "experts" and user group managers suggested that the system administrators program the FuseTalk software so that "newbies" in the community would be prohibited from posting messages until they had actually conducted a search of the online archives. They were so sick and tired of "newbies" asking the same questions over and over and over again that they wanted to force them to look for answers to frequently asked questions on their own. Of course, this Draconian abuse of "newbies" didn't get much traction and the community managers explained why victimizing new members of the community in this way would be inappropriate. Still, the dynamic between experts and novices is there and, if left unaddressed, is potentially destructive.

One technique that can be used to help new members have influence in the community and avoid the negative stigma attached to their initial attempts to participate in the group is to create a special area or special events intended exclusively for new members of the community. Your Leaders and Elders can create webinars, Second Life gatherings, special forums, and other events where new members of the community can connect with other new members of the community and get answers to their special questions while still benefiting from the institutional memories of Elders and Leaders.

12. GIVE ELDERS OPPORTUNITIES

Just as novices need a special place to avoid being ridiculed as "newbies" and still have their influence needs addressed, Elders also have influence needs that need to be addressed. As Kim says, it's important to "honor your elders" ([2], 147). Unfortunately, Elders can become a bit of a bore in a community if they aren't given sanctioned opportunities to have influence. They can tell the same stories over and over, damaging both themselves and other members of the community or, worse, they can turn into morality police and inappropriately chastise other members of the community for failing to live up to the cultural and social norms of the group. They can even undermine and challenge the authority of advisory councils if their influence needs aren't being met. Fortunately, there are many extremely positive ways you can find for Elders to contribute and have influence in the communities. For example, I have created interviews and podcasts with Elders in communities that I have maintained in order to draw attention to the contributions of some of the Elders in the community. Although my communities are usually closed and private communities, a good example of these is Tamara Adkins' online interviews with leaders in the user experience community (Figure 5.13).

Because Elders are interested in maintaining relationships with others in their fields rather than focusing on content-oriented conversations, posting Second Life meetings, online chats, cocktail parties at professional face-to-face conferences, and other similar events is an important means of giving Elders opportunities to have their influence needs met.

13. DEMAND RESPECT

The leadership in the community, the Elders, the administrators, and anyone charged with monitoring the tone of messages that are exchanged, must demand at all times and without equivocation that members treat other members with respect. Trust is the glue that holds communities and social networks together, and disrespect dissolves the glue of trust more corrosively than any acid. You must train your Leaders, your advisory council members, your moderators, and your system administrators to respond immediately to disrespectful language.

Recently, one of my advisory councils and I had to address a situation that broke out in a listserv community that we've been maintaining now since the

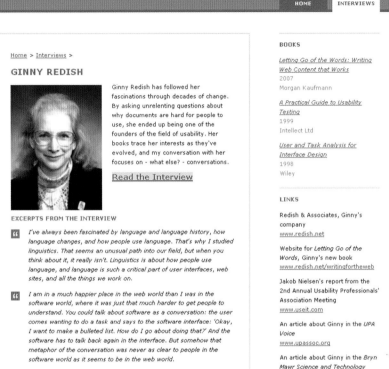

FIGURE 5.13
Tamara Adkin's UX
Pioneers interview with
Ginny Redish [1].

mid-1990s. Obviously I can't use names here to protect the innocent; however, the situation that occurred was the result of a fairly passionate discussion about an issue that had significant professional stakes for a large number of members in the community.

Because of the importance of this topic to the members, the participants in the discussion were tenacious about their respective points of view. As they argued back and forth about the topic (which was of tremendous benefit to the entire community), they finally got to the point where they realized that they weren't going to resolve the discussion without agreeing on what forms of evidence they could bring to bear on the argument. Neither side had the kind of evidence that both sides would find compelling, yet neither side was willing to give up the debate. In frustration at their inability to make progress, one of the participants used profane language and addressed another

> **TIP**
> Trust is the glue that holds communities and social networks together, and disrespect dissolves the glue of trust more corrosively than any acid.

member involved in the debate using dismissive and demeaning language. Not only did he use profanity and drop the "f-bomb" in his response, he used sarcasm in an attempt to publicly humiliate his opponents and used the logic of *reductio ad absurdum* to belittle them.

His comments were so unprofessional and abusive that, within minutes of his posting, I had already received multiple e-mail messages from other members of the community demanding that the advisory council take action and kick the poster out of the community. These members wanted his head on a spike, and the knee-jerk and easy response here would have been to send an e-mail message to the whole community criticizing the behavior of the individual in question and then possibly cyberexecuting the offender. And indeed, this is probably what I would have done back in my early days as a sole listowner, and it is what I see many community managers doing today. It seems logical because it seems like you're protecting the community by making an example out of someone behaving disruptively.

However, this isn't what I mean by "demand respect from everyone" involved in these situations. As community administrators, you and your council members have to demand that *you* also respect the person who appears to be creating the problem. Even though publicly humiliating the offender might feel personally satisfying because of the amount of grief they caused you, really it would only have the more general effect of telling other members of the community that they might also be humiliated if they accidentally overstepped the bounds of polite, professional discourse. In this case, despite the demands of a few enraged souls, a public cyberexecution wouldn't help create a "safe" space. Instead, it gives the impression that the leadership in the community isn't willing to listen to voices of dissent, it suggests that the community can't tolerate potentially uncomfortable discourse, and it implies that the leadership isn't willing to give someone a fair hearing or the opportunity to correct the potentially unacceptable behavior. In other words, no one really wants "blind justice."

So what do you do in this situation? The concept of "play" demands that you set boundaries and restore order and direction on the one hand, but it also demands that you need to balance rigid boundaries with tolerance for playful misbehavior on the other. So in this particular case, we didn't respond publicly to the offender or his victims. Instead, we sent a private message to all of the members who complained about the offender's misbehavior indicating that the council was taking action behind the scenes. Without telling them specifically what action we took in order to protect the privacy of all the parties involved, we nevertheless let them know that their messages to the community's leaders had influence.

Next, we sent the following private message to the person who had cursed at and sarcastically ridiculed others in the community.

Dear Mr. [name removed]:

The Advisory Council has received several complaints from members about the tone of your recent messages.

Community members have complained about your referring to another member as [expletive with f-bomb deleted], dismissing other members' arguments without addressing their substance, referring to people who disagree with you as "kids," and other examples of your using sarcasm rather than participating in the conversation politely.

These complaints are all saying that you have been disrespectful to other members of the community. We value your contributions to the conversation when they are constructive; but, as one person put it: "I do not enjoy reading messages that sound very much like middle-school boys at lunchtime."

The tone of your recent messages damages not only your reputation in the community but also harms the entire community. If people are put off by the tone of the conversation and, therefore, don't join the conversation, we all suffer by losing their contributions.

Tone down the sarcasm. Please contribute constructively without the sarcasm.

On behalf of the Advisory Council,

By handling the situation privately and outside the earshot of the rest of the community, we were able to demand respect from everyone involved. We let the person know he had overstepped the acceptable boundaries. By contacting those who had complained, we let them know that we respected their input, but that we also respected members who made a poor decision and slipped into indiscretion.

14. PUBLISH AND ENFORCE SAFETY POLICIES

People are looking for a safe space. They want some assurances that ideas they put out for discussion are treated fairly. They need to be confident that their idea is not satirized, dismissed sarcastically, recontextualized in some way that will cause them to be embarrassed professionally, or quoted out of context in another public forum that might harm their job or damage them in some other setting. Part of influence is how people control that safety factor. You need to have clearly established and actively enforced policies that members of the community will recognize as offering them that kind of protection.

I use two different kinds of policies for the online communities I maintain. The first type is what I call "netiquette policies." These are policies that describe some simple practices members should use when they create and respond to messages; they mainly involve simple practices that help members avoid stepping on others' toes. Figure 5.14 shows a sample of netiquette policies I use for e-mail-based discussion groups.

The second type is what I call "special policies." These policies address issues involving questions of how the members' communication should be used. They seek to address issues such as members' ownership of their messages, whether messages can be archived publicly, and conditions under which messages may be quoted. These special policies also address what types of messages may be posted and how the community itself may be used. These policies address issues such as whether commercial advertising is permitted, whether the community is open and public or closed and private, what types of general announcements are permitted, whether cross-posting is allowed, whether surveys and questionnaires can be distributed to members, and so on. Again, these policies basically seek to create a safe space where members can have confidence that they have control over their participation in the community and how that participation will be used.

The following is an example of the special policies used in a closed, private e-mail community that has been operating successfully since 1993. Because of its status as a closed community, I have changed the actual name of the community to USERTOPOI.

Most of USERTOPOI's policies are based on common "netiquette" or network etiquette practices; however, USERTOPOI does have some unique policies that result primarily from three principles:

1. USERTOPOI is a *closed*, *private* community.
2. USERTOPOI seeks to maintain the highest possible "signal-to-noise ratio."
3. Membership in USERTOPOI is a *privilege*, not a *right*, and this privilege can be revoked by decision of the Listowner and/or Advisory Council.

These "special policies" described in Figure 5.15 have been developed over several years by the Listowner and the USERTOPOI Advisory Council in an effort to protect USERTOPOI subscribers from external abuse. Thus, membership in the USERTOPOI community is contingent upon adherence to these policies. The policies are simply stated; the rationales for many of these policies are described on the USERTOPOI Web site.

Please remember that USERTOPOI is run entirely by voluntary effort and that we do not have the benefit of teams of lawyers who can draft a loophole-free set of rules. This is why we prefer to call them "special policies" and urge members to consider the spirit rather than the letter of the law. If you are in any doubt about whether your post is written appropriately for the list, then please either (a) send it off-list or (b) ask the listowner for clarification.

1. Keep your messages short. Email users are often bombarded with messages from lots of different groups, and they are more likely to become irritated with long messages than just about anything else. Short, pithy, substantive messages go a long way toward creating good will, as well as reducing the amount of disk and memory space you'll use.

2. DO try to respond to other people's messages; DON'T BE A "LURKER." When you join a group, you have an ethical responsibility to that group; you are, in effect, making a promise to participate, to give back to the group as much as you get out of it. If somebody takes the time to share his/her thoughts with you, it's rude to ignore the gesture. Keep mind that the only compensation the writer is likely to get for his/her efforts is your response. This doesn't mean that you should respond to every message you read, but you should consider how discouraged you would feel if no one thought that something YOU wrote was worth discussion.

3. Stick to one subject. Messages on the computer screen don't lend themselves to careful reading or exhaustive interpretations. Most "electronic audiences" are only reading to get the main gist of your message, and introducing several unrelated topics just confuses your reader. If you have different topics to discuss, you're more likely to get a "fair" reading if you put each topic in a separate message.

4. Use clear subject headings. Many "e-readers" decide what they want to read by the subject line in the message header and become quite irksome when the message doesn't meet their expectations. Some conventions here include using the same subject heading with an "Re:" in front of it when responding to someone else's posting. E.g., to respond to a message on "Mail Manners," you would type on your subject line "Re: Mail Manners." If you're departing from an old subject but the new subject is still related, consider using the header "[new subject] was [old subject]." Finally, try to keep your subject lines less than 10-15 characters long.

5. Read ALL your mail before responding to a message. Often you'll find that someone has already said what you were planning to say, and it's very irritating (not to mention a waste of valuable resources) to have to read several messages with the same content. An additional advantage of reading all your mail before you respond is that you will often find that your emotions will have a chance "chill out" or that you'll discover that you misinterpreted the message in your original reading.

6. Offer a *brief* context for messages to which you respond. "E-readers" usually don't read their mail everyday and/or forget messages that they have read, so quoting a *small* excerpt from the message to which you're responding helps refresh their memories. There's nothing so frustrating as reading a message like, "Yes, I agree," when you don't know what the author's agreeing to. Remember, however, to keep your quotes *small* since it's just as frustrating to have to re-read an entire message you just received.

7. Be sure to "sign" your messages. In many cases, your name will not appear in the message header, and, in any case, few mail programs allow the reader to scroll backwards so she can read the header; thus, putting your name at the end of your message makes it easier for the reader to identify you. Usually, your name is enough of a "signature." In some cases, you may also need to give a return address as well, but you should ALWAYS avoid long signature files which take up more than two or three lines. Long signatures not only waste valuable disk space, but most e-readers view them as little more than infantile gestures aimed at grandstanding. Also, long signature files advertising products or services may be considered "spam" (which is a violation of Special Policy #2) and may result in your removal from the list.

8. Always remember that you're communicating with at least one other human being. Research shows that new users often seem to forget that they aren't talking to a computer and are more likely to engage in emotionally revealing behaviors than they are in face-to-face

FIGURE 5.14
Sample netiquette policies.

(Continued)

communication (see Sara Kiesler et al, "Affect in Computer-Mediated Communication." _Human-Computer Interaction_ 1 [1985]: 77-105). Don't say or reveal something you're likely to regret later; e-mail has a way of spreading much farther than you may have intended and is much more permanent than oral discourse.

9. Bear in mind that humor and irony don't work well in e-mail messages and are misinterpreted more often than not. This doesn't mean you shouldn't be humorous, but you should make it clear that you aren't being serious. Experienced users use a smiley face tipped on its side -- (:-) -- when they wish to indicate that they are being humorous or ironic. Other conventions you may see where writers wish to convey emphasis include: _underlining_, s p a c i n g, UPPERCASE, and a*s*t*e*r*i*s*k*s. Also, you should try to limit the use of these conventions (especially the use of uppercase) to occasions when you wish to convey emphasis. DON'T WRITE YOUR WHOLE MESSAGE IN UPPERCASE, and try to remember that the first person singular pronoun is "I," not "i."

FIGURE 5.14—CONT'D

Members of a community don't even have to experience unfair treatment directly in order to abandon a community. All they need to do is to see someone else treated unfairly and abusively in order to leave the community. I've had situations where I've lost 10% of the membership in a listserv community because a flame war was started and I (the sole listowner) was on vacation and didn't intervene quickly enough to assure other members of the community that the antiflaming policies were being enforced. The Purtopoi community, which was the subject of the *Rhetoric of Electronic Communities* in 1992, actually died because I, as the listowner, failed to intervene when one of its members engaged in libelous slander against three other members of the community.

In this particular case, I didn't have special policies in the community that stated explicitly that the kind of behavior in which this individual was participating was prohibited, nor did I have a statement stating that "membership is a privilege not a right," such as the one that appears in Figure 5.15. As a result, I didn't have the legal authority to dismiss this disruptive individual from the community. In fact, when I tried to dismiss him, he threatened to file a lawsuit on the grounds that I was violating his free speech rights. Conversely, the people whose publications and careers he had slandered also threatened to sue me because they had been slandered and I hadn't acted on their behalf. At that time, it was unclear whether a listserv list could legally be considered a "publication" and thus my role analogous to that of an editor, which would have made me legally responsible for the libelous messages, or it could have been argued that I was simply a distributor and, thus, no more culpable than, say, the post office for the delivery of information.

In any case, the upshot here is the lack of policies made me legally vulnerable, and my lack of enforcement of any policy killed the community; even though there were still "subscribers" to the e-mail list, no one would post any more for fear of being savaged.

1. The topics and content of messages sent to USERTOPOI must be consistent with the purpose of the list. Those messages judged inconsistent with the list's purpose may result in expulsion from the list. Messages which are illegal, morally unacceptable, or unprofessional in content may not only result in expulsion from the list, but the listowner and/or Advisory Council may also forward such messages to the appropriate authorities.

2. Unsolicited messages that advertise any commercial products or services on the USERTOPOI list are strictly prohibited, even if the products or services are owned or hosted by a not-for-profit institution. As a general rule of thumb regarding what is or is not a violation of this policy, ask whether profit is made on the product or service being described. If a profit is being made, then it's probably a violation of the list's policy.

3. We value vendors and consultants who develop tools or offer services to the usability community. Thus, postings which include commercial information in ***direct reply*** to a question or in the context of a discussion thread are permitted, but they must not be advertising copy, brochure-ware, or promotion in another guise.

4. If you wish to announce not-for-profit conferences, meetings, email lists, websites, calls for papers, surveys, or **any** other type of not-for-profit meeting, product, or service then contact the listowner (*tharon@clemson.edu*) for review by the USERTOPOI Advisory Council.

   Announcements should be short (less than approx 2000 characters or roughly a screenfull of text).

   Your request to post must include the **complete** text of the announcement.

   You must report results of surveys, questionnaires, and the like to USERTOPOI when your results are available (see Policy 17 below).

   Please allow 7-10 working days for a representative of the Advisory Council to respond to your request.

   Please do not assume that your next announcement will be approved even if you have always been approved before.

5. USERTOPOI may not be used to let the community know that you are seeking a job. Posting resumes and/or sending inquiries about job opportunities is strictly prohibited.

6. Ads for job openings are permitted, provided they include geographical and contact information and are less than approx. 2,000 characters or roughly one screen full of text.

7. Collecting or "harvesting" addresses from the list in order to distribute resumes, commercial ads, announcements, etc. is strictly prohibited and will lead to immediate expulsion from the community.

8. Do not "advertise" the existence of USERTOPOI in **any** public media such as newsletters, journal articles, web pages, USENET groups, conference presentations, other listservers, books, etc. without written permission from the Listowner or Advisory Council. You may, of course, tell colleagues and co-workers about the list via private media such as email or conversations. However, tell them to contact Tharon Howard (*tharon@clemson.edu*) for more information, and do not attempt to provide any alternative subscription method.

9. Only INDIVIDUALS may subscribe to USERTOPOI. You must subscribe from your individual email address -- either an address supplied by your organization or one that you have obtained on your own. No address that is accessible to more than one person may be

FIGURE 5.15
Sample special policies.

(*Continued*)

used. This specifically excludes redistribution servers, archive systems, and groups such as college classes (although individual students may apply for membership).

10. If you save USERTOPOI messages, they may only be used in a ***private*** archive for your own, personal use. If you create such an archive, you are personally responsible for the security and integrity of your private archive. Archives may not be shared with non-subscribers under any conditions (this includes students, co-workers, and the possibility that you have left your private archive where non-subscribers may easily find it.)

11. If you or your company make USERTOPOI's messages available to anyone who is not currently a USERTOPOI subscriber in any medium, then you are effectively functioning as a "redistribution server" and will be expelled from the list. Educators may ***not*** share USERTOPOI's messages with classes (except as noted in Policy #12 below).

12. Single messages from USERTOPOI may be quoted elsewhere so long as:
    1. you have the authors' consent to quote or cite their messages
    2. you do ***NOT*** use the USERTOPOI email address in your citation or quote.

    Please note that sometimes USERTOPOI messages contain an interleaved dialogue between several subscribers or mention subscribers by name. In these cases you must contact every USERTOPOI subscriber included in the message for their consent before quoting. Also, should you need to refer to the USERTOPOI list in your text, you should not use the term "USERTOPOI." Instead, you should describe the list as "a professional, private Internet discussion group."

13. Substantive debates and even extreme disagreements are encouraged since such discussions are often highly productive. However, the tone of the messages must be maintained at the highest level of professionalism; flaming, sarcasm, or personal attacks will not be tolerated.

    Also, comments and complaints about the lack of professionalism or appropriateness of other subscribers' messages should ***never*** be sent to the entire USERTOPOI community. Instead, comments and complaints of this nature should be sent to the Listowner directly at *tharon@clemson.edu*. To prevent flame wars and unnecessary embarrassment to the parties involved, such issues are resolved in private and off the list by the Listowner and the USERTOPOI Advisory Council.

14. If your e-mail account begins generating delivery error messages or automated messages, then unfortunately, your address will have to be unsubscribed from the list. Please contact the Listowner at *tharon@clemson.edu* if this happens. If your email address consistently generates error messages over a period of time, it may be permanently blocked from any future attempts to subscribe to the USERTOPOI list.

15. The use of auto-reply mailer daemons is prohibited on USERTOPOI. Auto-reply daemons are programs that many people use to automatically respond to incoming mail messages when they are out of town or on vacation. For more information on how to prevent an auto-reply mailer from disrupting USERTOPOI, see the NOMAIL command on the help page.

16. Please note that attachments should not be sent to USERTOPOI. Also, if you offer to distribute a document in a USERTOPOI message, make sure that you have permission from your client or the group in your company responsible for approving public distribution of documents. And if you receive a document from a USERTOPOI subscriber, remember that copyright is a "default protection" which applies unless the owner waives it, no matter how you got the document and even if it isn't marked with a copyright notice.

FIGURE 5.15—CONT'D

17. The unique composition of the USERTOPOI community makes it an obvious target for surveys (the term "survey" includes questionnaires and any other postings seeking mass responses). Surveys must be sanctioned by the AC before being announced on USERTOPOI. Such surveys will only be permitted if they serve to articulate or progress the goals of the community and display an appropriate level of professionalism. The surveys themselves should NOT be posted to USERTOPOI. Proposers of surveys must state their commitment to sharing the results with the community when they become available (either as a posting on USERTOPOI, or as a URL to a separate site where the results may be accessed free of charge by the USERTOPOI community).

The special policies above are considered essential for the protection of the USERTOPOI community. However, in addition to the special policies above, USERTOPOI also has "netiquette" policies because any message sent to USERTOPOI is automatically redistributed to well over 1,000 other people. Please see USERTOPOI's Netiquette Policies for a listing and discussion of these.

FIGURE 5.15—CONT'D

CONCLUSION

This chapter discussed how you can develop policies and practices for managing your social networks and communities that maintain a productive "play" between users' need to have individual influence and control over their environment on the one hand, while still providing boundaries that help individuals understand what the group will find productive on the other. We also looked carefully at the different types of members that exist in social networks and communities in order to understand how each membership type has different influence needs that should be met in order to achieve long-term success. Finally, we examined some techniques that can be used to find a balance between the competing influence needs of the various membership types. You'll need additional techniques to manage your own community or to maintain a network; however, the techniques here are some of the best practices I've used as the core around which I've built successful long-term communities.

WORKS CITED

[1] Adlin T. Ginny Redish. UX Pioneers 14 Feb 2009. http://www.adlininc.com/uxpioneers/original_pioneers/ginny_redish.html.
[2] Kim AJ. Community Building on the Web. Berkeley, CA: Peachpit Press; 2000.
[3] Lave J, Wenger E. Situated Learning: Legitimate Peripheral Participation. Cambridge University Press; 1991.
[4] Li C, Bernoff J. Groundswell: Winning in a World Transformed by Social Technologies. Boston, MA: Harvard Business Press; 2008.
[5] Nielsen J. Participation inequality: Encouraging more users to contribute. Alertbox. 9 Oct 2006. 15 Jan 2009. http://www.useit.com/alertbox/participation_inequality.html.
[6] Nonnecke B, Preece J. Silent participants: Getting to know lurkers better. In: Lueg C, Fisher D, editors. From Usenet to CoWebs: Interacting with Social Information Spaces. Springer; 2003.
[7] Virtual Community. Wikipedia. 18 Jan 2009. http://en.wikipedia.org/wiki/Virtual_community.
[8] Wenger E. Communities of Practice: Learning, Meaning, and Identity. Cambridge University Press; 1998.

CHAPTER 6
Belonging

DESIGNING THE EXPERIENCE OF BELONGING

SYNOPSIS

What does it truly mean to *belong* to a community? How does someone know when they really have "made it" into a community and, perhaps more importantly, how do leaders in the community help them achieve that sense of accomplishment? This chapter explains that belonging is a sense of one's "social presence" in a community; it's a feeling or awareness of the shared bonds a member has with others in the group. This chapter begins by discussing how initiation rituals and "stories of origin" provide mechanisms that allow members to bond. It shows how real world organizations such as the Navy Seals use initiation rituals in order to build a sense of camaraderie and *esprit de corps* among its members and then extends those techniques into virtual spaces.

This chapter also talks about the benefits and potential pitfall of "leveling rituals," or advancement through the ranks or classes in a community. It provides alternative methods for ways of creating ranks without creating classification systems and potential hierarchies. It then talks about mythologies and how creating "secret handshakes," audiovisual symbol systems, and insider stories or local myths can all be used to help members understand how they're expected to interact with one another and how to respond to particular types of social situations. This chapter also discusses rituals, schemas, and protocols and how these standardized procedures are processes for behavior that, once again, help members understand how they're expected to respond in specific situational contexts.

Again, the chapter ends with examples of specific techniques from existing communities which can serve as a springboard for your own social networks and online communities.

INTRODUCTION

Of the four RIBS, belonging is by far the most fun for me as a community and network designer. Belonging is, of course, the techniques or mechanisms by which we help members of the community develop the sense of "social presence," a sense that they belong in that community, that they identify with it, and that they share a bond with its other members.

Belonging is created in a community through shared mythologies, shared stories of origin, shared symbols, and the cultural codes embedded in those symbols. As designers, we create rituals of membership that serve an epideictic function in our communities, that is, they celebrate the "brand identity" of the community. We celebrate through these rituals shared values, shared commitments, and a shared interpretation of a common history. Consequently, what makes working with the belonging elements in community design so much fun is that you're creating events and ritualized experiences for your users that bind them together and help them feel as though they truly belong. Unlike the influence element, which (although critical) can be a bit of a downer because it deals with how you're going to administer and govern your community, belonging is much more fun to think about and to plan because you're creating social experiences that are active and engaging to your users.

CEREMONIAL SPEECHES OF BELONGING

The term "epideictic" is used by classical Greek and Roman rhetoricians to refer to "speeches of praise and blame" used during Panegyrics and festivals meant to bind the polis together. Leaders of the Greek cities would hire famous orators called sophists to give public speeches during festivals, and these epideictic speeches would either praise a hero or beloved historical figure or vilify a common enemy of the community. The effect of epideictic speeches during these civic festivals was to celebrate a common history and shared values in order to bind members together.

INITIATION RITUALS

So what are a few examples of these stories of origin and epideictic rituals? One obvious kind of ritual is the hazing rituals of initiation that many experienced in their fraternities and sororities. Navy Seals share a bonding experience where they undergo what they call "Hell Week" where they suffer collectively as a team through experiences such as immersion in freezing cold water. Graduate teaching assistants in the Freshman Composition program at my university have a similar bonding experience that they also call "Hell Week." For an entire week all day, every day, the new graduate teaching assistants (or GTAs) undergo training in the skills that they all need in order to become effective composition teachers. They learn how to interpret the grading scales used in the program in the same ways so that the grades that students get in the program have a greater degree of interrater reliability. They learn procedures for dealing with troublesome students. They learn how to deal with plagiarism cases and so on.

Although it's not unpleasant and certainly not the same sort of painful hazing rituals used in some tribal societies, the GTAs always treat it as though it is. It's essentially a test of mettle—and since the most familiar ones are physical in our culture, the GTAs treat it that way. However, more often than not, initiation rituals today involve an emotional, psychological, professional, or intellectual challenge that every member of the community has to overcome in order to achieve membership status and be recognized. Hence the GTAs are really only challenged professionally; they only have to demonstrate that they have learned the skills necessary to be composition teachers to be accepted into the community. Nevertheless, clearing that very public hurdle and overcoming their fear of failure provide them with a sense of accomplishment and pride that binds them closely to their peers and sets them apart from those who have yet to attempt the challenge.

FOCUS ON TECHNIQUE

See the last entry in the Techniques section at the end of the chapter for an example of how to turn an application for membership in a network or online community into a type of initiation ritual.

Interestingly, this initiation ritual doesn't merely bond the cadre of new GTAs to each other. It certainly plays that role as they learn to collaborate in order to help each other complete the experience, but because it's a ritual of membership that is repeated year after year after year, it also binds the new members of the community to older members. When first-year GTAs meet second- and third-year GTAs who also endured "Hell Week," usually the first thing that they talk about is their shared experiences as survivors of "Hell Week." They talk about what was the same between their experiences and what was different about their experiences, which creates a bond and a sense of belonging between both groups.

SPARTAN INITIATION RITUALS

In ancient Sparta, once boys reached the age of 7, they were enrolled in the *agoge*, a state-sanctioned initiation ritual designed to produce tough, disciplined solders willing to sacrifice themselves in defense of Sparta. According to legend, young Spartan boys were deliberately starved. In order to demonstrate their skill in stealth and their military prowess, Spartan youths were required to feed and sustain themselves by stealing food from the Helots, who were the lower, slave class in Spartan society.

STORIES OF ORIGIN

Stories of origin are another way to initiate new members into a discourse community and to help them understand what it is that the community values. One example of this that I had to learn about in order to function effectively with the Boys and Girls Clubs of America (BGCA) professionals is the story of how BGCA got its start. I could not be effective as a community manager until I learned the story of the little old ladies in New England back in the 1800s who started serving tea and cookies to the hooligans running around their neighborhoods. Whether or not this actually happened as reported, every BGCA member knows that because these New England adults began having positive relationships with young boys in their communities, the levels of theft, vandalism, and other misbehavior in those neighborhoods dropped. The Boys Club (which later became the Boys and Girls Clubs) started as a result, and its goal of cultivating positive, lasting relationships between adults and youth continues to this day. This story of origin is critical because it's how the strategic mission of the BGCA movement is communicated between its members.

FOCUS ON TECHNIQUE

For examples of how stories of origin and initiation rituals can be used as techniques in social networks and online communities, see Techniques #1 and #2 in the second half of this chapter.

Internalizing this story was actually critical for me and for the social network that my staff and I were developing because what we were attempting to do was to give youth development professionals a place where they could have influence and feel like they belonged to the organization and had an impact on the organization. BGCA was experiencing a turnover rate among the youth development professionals who worked directly with the kids approaching 101% annually.

Now if you know the story of origin for BGCA and from it you develop the understanding that the goal of the organization is to develop long-term, lasting relationships with youth, it becomes clear how the development of an electronic community and anything that could be done to improve the retention rate in the movement was mission-critical. Many of the kids served by BGCA are from broken homes, and the youth have already suffered because they don't have the constant presence of an adult in their life. Having a high turnover rate among youth development professionals failed the kids from broken homes and was antithetical to the organization's goals. Consequently, retention and recruiting of youth development professionals became the mission of the Virtual Conference Center developed for BGCA members. More specifically, the mission of the Virtual Conference Center became helping BGCA professionals help each other sustain their careers in the movement. In other words, we leveraged the story of origin for the existing community in order to create a new one for the electronic community.

Stories of origin work for every size of virtual community or network. The Virtual Conference Center was actually a social network designed to support the 35,000 members of the BGCA's movement. However, stories of origin can work for smaller communities such as a software development team. For example, one of my former graduate students was hired at Microsoft to work as a user experience designer on the Microsoft Office 12 suite, which was eventually released as Office 2007. Office 12 is noteworthy because Office 12 is where Microsoft introduced the then-controversial ribbon interface. The team lead of the developers, Jenson Harris, used stories of origin in order to build the development team into a relatively cohesive group with a shared vision; you can see the story of origin that Jenson Harris told on his blog site at http://blogs.msdn .com/jensenh/about.aspx.

What Harris did was to tell the story of the Microsoft Office interface from its beginning up through Office 2003; more importantly, he told it in such a way that it focused on the relationships between functionality provided by the software and its users' experience of that functionality. He told the story of the buttons, menus, tool bars, and even "clippy" (the famous animated paper clip that thousands of users hated), and he told the story about how functionality in Office products (aka "feature creep") had grown so much that it was no longer possible to give users the kinds of experiences that the development team desired.

What's important about the story that Harris tells isn't the simple count of features creeping into the product and buttons that supported those features. What is important about the story in terms of the community of development that emerged as a result of the story of origin for Office 12 is the shared commitment that the team members came to understand that is presupposed in the story. In other words, just as BGCA's story demonstrated the commitment to long-term adult–youth relationships, the story of this team is about the commitment to user experience design.

WEB LINK

Jensen Harris: An Office User Interface Blog
**http://blogs.msdn.com/jensenh/
about.aspx**

We've seen how stories of origin can work for large social networks such as the BGCA and a relatively small group of developers working on a suite of products in a company, but stories of origin can also be used with medium-sized communities, such as a corporation or a university. At Clemson University, for example, every new faculty member at the university, regardless of rank, is required to attend a 2-day faculty orientation, much like the "Hell Week" we put our graduate teaching assistants through. During that orientation, faculty learn the Thomas Green Clemson story. We learn the economy of the South was devastated in the 1860s and 1870s as a result of what was then called the "War of Northern Aggression," more commonly known as the "Civil War."

CIVIL WAR JOKE

In addition to jokingly using the term "War of Northern Aggression," I've heard some faculty also use the ironic expression "the unfortunate incident" as a sly reference to the events of 1861–1865. The expression is ironic, as many of the people using it are not actually Southerners, but they use it nonetheless in order to show their sense of community.

Rebuilding South Carolina's economy was going to require an entirely new approach to the high-tech, agricultural practices of the day. Hence, Thomas Green Clemson, who had inherited John C. Calhoun's plantation by virtue of having married Calhoun's daughter, saw the need for a "high seminary of learning" where southerners could develop the skills and technologies to rebuild the "New South." As a result, he decided to use the Morrell Act and donate the Calhoun plantation to the State of South Carolina as one of the first land-grant universities in the United States.

Unfortunately for Thomas Green Clemson, members of the state legislature were mostly graduates of the University of South Carolina and didn't see the need for and didn't have the funding to support a second university in a small, rural state. As a result, it wasn't until the Supreme Court of the United States forced the state to accept Clemson's gift that Clemson University came to be. Yet, having been forced to accept such an outrageous gift that they did not wish to fund, the state legislature decided to show their displeasure by partially funding Clemson's operating budget out of a manure tax imposed on the very farmers that Thomas Green Clemson had wanted so badly to support.

The rivalry and odd local rituals that it has produced have become so popular that, ironically, television crews from Paris and other international sites also come to provide coverage on the event.

At this point, you're probably asking so why make a big deal out of this rather obscure history? The point is the effect that this story of origin has on Clemson's community building. One of the things that this story of origin does, which is tremendously valuable whether you're trying to mobilize an urban street gang or motivate a group of grant-getting faculty, is that it creates rivals or what psychologists call "negative reference groups." It lets you know who's on your side and who's not. If you've ever wondered why the Clemson–USC football game gets so much air-time on American TV, the story of origin just given hopefully explains part of that rivalry.

Both schools see themselves competing for the same resources in part because of this story of origin and because the administration of the university is able to use this story of origin to encourage faculty to pursue alternate forms of funding because we can't live on the "manure tax" the state legislatures provides. Clemson University's story of origin also provides an understanding of the university's mission and goes back to Thomas Green Clemson's altruistic desire to enhance the economy of South Carolina citizens through the development of that "high seminary of learning" that would produce research and scholarship needed for economic growth. It helps faculty understand that our mission isn't merely, as Matthew Arnold once wrote, "to protect culture for a generation which deserves it" but is instead to do the basic research necessary for new discoveries and then take the next step and apply those new discoveries for practical benefit.

As you can see, stories of origin work for social networks, large- to middle-sized communities, and even small communities within an organization. As Stephen Denning, the author of *Squirrel, Inc.*, has also noted, stories of origin can help you create a common vision among members of a community in the same way that the BGCA did.

They can also be used to motivate a team to understand a problem in a particular way and motivate them to tackle that problem using criteria *presupposed* by the story as Microsoft did by using the successful completion criteria embedded in the story being told. In other words, Microsoft's Office 12 team couldn't have developed a solution to their problem that failed to address their users' experiences with feature creep. Because of the story of origin that Jensen Harris told, the team simply had to address it. Finally, stories of origin define who is inside and who is outside of the community. Through the creation of negative reference groups and protagonists and antagonists in the story, they help members see and understand how they should feel about relationships with others outside the community.

For more information about Denning's Squirrel, Inc. *and how stories can be used in organizations, see the sidebar in the Mythologies section.*

LEVELING UP RITUALS

There are initiation rituals for new members—ways to help novices become part of the community, which is the role that initiation basically serves. But there are also rituals that demarcate other levels of membership within a community that you don't want to overlook. There are also leveling up rituals that you need to create so that members celebrate each others' progress through the "ranks" or levels in a community.

Upside to levels

Both of my sons were in Boy Scouts, and both achieved the rank of Eagle Scout. As is the case with video games, Boy Scouts motivate their members to move through the ranks through the curriculum and to become Scout, Second Class, First Class, Star, Life, and, finally, Eagle. The rank here is not as significant as the ceremonies that are attached to each. Parents, scouts, family, troop leaders, and even representatives from the regional council come together at a Court of Honor, which happens on a regular basis. Formally and ceremoniously the rank and privileges of that rank are conferred on the Boy Scout in the presence of all of his peers. Those who have already achieved the rank feel a bond and remember their own experiences in achieving the rank, and those who get to achieve that rank feel compelled to continue in the movement to go forward (Figure 6.1).

FIGURE 6.1
During the Eagle ceremony, scouts from every rank light a candle celebrating each step required for the achievement of Eagle Scout.

Again, what I'm trying to call attention to here is not the rank itself or the level itself, but the celebration and recognition that come with it. Without that celebration, without those leveling-up rituals, you lose the opportunity to build community.

THE ORIGINS OF MERIT BADGES

Lord Baden-Powell, who started Boy Scouts, used a curriculum and a reward system of badges that he originally designed and used for military scouts he trained as an officer during the Boer War. Baden-Powell found that his use of badges his men could wear on their uniforms motivated them to learn the material in his military training manual, *Aids to Scouting*. After the war, Powell used the same "leveling up" technique in the scouting movement. In 1910, Juliette Gordon Low, an American friend of Baden-Powell, used the same badge and leveling up strategy for the Girl Scouts of the United States.

This not only works in youth organizations but in business settings as well. Take, for example, the very popular Six Sigma organization. Six Sigma is a quality-control program used mainly by manufacturing companies, such as Magnavox, in order to reduce the number of errors in the manufacturing process by as much as six standard deviations (hence, the name Six Sigma). Individuals in the company who go through the training programs for the Six Sigma curriculum earn ranks in the same way that students in a karate school earn different colored belts. Thus, in Six Sigma, a "champion" of the cause may have a yellow belt, a brown belt, or even a black belt. Obviously, the desire to achieve a higher level belt, which comes with other benefits in the work environment, motivates employees to work through the curriculum.

ACADEMIC RANKING GAME

In a university, similar ranks are achieved. Tenure-track assistant professors have to undergo a 7-year probationary period traditionally during which time they're required to contribute to the community through their publications, research, teaching, and service on various academic committees. If after 7 years, they've demonstrated and built up a suitable record, a committee of their peers recognizes them by giving them the rank of associate professor. After 7 years, at the same level of service and achievement, they can earn the rank of full professor. Members who achieve these ranks are celebrated. Departments recognize them at departmental meetings, private parties are usually hosted, and their ranks are also recognized and celebrated at the college level where they are announced. And, of course, there's also an increase in salary that comes with advancement. They're also able to serve and have input into the community in ways that they weren't before. At some schools, junior faculty at the assistant professor level are not eligible to teach seniors or graduate students. Only associate and full professors are allowed to chair doctoral committees and so on.

Downside to levels

From a sustainability perspective, there's a downside to levels. The ceremonies and rituals that you're able to provide the community are useful, but they have the potential for creating jealousies within members when members aren't allowed certain privileges because they don't have the appropriate level or rank, for example. There's a danger that people will feel disenfranchised and leave the community. This is something that often happens among academics and at institutions where "rank has its privilege." Among academics at universities, an assistant professor typically has to serve the community for 7 years, providing excellent teaching, publishing, scholarship, and research and serving on various academic committees and community outreach projects. At many institutions, you have to hold the rank of associate professor before you are granted the privilege of teaching senior undergraduates and/or graduate seminars. As an assistant professor you can't chair a doctoral dissertation, for example, and work with graduate students on their research projects. Because it takes so long and is so difficult to achieve higher rank, many academic departments suffer from political infighting and petty jealousies.

FOCUS ON TECHNIQUE

For a discussion of how leveling ceremonies can be used in online environments with social media such as podcasts, see entry #5 in the Techniques section.

A second problem with leveling up, as gamers certainly know, is once you've achieved the highest level it's no longer any fun to play the game or to be a member of the network or community. World of Warcraft (WoW) had 60 levels in its original release and once gamers achieved the highest level, they lost interest because there was no challenge left for them. WoW had to evolve to provide new challenges for members who had achieved the highest level in the community. One of the ways Blizzard did this was by creating guilds, by allowing members to earn "honor points," and by allowing members to pick up new battle gear, more powerful weapons, articles of clothing, magical spells, and mounts. A similar problem exists in Boy Scouts. Once a scout has achieved the rank of Eagle a significant number of them lose interest in scouting and move on to other things and actually leave scouting. Although the Boy Scouts have created Eagle Palms and achievements beyond Eagle Scout, they still lose a lot of boys.

Using levels

In my own communities and social networks, I generally try to avoid having ranks beyond the fairly simplistic novice/apprentice membership rank and leadership rank. However, most of the communities in which I'm involved are professional communities where members consider themselves to be peers and colleagues working toward common goals. Having levels of membership in those communities create the kinds of dissention and political infighting that I mentioned among many academics. However, it is possible to achieve the same sorts of motivation among members without having to resort to levels of membership. You can still design communities and social networks that take advantage of the collecting motivation that leveling up provides and the opportunities to have ceremonies without the rank issues. This is done through the creation of membership roles and services.

Basically, the thinking here is to create a type of service that a member can provide for the community for which they must receive training and earn that badge or title that can then be celebrated and yet still hold the rank of member. Members in a community may, for example, learn how to become an electronic mentor to new members. They would, thus, undergo the initiation, training in the practices of becoming a mentor and then be celebrated, in front of the whole community, once they achieve it.

Every parent around the football team is a member, and they all share a common goal of helping the boys develop as young men. But there are additional roles they can take on in the Athletic Booster Club or additional services they can provide. For example, there is always a need for people who can drive buses. They may have to get a chauffer's license, which requires a number of serious training programs, and they're not considered higher rank than anyone else in the organization, but they are respected for taking on that additional responsibility. Similarly, there are people who receive training in CPR and other medical kinds of support who can take on roles of helpers and managers. There are people who serve the football players breakfasts and dinners, as many of the boys need to bulk up and need a lot of energy but don't always come from homes that promote those kinds of positive eating behaviors. All of these roles are recognized, valued, and celebrated during half-time, at dinner, and other events. But they don't require special rank or special privileges in order to obtain them within the community.

MYTHOLOGIES

These are shared histories (real or imagined) that express values of the community. For Americans, one of the best known of these is George Washington cutting down the cherry tree and then confessing that he was the culprit. The story, which probably never happened, celebrates the importance of honesty and taking responsibility for one's own actions.

Using mythologies

Communities use these stories to illustrate values and to inspire desired behavior. Like stories of origin, they are able to help members know what their attitudes are supposed to be toward certain issues and how they're supposed to behave in the community. They provide members with a moral compass in situations that are important to the community. For example, the ancient Greeks tell the story of Icarus who, in an act of overexuberant passion and hubris, flew too close to the sun and melted the wax wings his father, Daedulus, had made, thereby crashing into the sea and drowning. The Greeks used the story to show that (1) technological achievements are not God-like and should never undermine the religious values of their culture and (2) the passions of youth need to be tempered by the deeper understanding of the elders in a community.

In modern times, we still use mythologies to show members of a community what they should value. Democrats in the United States, for example, will point to Lyndon Johnson and his efforts to build a great society in support of their civil rights agenda. Britons point to Winston Churchill and his dogged defense of the country during World War II to celebrate national pride.

These are moral compasses where we're "painting with a big brush," but mythologies are important in social networks and electronic communities because they express some sort of religious or political correctness (though they do do that). From a designer's perspective, they're more important because they can be used to help members of the network and community understand how to respond in particular kinds of situations and how to interact with others.

DENNING'S SEVEN TYPES OF STORIES

In his delightful and insightful book, *Squirrel Inc.*, former World Bank executive Steven Denning creates a mythological company populated by talking squirrels. The squirrels tell each other stories in order to affect change in their company. Denning identifies seven kinds of stories that the squirrels use:

- A story to ignite action—a springboard story—is likely to require a true story with a positive tone, told in a minimalist fashion.
- A story to share knowledge is likely to be a true story with a negative tone, focused on a problem and presenting the context, the solution, and an explanation of the solution.
- A story to get people working together will be a moving story and will spark similar stories from the audience.
- A story to lead people into the future will be an evocative story, told with minimal detail.
- A story to neutralize bad news will be a true story that satirizes the bad news itself or the author of the bad news.
- A story to communicate who you are will tend to be a story in a traditional form, with context, characters, and a plot.
- A story to transmit values will likely be a believable story describing how organizational leaders dealt with adversity.

Adapted from Denning [2], 47

Among members of the usability and user experience design community, there's a collection of stories that its members often share to express the importance of what they do for society. The stories have been collected in an anthology that has been put together by Steven Casey known as *Set Phasers on Stun*.

FOCUS ON TECHNIQUE

See entries #3 and #4 in the Techniques section for a discussion of strategies and specific examples you can use to encourage the use of mythologies in communities and networks.

The book is called *Set Phasers on Stun* because the first story that the book tells is that of Voyne Ray Cox, who was accidentally given a lethal overdose of radiation because the interface that had been designed for his Therac-25 cancer radiation therapy machine had such significant usability flaws that it was possible for medical technicians to give an overdose. Mr. Cox laconically remarked when he learned of the lethal overdose he had received that he guessed "Captain Kirk forgot to put the machine on stun" ([1], 20). These kinds of stories bind the community together around a common set of values. In this case, *Set Phasers on Stun* tells usability specialists what they should value and what they should always guard against. Our failures can cost lives. Our successes protect them.

SYMBOLS AND CODES

Belonging can also be expressed through visual elements in a design. Oftentimes these are tacit and they're not expressed verbally, but we experience a sense of belonging when we encounter visual symbols or audio leitmotifs. Music can often function as a symbol, oftentimes just as powerfully. The kind of leitmotifs that you hear in a movie immediately jump out at you. Think about *Jaws*, for example, the music right before the shark attack still sends chills up the spine. The opening music of *Star Wars* or the music of the beginning of *Star Trek* immediately compels certain emotional responses from fans. Visual symbols have the same kind of impact and generate the same sense of belonging in a community.

FIGURE 6.2
A Red Hat Society member dressed for an outing on Fishman's Warf in San Francisco.

Consider the Red Hat Society for example. You don't even have to be a member to understand the power that wearing a purple dress and a red hat and going out with friends can have. For those unfamiliar with the Red Hat Society, it was started by mature women who decided they no longer had the time or interest in the petty politics of playing dress up for social gain (Figure 6.2).

While they wear their red hats, they don't have to care about what's in fad anymore; they don't have to care what other people think about them. If they want to dress up with a red hat and a purple dress, then the people who love them and care about them will still have fun with them. And so that's what they do. They dress up in red and purple and usually lots of feathers, they go out with their friends, and they enjoy each other because of who they are and not how they are dressed.

Corporate branding

Corporate branding is really just another type of symbology that attempts to achieve a similar effect. You see the golden arches anywhere in the world and you can pretty well predict what kind of food you're going to find at that location. AT&T is reputed to have paid nearly $2 million for its "death star" design because they put so much value on customers and employees being able to recognize immediately the corporate brand and to identify with it as soon as they see it. Although we tend not to think of them as such because they're made out of letters, the wordmarks for universities and corporations are really nothing more than symbols. When we read the wordmark Clemson shown in Figure 6.3, we don't phonetically sound each of the letters

FIGURE 6.3
Example of a wordmark.

when we see "C" "L" "E" "M" "S" "O" "N." Instead, we recognize the shape of the entire wordmark, tacitly understand its meaning, and recognize its identity.

Using visuals in electronic communities and social networks

While we've known for a long time that trademarks, symbols, wordmarks, and logos help with branding, in electronic communities and social networks, they can serve the same sort of function that colors and hand gestures play in gangs or that red hats play in the Red Hat Society. The look and feel, that is to say, the aesthetic design of your Web site or your interface, are critical parts of helping your members to feel a sense of belonging.

The WoW Oathsworn Guild, for example, uses black, symbology, and fonts reminiscent of medieval or gothic themes in order to evoke a sense of belonging in their guild. The guild is very much invested in symbols and creatures from Tolkien's *Lord of the Rings*, and the Oathsworn Guild members use that to its full advantage (Figure 6.4).

As you're thinking about your designs, you will obviously need to study the members of your community and understand their emotional and aesthetic needs in order to design accordingly.

PROTOCOLS, ROUTINES, AND SCHEMAS

Protocols, routines, and schemas are ritualized behaviors that members of a community use in two ways: (1) to identify and greet other members and (2) to understand the correct behaviors to use in different social situations.

Schemas

In the Western business community, these are very familiar to us. Consider what you do when you are introduced to someone who may become a business associate for the first time. You don't have a relationship with that person on a personal level yet, but you want to make a good impression. As you physically approach

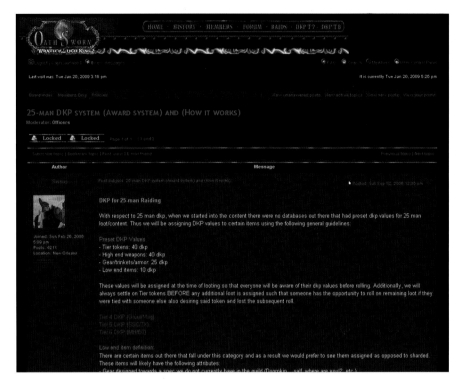

FIGURE 6.4
The look and feel of the Oathsworn Guild Web site build a sense of identity and belonging.

each other for the first time, chances are that you probably don't even have to think about what to do. Without consciously thinking about it, you're going to stick out your right hand, grasp that person's right hand, and shake hands firmly.

Why is that? Why is it that you don't have to think about "I need to use my right hand and I need to grasp the other person's hand firmly and shake it up and down three times?" The reason you don't have to think about it is because you've internalized the "schema." Schemas are sets of preprogrammed procedures used in potentially difficult social situations to keep those situations from embarrassing us. Imagine what would happen if instead of shaking hands with your new business colleague, you slapped her hand. That *faux pau* would almost certainly damage the social relationship and your chance of doing future business.

HANDSHAKES AND SALUTES

The handshake supposedly began when warriors would meet on the battlefield. In order to show that their hands were empty and that they didn't have any concealed weapons, they shook hands. The military salute similarly came about during medieval times because knights were mounted on horseback and wore so much armor that it was almost impossible for them to shake hands. Therefore, they held their hands up by their face with their fingers extended in order to show that they were also unarmed. Because most humans are right-handed, we use our right hand for greeting and salute schemas.

We have schemas for all sorts of communal and social behaviors. For example, we have schemas for going to a restaurant and even for different kinds of restaurants. When you go into a fast food restaurant, for example a McDonald's, a Burger King, or a Subway, you don't have to think about the behaviors that are required of you. You walk up to the counter, look at the menu displayed, order off the menu with as little modification as possible, pay for your food, and then go stand and wait for it. However, when you go to a more elegant "sit down" restaurant, when you enter the facility you automatically look for the maître d' or hostess who will seat you at a table where the maître d' will hand you the menu, and you have to wait for someone to come and take your order. You know in advance that you don't have to pay before your food arrives and that you get the check at the end of the meal.

Protocols

Protocols are like schemas, but they're not tacit. Consequently, when two heads of state are going to meet for the first time, their staff have to get together and discuss the protocol for that first meeting. Where are people going to sit at the table? Who will speak first? What topics are appropriate for conversation and what topics should be avoided? Protocols are overt and conscious where schemas are tacit. Regardless of whether they're tacit or not, schemas and protocols tell you how to behave in social situations. They're like rules of the road.

> **FOCUS ON TECHNIQUE**
>
> See the discussion of the "Fight Club" protocol in the Techniques section for an example of ways that protocols can be created and introduced into online communities and networks.

Routines

Routines are also protocols; just protocols that are happening repeatedly. They're a bit like schemas in the making since, given enough time, they become tacit. Some examples of routines in workplace cultures are the gathering around the coffee pot at a certain time each day or going out of your way to greet your co-workers as you come into the office to let them know that you're there and available.

Routines are of particular interest to communitarian theorists and social engineers because we can use them to encourage the kind of behaviors in communities and networks that help ensure sustainability and minimize conflict. Schemas tend to be so deeply ingrained and imbedded that they are very difficult to change or modify. If you can find schemas that already exist that you can use in your community to help encourage certain kinds of behaviors, they are far more powerful than protocols and routines because they are so deeply imbedded. However, the likelihood of creating schemas from scratch or modifying them significantly is minimal at best. Protocols, because they are overt and because they are negotiated, are useful but they're not always well understood by a large portion of the community. Protocols usually require an elder or a leader in the community to explain them to other members. The social situations where we tend to use protocols in communities are usually particular and contingent and don't occur often enough to have become commonplace. Routines are commonplace, but because they're conscious in the same way protocols are conscious, they can be manipulated and can be created. Thus, routines are the ritualized behaviors that occur over and over and over again that guide the members of your network and community in how to behave.

An example of this happened shortly after I joined Facebook. It turns out that you can put your birthday on Facebook, and the system will let people whom you have "friended" know that it's your birthday. What's unclear in that social network is what you should do if it's your birthday. People post messages on your "wall" wishing you a happy birthday. But what's protocol? Do you respond to each person individually? Should you respond in such a way that all of the people who are your "friends" see that you responded or should you respond privately to each person who wrote on your wall in order to avoid potentially embarrassing those people who didn't wish you a happy birthday? Users need schemas, protocols, and routines to show them how to behave in such situations, and as managers and designers, it's our job to find ways to provide them so our users/members have positive social experiences.

TECHNIQUES

Previous sections of this chapter showed how a sense of belonging is created often using examples from real life rather than online experiences. The following techniques or strategies have been successful for online communities I've built or which I've observed.

> **CHECKLIST OF TECHNIQUES**
> 1. Create and distribute a story of origin
> 2. Create an initiation ritual
> 3. Encourage your leaders and elders to share mythologies
>   ▪ Use negative myths
> 4. Encourage members to share myths and stories about themselves
> 5. Create leveling up ceremonies
>   ▪ Use podcasts
> 6. Establish routines and protocols
>   ▪ "Fight Club" protocol
> 7. Establish symbols, colors, and visual identities
> 8. Use a membership application as an initiation ritual

1. CREATE AND DISTRIBUTE A STORY OF ORIGIN

Although Facebook doesn't actually require that its members know its story of origin, the fact that Facebook's story is well known and highly publicized has probably contributed a great deal to its success. So many people have heard the story of how Mark Zuckerberg started Facebook with several of his college friends at Harvard University that new users come to the site with their expectations of the network's purpose and potential uses already well formed.

A significant number of people know that the Facebook site began as a place where college students could keep track of friends and who those friends were dating. They also know that Facebook was initially limited to college students, then high school students, and then only much later opened to anyone aged 13 and older. As a consequence, users tend to come to Facebook with the expectation of experiencing a culture already saturated by college-aged interests and agendas. Indeed, this probably accounts for some of Facebook's success since, despite its sometimes questionable morality, college culture is celebrated both by teenagers who are looking forward to experiencing it and by working professionals who look back on their college days with affection. But its story of origin also helps users understand and even appreciate the idea of "poking" someone else in the network.

TIP

On Facebook, friends can "poke" one another virtually in the same way that teenagers in a group sometimes poke each other with a finger as a means of saying, "I'm still here and I'm thinking about you."

2. CREATE AN INITIATION RITUAL

On Web-based communities, the ability to require a login and then the ability to track and collect data on a user enable you to create some fairly elaborate initiation rituals. One type of initiation ritual used by many WoW guilds, for example, is the trial membership initiation. Among members of the Oathsworn guild, individuals wishing to become new members must first attend a few trial raids with the guild and prove to its members and officers that they have the skills needed to be a healer, tank, or other service required by the community. Because statistics are kept on each raid and posted publicly, it is fairly easy for guild members, particularly the guild's leaders, to review the performance of an initiate so the guild can decide whether to admit the initiate as a full-status member.

In corporate settings, initiation rituals often involve some sort of training or professional development program that new members undergo, and if you build your Web site using tools such as MySQL and PHP, it's fairly easy to use the MySQL database to track which elements of a training program novices have completed. For example, we created an online community for industry professionals who participated in a leadership program for online professionals called "ONELead" (Online Network Enhanced Leadership program). ONELead was designed to help project managers learn to take advantage of online collaboration tools to build and lead virtual teams, and once individuals had gone through the training program, they were able to connect with other members of the ONELead community in order to continue sharing ideas and strategies for leading teams in online environments. Because some of the training program involved a series of online modules we had developed in Cascade, we were able to require that participants take quizzes that they had to complete with 80%

Reporting statistics on WoW characters was illustrated in the Remuneration chapter's discussion of showing the value of members' contribution to a network or community.

accuracy before they would be allowed to participate in the ONELead community. In other words, ONELead used its initiation ritual to help ensure that members of the community shared a commitment to online leadership and helped them learn to speak a common language.

3. ENCOURAGE YOUR LEADERS AND ELDERS TO SHARE MYTHOLOGIES

The stories members tell each other are important because they guide behavior in the network or community, and as a result, you will want to encourage leaders and elders in your community to tell the stories you want to serve as models (both positive and negative) for your organization. For example, in the case of the social network we built for the Boys & Girls Clubs of America, one of the most popular and successful ways we did this was to create a "Share Stories Archive" where we asked members to share stories that they thought others in the BGCA movement needed to hear. Behind the scenes, we asked some of the leaders in our network to "seed" the discussion by sharing some of their personal stories. People shared many kinds of stories, but the most popular and dynamic of these was the "YDP stories—Saving Souls" area. YDPs are "Youth Development Professionals," and they are "the sharp end of the spear" in the BGCA movement; they're the people who work directly with the club kids on a regular basis. Nearly everyone in the BGCA has, at some point in their career, worked as a YDP and has some story to share about a youth who has touched and been touched by the efforts of a YDP (Figure 6.5).

Once the leaders in the network began sharing stories about their work as YDPs and about the impact their experiences had had on their careers in the movement, members of the network instantly recognized the mythological character of the narratives and began contributing their own stories, using the first stories and themes produced by the leaders as their models. The resulting body of stories and the organizational goals and professional objectives expressed by those stories became a central hub of the network.

BREADLOAF MYTHOLOGIES

Mythos has also been used by educators working across disciplinary boundaries in order to build communities. The BreadLoaf Rural Teacher Network is part of "BreadNet," one of the oldest online communities of educators in existence, which dates back to the early 1980s. BreadNet and the BLRTN run on FirstClass, a client-based content management system, which supports modem dial-up connections that many rural teachers still have to use in order to take advantage of online communities. Dixie Goswami, one of the original founders of BreadNet and BLRTN, encourages K-12 teachers to tell about their successful student-to-student collaboration stories on BreadNet as a means of helping them see how they can use online communities to teach successful writing skills in their language arts classrooms. Through the stories they tell each other, these K-12 teachers provide both the emotional support and professional motivation they need to risk putting their students' writing online.

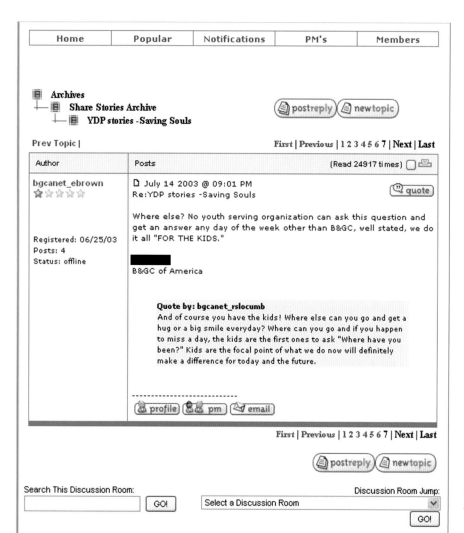

FIGURE 6.5
An archive of most important stories/ mythologies.

Use negative myths

Your community elders and leaders can also use negative myths to warn members against prohibited behaviors. For example, in one of the closed, private listserv communities I maintain, the members are all practicing professionals who have an extremely low tolerance for "noise" in the community. Additionally, members are expected to avoid emotional outbursts and *ad hominem* arguments during debates. Some years ago in this particular community, the author of several of the field's important and possibly even seminal books joined the community. In order to protect the innocent, I can't use his actual name, but let's call him JJ. Because of the importance of his works, JJ's books were often discussed by members of the community, and JJ was fine with this since, generally speaking, he used these conversations about his work as an opportunity to go into more detail about an idea or to describe how different ideas were related. It also didn't do any harm at all to JJ's professional consulting business to get all the free publicity in an influential professional community either.

One day, however, a member of the community challenged one of the major principles upon which JJ's most recent book was based. JJ tried to defend the work and attempted to explain why his comments in the book were still valid for the profession; however, the member continued to express discomfort with JJ's points. Frustrated by his inability to silence his opponent in the debate and incensed by the potential damage being done to his reputation, JJ launched a scathing attack on the community member, sniping at the person's failure to publish anything in the field, and JJ began ridiculing him by speculating about his poor education and impoverished training in the profession. In netiquette terms, JJ essentially "flamed" the guy, which was a flagrant violation of the community's published policies. As a result, he was contacted about his behavior off list and offered a number of options to rectify the situation. However, this only angered JJ further and, in a fit of piqué, he cursed the entire community publicly and unsubscribed himself from the list.

Because of his abysmal behavior and, ironically, because of the status his books afford him, JJ's story has become a myth in this professional community. Elders in the community tell the story as a reminder to members that no one in the community, regardless of how famous they may be, has the right to treat anyone in the community disrespectfully. Like the story of Icarus whose excess of passion and pride led him to fly too close to the sun, melting his wings, JJ's myth has become a kind of cautionary tale for those who might slip into flaming, sarcastic, and disrespectful behavior.

4. ENCOURAGE MEMBERS TO SHARE MYTHS AND STORIES ABOUT THEMSELVES

Just as community leaders can use *mythos* to help members of a network or community to better understand how they can interact with others in the collective, individual members can also use the same storytelling technique to create a persona for themselves within a community. Indeed, these can be either real or imaginary personas and either true or fictional stories, depending on the needs or goals of the community. On Second Life and on "role playing" WoW servers, for example, the whole point of *being* a member of the community is often to adopt the character of an "alter ego" and to experience a "second life." In fact, World of Warcraft has whole servers dedicated solely to characters who have fictional personas created entirely by their real players. Inside the immersive world of WoW, players live vicariously through these characters, creating friendships with others within the social network made possible by these servers and becoming members of guilds or online communities on those networks.

Paul Gorton lives in the United Kingdom and is a member of just such a guild whose members meet regularly on a dedicated role playing server. And like most guilds on WoW, Paul's guild has adopted some of the cultural practices and symbols of medieval society, as the world in which WoW is set is "Tolkienesque." Indeed, use of the term "guild" to refer to the community is itself an example of the practice of borrowing from medieval traditions and symbology. As a result, it's not surprising that Paul's guild has a "bard" who, like the medieval bards of old, has the responsibility of collecting the stories of the group. The bard, who happens to be Cynthia Haynes in the case of Paul's guild, plays an important role in the building of community because she is charged with both soliciting and delivering stories from community members that entertain the guild members as they sit around the "virtual campfire" and relax. Beyond the entertainment value, however, the Web site and stories Cynthia maintains are critical to guild because the stories establish the identity of the members.

BARDS IN OTHER COMMUNITIES

The role of "bard" isn't unique or limited to WoW guilds. I've asked members of professional communities to play the same role and to collect stories of members. We also saw examples of this when we discussed Tamara Adlin's celebration of elders' stories in the chapter on Influence.

The following is a short excerpt from one of the stories Paul wrote for Cynthia and their guild. For those who are unfamiliar with the intricacies and backstory behind World of Warcraft, however, it's important to note a couple of pieces of information. First, at its core, WoW is a game where players use swords, axes, and other medieval weapons to contest against and hopefully to slay opponents in order to obtain jewels, gold, higher quality weapons and armor, and reputation points among allies.

Second, to be successful, players really need to partner with other players and to collaborate in the same way that members of a product development team in industry need to partner. And just as product development team members have to have clearly defined roles in order to collaborate successfully, the roles each player adopts in the game need to be articulated very carefully and clearly in order to avoid seriously stepping on each others' toes, e.g., stealing someone else's kill is just as destructive to a relationship in the WoW as stealing credit for a great idea is in business.

In WoW, one of the ways players collaborate is to adopt the roles of "tank" and "healer." One player will allow another player to attract the attention of opponents and to absorb their attacks (which is called "tanking") while the other player hangs back and usually plays the role of "healer" for the tank by using long-range weapons such as the bow Justus carries in the following story to damage opponents, while also casting magical healing spells for the tank.

FIGURE 6.6
The character Justus.

Paul's WoW character is named Justus, and Justus and another player named Kihara met online and have been collaborating for a very long time. Justus can be seen in Figure 6.6.

Unthinkable Motion

The small deer twitched, shivering in the cold night air of the forest as it fed on the sparse undergrowth at the base of the tree. Her brown fur was slightly dulled, she seemed a little slim, and to a trained eye it was evident that she seemed too young to be away from her herd, especially at such a late hour.

The trained eye that watched the doe feed did not really care about these things; all that it was interested in was that the creature was a source of meat and hot, gushing blood.

The worgen crept silently forwards through the brush, tensing its muscles as it prepared to charge the distracted forest animal. It waited for the most opportune moment, the one that guaranteed the success of the kill.

Unable to control itself, a sliver of hot, steaming drool emerged from its feral mouth, sliding down the greasy fur to pool about its forepaws.

The doe, inexperienced as to the ways of these woods, seemed oblivious and reacted slowly as the crashing of the bushes to her left and the bone-chilling snarl that followed interrupted the peaceful melody of the night. As her head came round, panicked eyes staring straight into her doom, a sharp swish of displaced air was heard a moment after a long straight arrow thudded into the wolf-like humanoid's torso, spinning it in midair to crash metres away from her. Instinct took over, and with a bound of her powerful hind legs she fled into the deep forest.

(Continued)

Unthinkable Motion—cont'd

Leaping to all fours, the worgen spun, peering into the gloom with its heightened senses, searching for the source of the feathered shaft that was buried between its ribs. Spotting a lone figure readying a bow for another shot, the beast hurled itself forwards with preternatural speed towards its new prey. The large figure looked up, and for the last second of its unnatural existence, the worgen wondered why a savage grin was plastered over the human's face as it felt the pain of two hatchets burying themselves into its back, crushing its spine and its connection to life at the same time.

Kihara grunted slightly as she placed her armoured boot onto the dead worgen, and yanked her axes out of its body, buried deeply with her unusually powerful blows. She looked up and noticed the eyes of the big man upon her, his face lit by the rays of the full moon breaking through the forest canopy.

"Are you alright, Kihara?" Justus asked, in grim, quiet tones as he slipped the vile, skeletal bow back over his shoulder.

Kihara nodded curtly in reply as she cleaned the blades of her twin axes against the dark mottled fur of the creature at her feet.

"Any reason I shouldn't be?" she returned as she rose to her feet and followed the ranger towards the roadside where they were to meet their companions.

Staying silent, Justus hesitated for a moment before shaking his head and continuing forwards through the gloomy night.

by Paul Gorton

For members of Justus' guild, "Unthinkable Motion" is an extremely revealing story because it helps them better understand the special collaborative relationship that Justus and Kihara share. Many of the players in the guild will have also attempted to kill the mythical beast called "worgen" because there is a popular quest called "Worgen in the Wood," which occurs early in the game, so they will recognize this shared experience with Justus and Kihara. And because they will recognize the particular killing technique that Justus and Kihara used to attract the attention of the worgen so that it could be killed more easily, the story identifies the pair for the guild members. It enables them to understand how they can relate to and collaborate with Justus and Kihara.

On Facebook, there are a number of applications designed explicitly to encourage this same kind of sharing of stories and to serve the same role that Cynthia plays as the bard for her guild. An example of one of these is "25 random things," which friends can use to share information about each other. Although I personally found it hard to come up with 7 random stories about myself that I was willing to share, people in my circle stopped playing this application because telling 25 stories became too onerous. However, when the idea was to share 7 random stories about yourself that other people wouldn't be likely to know, the people in my circle did tend to bond and began talking to each other more than they had before these "random things" applications became popular (Figure 6.7).

Application:	25 Random Things	View Application
Developer:	Inherently Viral	
Description:	Rules: Write 25 Things about yourself, and then tag your friends. Read your friends' 25 Random things and comment on them. It's not just 25 things about me it's 25 random things about us	
Users:	48,969 monthly active users	
Matches:	Application Name and Application Description	

FIGURE 6.7
The 25 random things Facebook application.

Another popular application on Facebook that had a similar impact on encouraging my circle of friends to share was the "Where should you be living?" quiz. The quiz asks the user seven different questions, such as "What do you do to relax?" and then gives you four choices for your answer.

The quiz is easy to take, programming such a quiz is relatively simple, sharing and discussing the results are fun for the users, and, of course, the application encourages members of Facebook to share their stories with each other in order to increase their sense of belonging. What's more, this "quiz" technique can be adapted easily to use in listserv communities, chat forums, and other Web sites (Figure 6.8).

 Tharon Howard took the "Where should you be living?" quiz and the result is: Seattle

 Tharon took Where should you be living? quiz and the result is Seattle
You are tired of the scorching sun and the heat. You want to go somewhere were you can enjoy the rain and the ocean and feel like you are at home. You want to go to the top of the space needle and see everything around you. You have an adventurous spirit that is itching to explore.

☐ 10:12pm · Comment · Like · Take this Quiz · See other Quizzes

FIGURE 6.8
Feedback from a Facebook quiz.

5. CREATE LEVELING UP CEREMONIES

It's surprising how many networks and communities have levels of membership in them or different ranks for members to achieve, yet they don't have any recognition rituals or celebrations attached to them. As a community architect, you miss a tremendous opportunity if you don't create some ritual or ceremony that *publicly* recognizes your members' achievements. In professional communities such as a department of colleagues or in professional development communities, these ceremonies are particularly useful because they help members understand what the profession values and what goals they need to set for themselves.

One simple technique for recognizing achievement in e-mail-based communities is, of course, to send out a regular announcement of members' achievements; I've found that it works really well to have the responsibility for compiling and distributing the announcement assigned to a special leadership role in the

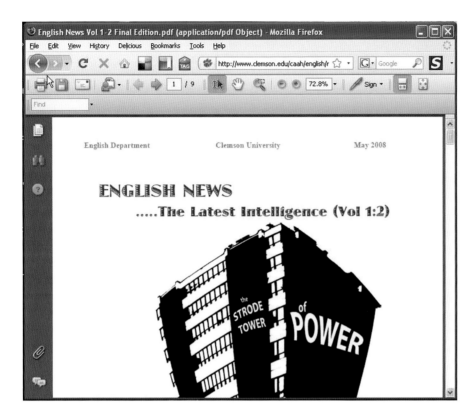

FIGURE 6.9
Departmental recognition
of achievement.

community. For example, in the Association of Teachers of Technical Writing (ATTW) community, Marge Hovde takes responsibility for compiling and sending out a quarterly message that lists recent book publications of members, award recipients, guest editorships, and other notable professional accomplishments by ATTW members. Many departments in organizations have similar kinds of arrangements. In my own department, for example, Steve Katz and Grace Ammons compile a similar collection of achievements by members of our department that are distributed ceremoniously via e-mail and are posted on the department's Web site each Spring and Fall (Figure 6.9).

Use podcasts

Creating a special Web page where members' achievements are recognized is a good thing, but using podcasts to recognize members is another useful though less often used means of celebrating a member's achievements. For example, one of the services I provide for my own department is to conduct interviews with colleagues who deserve recognition in the departmental community because they recently completed a new research project, published a book or article, obtained a grant, created an outreach program for the community, developed a new course for students, and so on. Basically, these podcasts celebrate the routine work these individual members perform, but they do so in a way that reminds the entire community what it values, thereby increasing a sense of belonging. However, what's particularly interesting about these podcasts is how useful we're finding them for recruiting new students and new faculty and for explaining and justifying what the department does to administrators outside the department. Perhaps it's because community-based podcasts are still considered novel, but in looking at who is downloading and listening to them, we're finding that potential members of the community are a far more significant portion of the audience than we anticipated when we started the ritual (Figure 6.10).

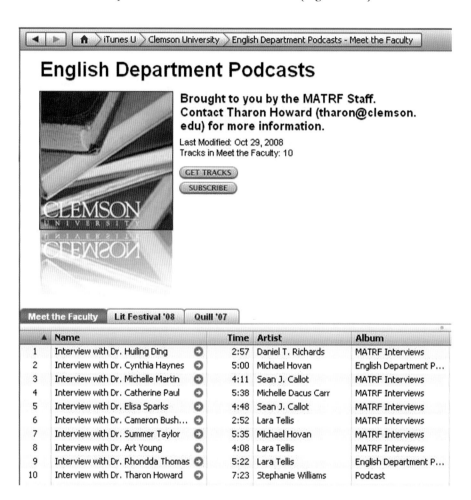

FIGURE 6.10
Podcasts of interviews celebrating members' achievements.

6. ESTABLISH ROUTINES AND PROTOCOLS

Most of my personal experiences with communities have been as a manager for one of my own networks or as a consultant helping design community architectures for corporate clients. As a result, I'm required to spend much of my time dealing with conflicts that inevitably emerge when, for example, members of a virtual team are trying to hash out the design of a new Web site. Most of my thinking about routines and protocols has thus focused on finding protocols that will prevent flame wars and emotional conflicts before they get out of hand and destroy the sense of trust and respect members need to feel for others in order to experience a sense of belonging.

"Fight Club" protocol

One of the protocols I've used over and over with good effect is what I call the "Fight Club" protocol. I probably need to come up with a better name for this protocol, but the reason I called it "Fight Club" goes back to a particularly challenging group I had when the movie *Fight Club* was popular [3]. The group with which I was working was a department composed of very successful and very strong-willed professionals who were used to managing projects on their own without oversight and supervision. Most of them were regional directors for a large organization and, as such, traveled a great deal in order to visit the various units in their regions. Being able to collaborate online was a tremendous asset to them because they couldn't afford the time away from their region or the expense needed to travel to the national headquarters. Furthermore, because they were trying to work on a strategic plan that all 16 regions in the organization were going to use and because the development of that plan was scheduled to take several months of work, they all needed to have input over a long period of time.

This particular group was mostly male, and it was fairly obvious to everyone concerned that much of the group's inability to make progress when they met both online and face to face was their inability to resolve conflicts. As one member of the group told me, "We've just got too many big egos suffering from too much testosterone poisoning to get things done." In talking to members and doing my preliminary research, it was clear that members could easily spot when a conflict was getting started, they just didn't know how to resolve it. They needed a protocol for "defanging" members who were starting to have an unproductive disagreement.

For those who haven't seen *Fight Club* or read the novel, its themes worked particularly well for this group because it is a black comedy that deals with a bored, white collar cubicle slave who believes that his position in society has left him hopelessly emasculated. The protagonist, played by Edward Norton, believes he finds purpose in his life when he meets Tyler Durden who makes his living selling soap made from fat he steals from successful cosmetic surgeons. In order to help Norton's character escape from the boredom and purposelessness of his life, Tyler Durden picks a fight with the protagonist. Ecstatic at having demonstrated their masculinity through conflict, the two repeat the experience, are observed by other socially castrated men, and ultimately end up creating "fight club." Fight club becomes a kind of bizarre psychological support group where bored and emasculated white collar males pummel each other in bare-knuckle fisticuffs.

In the novel and in the movie, what makes fight club work so well is the protocol Tyler Durden lays out for each night's fight ([4], 48–50):

1. You don't talk about fight club.
2. You don't talk about fight club.
3. When someone says stop, or goes limp, even if he's just faking it, the fight is over.
4. Only two guys to a fight.
5. One fight at a time.
6. They fight without shirts or shoes.
7. The fights go on as long as they have to.
8. If this is your first night at fight club, you have to fight.

At this point, we can return to the problem the regional directors' group was having with fights getting started that everyone on the team agreed were unproductive, but which no one really knew how to stop in a socially acceptable way. Basically, what happened was that we created a parody of Tyler Durden's protocol for fight club. We created a set of step-by-step procedures for dealing with conflicts before they got out of hand. And because we did it as a parody of a scene from a movie that was already a black comedy, we were able to use humor to defang the situation.

When someone on the team recognized that another member was starting an argument, the person starting the argument would get the "fight club soap bar." Receiving the soap bar meant that whenever that person posted a message to the discussion board, he was required to attach a small picture of a soap bar with the word "Fight Club" carved in it. The soap bar became, in effect, a badge of shame that the person would have to keep until someone else on the team "earned" the soap bar.

The official "fight club protocol" that the regional directors used was as follows.

1. Anyone on the team can nominate someone for the soap bar except the person who currently has it.
2. Someone has to second nominate the bar to be awarded.
3. If nominated, you can't explain why you don't deserve the soap.
4. If you are awarded the bar, you have to accept it.
5. You have to use the soap bar on all postings for 5 days or until someone else earns the bar in your stead.

The protocol worked for the regional directors because it was introduced to them in a way that made it funny and palatable to them. Later, once the humor and novelty wore off, it continued to work even though several of the members stated bluntly that they thought it was a "stupid game" and stated that they would refuse to use the soap bar on their posts. Nevertheless, it continued to work because just being nominated sent members the signal that they needed to hear. Furthermore, once the protocol was in place, earning the soap bar and not using it showed a degree of contempt for the entire community that few in the group were willing to risk. As a consequence, they worked hard to keep from being nominated in the first place, which was, of course, the whole point.

The fight club protocol doesn't need to refer to the movie *Fight Club* or to use a soap bar from the movie, however. I've used it with other communities, only I've changed the symbols to suit the occasion. In the case of BGCA teams, we used an animated gif of one smiley smashing another smiley on the head with a hammer and referred to it as "earning the hammer."

FIGURE 6.11
Hammer-beating and chair-bashing animated emoticons.

For another group, I used an emoticon which showed a red-faced smiley bashing a folding chair on another smiley. We called that one "getting sent to the chair," while in yet another community, the award was a rubber chicken. What matters most is the fact that your community has established a protocol for dealing with situations (Figure 6.11).

7. ESTABLISH SYMBOLS, COLORS, AND VISUAL IDENTITIES

Giving users the opportunity to use symbols to create an identity and sense of belonging in a community doesn't necessarily mean that you have to use visual symbols. Community members can find some tremendously innovative ways to let other users know how to respond to them. For example, members of the ONELead community have learned to use numbers instead of icons to represent themselves to other members.

ONELead members have all gone through a professional development program intended to help them learn to become more effective leaders in online environments, and an important element of the program involves "DISC profiling." DISC is a commercial psychometric profiling tool based on William Moulton Marston's observation that personality traits and communication styles can be roughly located into four different categories:

- Dominance—need to assert control and desire decisive, active responses to problems
- Influence—need to influence others in social situations and are concerned about emotions
- Steadiness—need a steady, clear plan of action without a lot of emotional drama
- Conscientiousness—need a rule-based and perfectionist approach to problems

As with the popular Myers–Briggs personality trait profile, individuals learn their DISC profile by responding to a series of test questions. Their responses to the questionnaire are scored on a seven-point scale according to each of the DISC categories. For example, someone scoring a "7" on the D or Dominance dimension is a "high D" and is likely to be aggressive, proactive, and forceful in her leadership style. Someone scoring a "1" has a "low D" and is likely to have a more cooperative, agreeable, and cautious leadership style. ONELead members all take the DISC assessment of their leadership and communication styles, and they all receive a four-digit score. A score of 7117 would be someone who has the highest possible D and C characteristics and the lowest possible I and S characteristics.

Now, among ONELead members who have gone through the community's initiation rituals and who have learned how to use DISC to adapt their communication styles to meet the needs of different profiles, knowing that someone scored a 7117 on their DISC assessment is valuable information. It tells you that you're dealing with a person who values direct, to-the-point, and completely accurate information. A 7117 doesn't want you to tell them the long backstory behind a situation and definitely doesn't care about all the social drama. Instead, they want a definition of the problem and what measures will be used to assess the quality of any potential solution to it. Also, knowing that you're dealing with a 7117 also helps you avoid stepping on the person's toes inadvertently because you know that people with high C's respond very badly if you even hint that the quality of their work is substandard and high D's respond badly to any challenge to their authority or ability to control situations: i.e., you're probably dealing with someone who tends to take criticism personally.

Because members of ONELead share this understanding of DISC, they use their four-digit DISC scores as symbols in the community intended to help each other understand their respective communication needs. Members in ONELead will, thus, sign a message posted to the forums as:

```
Sincerely,

Tharon (7117)
```

Alternatively, they might use the DISC symbology at the beginning of a message in order to justify why they are asking a particular question. For example, in responding to a high-D user's message requesting feedback on a problem the group was trying to solve, a member wrote:

```
Tharon, I understand the problem you want us to solve,
but please remember that I'm a 6-S, and I really need
to understand the steps you think we need to follow
before I can give you a substantive response. . .
```

Members of ONELead have found the DISC symbols so valuable in helping them explain their communication needs to each other that I've also found it's worth the time and energy to explain DISC and to teach the same symbol-usage techniques to my graduate students when I assign them to work on collaborative projects in our seminars. Although they can't afford to take the commercial version of the DISC test, they do a self-assessment of their DISC profile and use the letters D, I, S, and C as symbols rather than numbers. The effect is the same—the symbols allow them to identify themselves to others in the community in a way that helps people better understand their communication needs.

Using visual symbols to guide social interaction

But while using letters or numbers in text-based communities is useful, visual symbols in three-dimensional worlds and immersive systems require far less explanation and training for your members and have an immediate effect. For example, in World of Warcraft, users have a powerful means of communicating their status and identity in the system through the use of what are called "mounts."

Mounts are animals and mythical creatures that members of the network can ride as they move around the three-dimensional space of WoW. Having a mount is extremely desirable because riding a mount can reduce the amount of time a player spends traveling from one area to the next by as much as 200%. Beyond their utility, however, mounts serve as symbols of a player's level. Players can't purchase a ground mount until they have reached Level 30 in the game. Reaching Level 30 is a significant achievement in and of itself, but obtaining enough gold to buy one of the more desirable mounts is even more testimony to the player's skill in the game. Figure 6.12 shows a very desirable ground mount, but the white tiger shown in Figure 6.13 is an example of an even more costly mount.

Having a ground mount in WoW is an important symbol, but there are two additional types of mounts that players recognize as even more impressive. In addition to ground mounts, there are "epic mounts," which only Level 60 players can obtain. As its name suggests, a player on an "epic" mount has reached the same heroic status as warriors in great battle epics. Indeed, originally Level

FIGURE 6.12
Level 30 ground mount.

FIGURE 6.13
Level 30 ground mount.

60 was the highest level that a player could reach in the game. Hence, when you encountered a player on an epic mount such as the one shown in Figure 6.14, you knew you were interacting with an elite player.

Over time, however, it became commonplace to see players mounted on epic mounts, and while the symbolism of the epic mount was still a testimony to the player's skill and commitment to the network, it lost much of its impressive impact. Consequently, WoW's designers created more levels for players to earn, and a whole new class of mounts called "flying" mounts became available for players who were able to reach Level 70 in the game (Figure 6.15).

On a social network where one of the ways that members can interact is to engage in player vs player battles that allow both to earn "honor points," it's critical to have a visual symbol system that tells you who you should and shouldn't attack. Mounts are just one of the obvious visual symbol systems WoW's designers use to allow members to show that they belong to a particular community in the network space. As community or network designers, you can use visual symbols to allow your members to identify where they belong, and just as Blizzard had to create new symbols as its network changed and evolved, you'll need to track and provide new symbols to meet your members' visual identification needs.

FIGURE 6.14
Level 60 epic mount.

FIGURE 6.15
Level 70 flying mount.

8. USE AN APPLICATION FOR MEMBERSHIP AS AN INITIATION RITUAL

The importance of using initiation rituals to create a sense of belonging has already been discussed, and some techniques that will hopefully inspire you to create your own rituals in Web-based networks and communities have been offered. However, for community-based systems such as listserv, Major-domo, Lyris, Postman, Yahoo Groups, and other asynchronous, text-based communication servers, it can be a bit more difficult to see how to create an initiation ritual that will help new members better understand what it means to belong. It's a bit more difficult to create an online training package in Cascade, say, that will teach them DISC profiling principles.

The application form given here is one that members of one of my advisory councils and I created that you can adapt to meet your own system's needs.

The form was designed for a closed, by-invitation-only community, which communicated almost exclusively via e-mail.

Because of the private, closed nature of the community, the pseudonym "UserTOPOI" was used instead of the community's real name. For the same reason, please note that the URLs in the sample form also do not function.

The form was designed to drive new members to the Web site where they would find:

- information about policies for how the community's e-mail could be used
- samples of how to post effective messages
- a history of how the group originated
- a list of individuals who would serve as mentors
- recent books published by members
- podcasts profiling the professional work of members

```
Dear [insert name]:

Thank you for your interest in UserTOPOI.

--------------

WHAT IS UserTOPOI?

--------------


UserTOPOI is a closed, private community for usabil-
ity professionals. UserTOPOI exists to promote new
usability methodologies, increase general knowledge
of HCI practices among members of the usability pro-
fession, and to facilitate healthy, productive discus-
sions among members while protecting their privacy and
intellectual property rights.

You can learn more about UserTOPOI at:
```

http://people.clemson.edu/~tharon/UserTOPOI/

JOINING UserTOPOI

To join, you must:

A. Read the UserTOPOI policies.

- Special policies at

http://people.clemson.edu/~tharon/UserTOPOI/policies.
html

- Netiquette policies at

http://people.clemson.edu/~tharon/UserTOPOI/npoli-
cies.html

B. Agree to abide by these policies.

C. Answer *ALL* of the questions below, to help us
understand whether you will be a valuable member of
the community.

- Be sure to provide more than just a one-word response
to questions 4, 5, and 6.

- Avoid blank, inappropriate, or inadequate responses,
which will cause your subscription request to be
rejected.

D. Email your answers to Tharon Howard [THARON@CLEMSON.
EDU].

QUESTIONS

1.What is your full name?

2.Have you thoroughly reviewed both sets of UserTOPOI
policies at the URLs above?

3.Do you agree to abide by these policies?

4. In a few sentences, please explain why you want to join the UserTOPOI community.

5. One of the differences between a public email "list" and a private "community" is that members of a community are expected to give back to and to support a community. Please explain how you expect to support and contribute to the UserTOPOI community.

6. In a few sentences, please describe your background. Include any experience you have with usability activities.

7. How did you learn about UserTOPOI?

IMPORTANT

-- Check to be sure you have not skipped any questions.

-- Send this application from the email address where you want to receive UserTOPOI messages.

Sincerely,

Dr. Tharon Howard,
UserTOPOI Community Manager

Although not directly related to developing a sense of belonging, questions 1, 2, and 3 on the form are important because members can't claim later that they weren't aware of a policy or practice in the community should you and your advisory council need to take some disciplinary action. The responses to these questions show that members went through the initiation rituals, learned the policies and practices of the community, and explicitly agreed to abide by them. Question 7 is important because this particular community is "by-invitation-only." Question 7 helps remind applicants that they already know someone in the community and thus have a connection. Question 5 is important because it helps new members understand that, if they really wish to belong, they are expected to participate in the community. This has implications, of course, for both remuneration and influence, but it's also an important part of the initiation ritual, as you want your new members to begin to see how remuneration and influence are logical consequences of belonging.

CONCLUSION

This chapter discussed how you can use epideictic storytelling techniques to create a sense of belonging in your networks and communities. Through your leaders' narratives about the origins of your organization, you can give purpose and meaning to members' participation in the group. And through mythological narratives that praise heroes of the group and vilify its enemies, you build *esprit de corps* and provide models of exemplary behavior you want to encourage in the group. This chapter also discussed creating rituals, routines, protocols, and schemas to guide your users' behaviors and to help them better understand what is expected of them in particular social situations. We discussed ways to use symbols, both verbal and visual, as ways of signaling to other users what kinds of protocols and routines would lead to effective communication.

Once again, these strategies for building a sense of belonging among your users are really just attempts to prime the pump of creativity. The techniques I've offered here are by no means exhaustive. However, now that you're familiar with belonging and how it functions in social networks and communities, it is hoped that you'll be able to use these suggestions as jumping off points for creative and innovative techniques in your own systems. I hope you find the challenge of creating the *mythos* and visual symbologies your members will need to signify their communication goals to each other as intellectually challenging and as stimulating as I do.

WORKS CITED

[1] Casey S. Set Phasers on Stun and Other True Tales of Design, Technology, and Human Error. Santa Barbara, CA: Aegean Publishing; 1993.
[2] Denning S. Squirrel Inc.: A Fable of Leadership through Storytelling. Jossey-Bass; 2004.
[3] Fight Club. Dir. David Fincher. Perf. Edward Norton and Brad Pitt. Twentieth Century Fox, 1999, DVD.
[4] Palahniuk C. Fight Club: A Novel. New York: W.W. Norton; 1999.

CHAPTER 7
Significance

BUILDING GRAVITAS, BRAND, AND RECOGNITION

SYNOPSIS

How does someone know when a social network or online community is significant enough to warrant their constant and long-term attention? Perhaps more importantly, how do leaders in communities help members develop a sense of the significance of the space? This chapter addresses the issue of how to make your members feel that participating in your system is not only remunerated but it is also important because— simply put—people are more motivated to join, to participate in, and to remain members of communities that they believe are significant.

The chapter begins by discussing what I call the "paradox of exclusivity," which basically recognizes that people want to participate in popular groups and yet also want to feel like they're getting exclusive access to something that the average member of the "crowd" can't obtain. In order to better understand how to manage the paradoxical nature of "popular exclusivity," we look at some historical examples and show how exclusivity has been used as a means of creating significance all the way from "invisible colleges" in the 17th century to Facebook and to the Obama presidential campaign in modern times. Our examination of historical examples will also reveal that the acquisition of "social capital" is a fundamental principle and driving force in the creation of significance.

After exposing the concept of social capital, the chapter describes how certain individuals will use their social capital to purchase a disproportionately large degree of "influence" in social systems. It discusses how these individuals, who are called "influentials" by marketing and public relations professionals, can be leveraged in order to spread information about the significance of your network or community throughout a marketing demographic or particular social system. It shows how Stanley Milgram's "small world phenomenon" can be used to understand how influentials distribute information throughout a networking system, and it provides specific strategies and tools that can be used to locate influentials.

Ultimately, the chapter concludes with two illustrations of how all of these diverse concepts can be used to build significance. It describes two case studies of using exclusivity, social capital, and influential theory to create significance first in an invitation-only community of professionals who work for diverse organizations. Next, it illustrates the concepts by discussing how significance was created in a social network designed for internal use in a large organization with 35,000 employees.

In addition to the techniques discussed in these two case studies, once again, the chapter ends with examples of some additional, specific techniques from existing communities that can serve as a springboard for thinking about how to create significance in your own social networks and online communities.

INTRODUCTION

Chapter 4 showed that users don't stay in social networks or communities long if they don't believe there's adequate remuneration for doing so, but if your users don't believe that your community is significant, they probably won't become a member in the first place, much less stay. In order to be considered "significant," your network or community needs to be:

- well recognized
- established as the "go-to place" for accomplishing your users' goals
- valued by people your users respect
- populated by people who are serious and passionate in their field
- distinguished as a reputable brand to your users

In short, significance occurs both inside your community and outside it, and it is about building your network or community's *gravitas*, brand, and reputation.

THE PARADOX OF EXCLUSIVITY

One of the things about significance and building the sort of reputation in your community that will attract people, which is always difficult for my clients and other community leaders to accept, is the idea of exclusivity. There's a really difficult paradox that social network and community designers have to overcome in order to take advantage of exclusivity and its impact on the significance of the community or network. Chances are that you have a passion about the issue or topic or concept on which your community or network is built and the reason that you are building it in the first place is so that you will attract lots of people to the community or network so that they can share your passion for the idea. But they won't come just because you build it. And your desire to populate your community with lots of people can be counterproductive.

People are perverse; they want to be part of group, but they don't want to be another face in the crowd. If they can become a member easily, they often won't value becoming a member. They want to be members of *exclusive* groups. They want to be part of the "in crowd." They want to be the first to know. They want the inside track, the scoop. As result, there's a really difficult paradox that you, as a designer, have to learn to address. You have to curb your desire to reach as many people as possible and to be as *inclusive* as possible in admitting members to your electronic community or social network. Instead, you need to create ways to make people feel as though they're participating in something exclusive.

One of the best examples of this occurred during Barack Obama's presidential campaign. Obviously a presidential candidate has a vested interest in getting as many people as possible to pay attention to his or her message. Thus, it would seem to be in Obama's interest to make his Web site and cell phone text messaging systems as open as possible. But Obama's community architects didn't do that. Instead, they played on the exclusivity angle by *selectively* releasing critical information *exclusively* to members of his community. The my.barackobama .com community became famous and established tremendous "significance" for itself by refusing to release information about Obama's choice for vice president to anyone outside of the people who had registered on the Web site shown in Figure 7.1. In short, Obama's community designers paradoxically created popularity and drove eyeballs to their site by promising exclusivity.

FOCUS ON TECHNIQUE

Managers can combine techniques like the my.barackobama.com site with:

- Create a contest, game, or video.
- Celebrate celebrities.

FIGURE 7.1
Screen capture of http://my.barackobama.com/page/s/firsttoknow [1].

USING EXCLUSIVITY IN PRODUCT USER GROUPS

One of the groups that I personally co-coordinate is the South Carolina Adobe Users Group (SC AUG). This same drive to be the first to know and to get an inside track is one of the major reasons that this group has been successful. People have many reasons to come to the SC AUG meetings, some of which have to do with simple remuneration issues. Many of our members are graphic designers, Web site designers, or instructional technology developers. They attend meetings and participate in the community in order to share information, strategies, and ideas about Adobe's development software, which they use every day in their professional practices. Learning how to create an animated gif in Photoshop or how to create widgets in Flash that can be used in other Adobe applications gives these busy professionals a significant advantage over their competition in the marketplace. That's the remuneration side.

But they also come because the Adobe users' group has a direct pipeline inside Adobe. The Adobe users' groups are sponsored by Adobe, and there are a number of demonstrations of prereleased products under development available during the meetings. Members of the group have exclusive access to videos from the product developers at Adobe describing the work that they're doing on, for example, Captivate or Flash. In short, as soon as information is no longer covered by a nondisclosure agreement and able to be released, then the members of the SC AUG get that information. They're the first ones to see. They have exclusive access to information they desire.

EXCLUSIVE COOKIES

Susan Weinschenk, in her book *Neuro Web Design: What Makes Them Click?*, described a 1975 study that asked people to rate chocolate chip cookies. The researcher took the same chocolate chip cookies from a package and put 10 cookies in one jar and 2 cookies in another. They asked people to taste cookies from both jars. The jar with the fewest cookies always was judged to taste better and received a higher ranking from participants in the study ([17], 45).

ACQUIRING "SOCIAL CAPITAL" AND SIGNIFICANCE

As a community designer, one of the first decisions that you need to make as you're building your community is whether that community is going to be private or open. And because of the paradox of exclusivity, a common mistake that many designers make is to open their network or community to the public so that anybody can join. They want to get big fast, and being open and minimizing barriers to participation seems like the obvious route to take. However, as discussed later in this chapter, being big isn't necessarily "better," and it's also often the case that starting off closed and private will get you bigger faster.

A classic example of this in operation is Facebook. Facebook's popularity didn't come from being an open-access, anyone-can-join system. Friendster took that approach, and yet it has lost so much market share that nobody takes Friendster seriously anymore. Facebook started out quite the opposite. Facebook's origins were very exclusive. Initially, people couldn't become a member of Facebook unless they attended a particular university. And if we look at Facebook's dynamics before it was opened to the public, part of the attraction of becoming a member of Facebook (even when it was limited to particular colleges) was that college students wanted to join friends of theirs who were in a particular clique.

In other words, college students would become members of Facebook and seek to collect "friends" who were in the particular social circles that they felt had significance. Sociologist Pierre Bourdieu has an excellent term that describes this "collecting" behavior that he calls "social capital" [2]. Just as an entrepreneur will seek economic capital in order to buy equipment or resources needed to produce products or services in a business, people will attempt to acquire "social capital" that will "buy" them access to individuals and conversations that will allow them to achieve their particular, individual goals. College students on Facebook befriend particular groups as a means of demonstrating their accumulation of "social capital." It was a way for them to demonstrate that they were part of the "in crowd."

FOCUS ON TECHNIQUE

Managers can take advantage of this desire to accumulate social capital with techniques such as:

- Listing members' accomplishments.
- Making connections with other leaders in social media.

See Techniques #2 and #5.

When Facebook went public, there was a huge outcry and protest among its established members because they felt betrayed. Making Facebook available to parents or anyone in the world meant that the significance of the social capital that they had accumulated was diminished.

I really like the term "social capital" when thinking about building the significance of a group because I think it does a better job of explaining people's motivation for wanting closed communities and networks than the concept of "exclusivity" alone. It's certainly the case that people want to have inside information and they want to feel like they're plugged into what Diana Crane calls "invisible colleges" [3]. Indeed, Crane's work and that of Robert Lomas in his book, *The Invisible College: The Royal Society, Freemasonry, and the Birth of Modern Science* [11], are instructive because they illustrate how, historically, the same forces have been at play since the 17th century when it comes to building significance in communities.

OBTAINING SOCIAL CAPITAL IN INVISIBLE COLLEGES

Most people have heard of the Royal Society, which was founded in 1660 and which is, even today, considered to be one of the most prestigious scientific academies in existence. To become a Fellow of the Royal Society is one of the highest honors that a research scientist can receive, as it is only awarded to individuals who have been elected by the existing body of Fellows. What is less well known, but which is interesting because of its parallels to today's online communities, is that the Royal Society's origins actually lie in something known to 17th-century intellectuals as "the invisible college." Back then, if you were an astronomer, biologist, or mathematician and wanted to exchange ideas with others, you had to do it by sending letters to other "natural philosophers" who were also interested in learning about nature through experimental research. During a period of history that saw Galileo tried for heresy and placed under house arrest by the Church for pursuing such dangerous knowledge, it made sense to keep your colleges "invisible."

Since the "visible" educational system of the day was mostly limited to training intended to promote religion and educate clergy, learning how to engage in scientific inquiry and learning about experimental discoveries being made by others were almost entirely contingent on your access to the letters being exchanged by scientists such as Robert Boyle, Johannes Kepler, Robert Hooke, Tycho Brahe, and others. In fact, using the phrase "man of letters" to describe a person of learning and intellectual prowess came about as a result of this 17th-century practice of exchanging and circulating letters. Back then, being a "man of letters" didn't only mean that a person was well read; instead, it was more a measure of the amount of social capital that individual had acquired.

Being a member of an invisible college in the 17th century meant that you were part of a network that was remarkably similar to the blogging systems of today. Back then, a scientist such as Boyle might conduct an experiment with his air pump or record his observations about the relationship among temperature, volume, and pressure in a letter that he would pass along to a colleague in the invisible college. His colleague would then make a few marginal comments on the letter and possibly append a letter of his own to the original. The packet would then be passed on to the next "link" in the invisible college's chain, creating the 17th-century equivalent of a store-n-forward network. Over time, the result would be a collection of letters that could be bound together into a journal or book, which were precursors of the modern academic journal. And of course blogosphere aficionados will immediately recognize their comment feature in the "marginalia" that invisible college members could write sparking off the same sorts of conversations and controversies that drive up reader interest today.

While it's fun to find 17th-century parallels to blogging in the invisible college, the connection breaks down as soon as we remember that the invisible college was invisible for a reason. Membership in the invisible college purchased individuals social capital, which gave them privileged access to information that set them apart from the "vulgar" crowd. They were able to use the social capital to purchase an education in how to become a successful scientist in the 17th century at a time when that information was exclusive and desirable (and therefore *significant*). What most bloggers and community designers forget when they're building their systems is that the people who read their blogs and join their networks aren't doing it so they can become another nameless face on your list of followers and friends—they are doing it so they can acquire the social capital they need to be *different* and to set themselves apart from others.

QUALITY VS QUANTITY

Being "significant" is often antithetical to creating homogeneity. And yet traditional mass marketing campaigns have tended to seek homogeneity by building on the lowest common denominator in a market. Indeed, if you think about it, the whole point of doing demographic analyses is to use statistical measures of central tendencies in order to locate those commonalities so that marketers can exploit the homogeneity in a segment. And yet this whole approach flies in the face of what I've been calling the paradox of exclusivity and the desire of community members to acquire social capital. The *Cluetrain Manifesto* [10] and Seth Godin's recent book *Tribes* have made it clear that traditional methods of branding aren't as successful in online social media as they were in print and television. The days of sticking a "brand" such as Coca Cola or McDonald's logo on a billboard or in some media channel where it will collect as many eyeballs as possible aren't accepted anymore.

Increasing name recognition by counting the number of times your company or organization is mentioned in the popular media isn't what we're talking about when we're talking about building significance. It's about building a conversation and a relationship with your customers now. Traditional marketing is passé in an age when the new marketplace is online and when potential customers use social media to learn about you instead of learning about you through commercial messages in mass media. This is not to say that getting name recognition with a large quantity of people is a bad thing, but it is naïve to equate quantity and name recognition with significance. The fact that many people know the name of your social network doesn't mean that they will want to have a sustained relationship with it. Name recognition doesn't equal significance. What we are talking about and what social media marketing is about is building significance for your community through *conversations* and through the quality of relationships you can have with customers and potential members of your network and community. It's less about the number of people you reach and more about helping them feel like they are earning social capital by connecting with you.

USING NODES AND CONNECTORS TO START THE CONVERSATION

If creating significance for your network or community involves establishing a conversation with potential members, this begs the question: How do you

The National Geographic Society has its origins in the Royal Society, and though many people don't realize it because of the popularity of its media outlets, originally, you couldn't become a member of the National Geographic Society simply by contacting the society yourself. In order to become a member of National Geographic, you had to be nominated for membership. The Society is another example of the paradoxical popularity of exclusivity.

contact them? How do you spread information about the significance of your network or community using social media? Thanks to Gladwell's *Tipping Point* [6], Ed Keller and Jon Berry's *The Influentials*, and Paul Gillin's book *Secrets of Social Media Marketing* [5], one answer is to attempt to find "influentials" or "connector nodes" in social media.

Gladwell's book returned to the now famous 1960s "small world experiment" by sociologist Stanley Milgram where Milgram sought to discover the average path length between individuals linked together by the American social system. Milgram was influenced by political scientist Ithiel de Sola Pool, who was interested in the flow of information and political influence through social networks. De Sola Pool had hypothesized that it might be possible to predict and possibly even control how influential political ideas spread through a society if it were possible to understand the interconnectedness of a particular social system.

Milgram's experiment took up this challenge by attempting to track one individual's attempt to contact another member of the same society. In several different studies, he contacted people in Wichita, Kansas, and in Omaha, Nebraska, as his starting points and then asked those individuals to contact a specific stock broker in Massachusetts (he chose these locations because the starting and ending points split the United States geographically and represented diverse cultural differences). Milgram's Midwestern participants were asked to send a packet to a target individual in Boston; however, they were required to send the letter to individuals whom they knew on a first-name basis. In this way, Milgram ensured that they had a particular kind of social relationship with the letter's recipient (i.e., Milgram's participants had the same kind of strong, first-level connection that we saw distinguished social networks from communities). Those who received the letters received the same instructions—they recorded that they had received the packet by signing it and then they forwarded the packet on to someone who they knew on a first-name basis, someone whom they speculated might be able to forward the letter directly to the targeted stock broker in Massachusetts. After several iterations, Milgram found that it took an average of 5.5 or 6 steps before the packet reached its target destination.

WATT'S REPEAT OF MILGRAM'S EXPERIMENT

Milgram's experiment has been critiqued because of his small sample sizes. His most-often cited example only used 160 letters. Of those 160 letters, only 24 letters actually reached their target in Sharon, Massachusetts. Duncan Watts used the power of the Internet to repeat the study. In 2001, Watts recruited 61,000 people and then asked them to transmit messages to 18 targets worldwide. Like Milgram, he found that average length of the chain was roughly six links.

Milgram referred to this predictability as the "small world" phenomenon; however, it's more popularly known as "six degrees of separation." A visualization of the six degrees concept is shown in Figure 7.2, which shows that even though the mass of circles or "nodes" in a network may at first seem chaotic, no two nodes are separated by more than six links or degrees of separation.

Milgram's small world phenomenon is useful because it suggests that influence does indeed appear to flow through a social system in a predictable fashion as de Sola Pool had initially speculated. However, it still doesn't get us much closer to understanding how to contact potential members about the significance of your online community. We need to have quality conversations with a few "nodes" in the network and so we need to be more selective about where to start having those conversations.

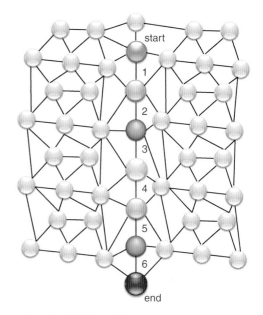

FIGURE 7.2
Six degrees of separation in social network with strong, first-person connections between members.

According to those who follow what Clive Thompson calls the "influentials theory" [16], to get closer to spreading our significance meme selectively, we need to understand that not all nodes are created equal. Gladwell identified three types of individuals who can "tip" a trend into a word-of-mouth viral marketing campaign. These are:

> **Connectors**—these are those people who seem to know everybody; they're the kind of people who want thousands of Twitter followers and hundreds of LinkedIn connections.
> **Mavens**—these are the enthusiasts and devotees in a subject matter area; they collect information about a subject and are thrilled to distribute it.
> **Salesmen**—these are the big idea brokers; they aren't only interested sharing information like mavens, but they're also interested in persuading people to act on it.

These three types of individuals have more impact on a networking system than the typical node, according to Gladwell. Because they function like a "hub" in the network, they offer a greater degree of interconnectedness than a typical node. In other words, they have the effect of shortening the number of links needed from six to as few as three.

FIGURE 7.3
Disproportionate impact of a hub on network topology.

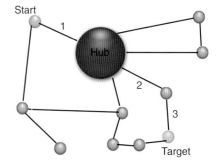

Figure 7.3 shows a network in which a typical node can only have, at most, three connections but in which a hub can have five or more connections. The impact of this hub (which in this case represents one of Gladwell's "connectors") is substantial because it suggests that you can ignore the "typical nodes" or the masses.

FOCUS ON TECHNIQUE

Managers can take advantage of the impact of hubs on network topologies with the following techniques:

- Participate in influential communities to create trails back to your own.
- Make connections with other leaders in social media.

See Techniques #3 and #5.

As Thompson says, "In modern marketing, this idea—that a tiny cadre of connected people triggers trends—is enormously seductive. It is the very premise of viral and word-of-mouth campaigns: Reach those rare, all-powerful folks, and you'll reach everyone else through them, basically for free."

INFLUENTIALS AND USER MANUALS

In her study, "Process, Product, and Profit: The Politics of Usability in a Software Venture," Barbara Mirel conducted an ethnographic study of software manuals and training materials in organizational settings. Mirel found that in large workplace environments, there are typically one or two "experts" who routinely use a software package. The rest of the employees depend on that individual for their technical support. When they have a question about a task they wish to perform, they typically will not look for their answers in the manuals and training materials; instead, they will go to their internal expert. Indeed, it's this internal expert who uses the manual in order to stay ahead of and retain their ability to support the needs of their colleagues [12].

DECIDING HOW TO CONTACT INFLUENTIALS

Whether your network or community is closed and accessible by invitation only or if it's open access and public, identifying and contacting those influentials operating as social media hubs are important and useful tactics for establishing the significance of your system. However, how you contact them and what you do once you contact them are contingent on the purpose of your group. Consequently, in order to illustrate how the principles of exclusivity, social capital, quality conversations, and influential network hubs all interact in order to create significance, the next few pages discuss two specific situations where these principles were used. First, we'll examine how significance was created in an invitation-only community of practicing professionals who work for diverse organizations. Next, we will consider the same concepts by discussing how significance was created in a social network designed for internal use in a large organization with 35,000 employees.

Invitation-only community of practice

Let's say, for example, that you operate a usability testing lab for your organization. You're passionate about your profession and you want to keep up with the latest trends and practices in your field. You want to talk to other professionals about the wide variety of problems you encounter on a day-to-day basis, but the local team in your lab is small and you're all too busy running studies and meeting with project managers whose development teams you support to be able to meet regularly with your other lab colleagues. You go to the UPA, CHI, and other professional conferences each year, and these are helpful. But they are also costly, they only meet once a year, and they run concurrent sessions so that you can't attend all the sessions you want. You decide that what you really need is an online community designed exclusively for serious, practicing professionals like yourself. But you've been around the Internet long enough to know that if you start an open access, public group on Yahoo Groups, Ning, or Usenet you're not going to attract and retain the kind of members you want. You've seen those groups before—college students get on them and nag you for help with homework projects or ask for help finding jobs; product vendors and consultants use it to hawk their wares; and newbies ask the same dumb questions over and over again or, worse, they try to wrangle free consulting and training out of the experts.

In this case, you want to build a "community of practice" where the significance of the community is based on the same kinds of exclusivity we saw in the 17th-century's invisible colleges. You know you need to recruit members, but you absolutely don't want to go "viral" with your marketing. You *don't* want to *get big*. The purpose of your group is about building high-quality and extremely strong ties between members. Focus on quality; that's your strength.

You need to take an invitation-only approach and you need to start by building a core of trusted colleagues who will share your vision, i.e., you start by building your advisory council starting with the social capital you, yourself have already accumulated in your community of practice. Chances are you already know who many of the people on your advisory council will be. Because you learned your profession from someone, one place to start is to talk to your mentors and the faculty members where you earned your degree. Ask them if they have colleagues who should be invited to participate in your community. Chances are that they'll direct you to influentials. You've probably also met other professionals and were impressed by speakers and presenters at the professional conferences you attended; these are potential recruits who can also help you identify hubs. Your colleagues at work will know other professionals whom they trust and whom they can recommend to you.

Of course, the authors of books and journal articles you admire are obvious choices of folks you will eventually want to recruit and contact, and then there are "technorati" in the social media you'll probably want to invite by contacting them directly (see Table 7.1 for a list of ways to locate technorati). Before you do, however, it's critical that you have *created a story* that will share your vision for the community with the people you contact. In other words, you want to share with them the same type of story I provided earlier. You need a story of "belonging" that helps them understand the problems your community will address,

Table 7.1	Some Useful Tools to Search for Influential Technorati in a Topic Area
Google's link:[URL]	On Google's search bar, type "link:[URL]" to obtain the number of pages that link to the URL specified. For example, "link:www.clemson.edu" will provide the number of links other sites make to Clemson's homepage.
Del.icio.us	Popular social bookmarking site that shows most popular sites for a particular topic.
Digg	Popular social news site where Digg members can identify or "digg" a Web site and locate it in a category such as "technology" or "sports" so that others can find it.
Mixx	Mixx combines and "mixes" traditional news feeds from outlets such as CNN.com and Reuters with a social news markup tag such as Digg by allowing members to vote and comment on stories.
StumbleUpon	This site allows users to "stumble upon" Web pages recommended by friends and peers. This service "automates the 'word-of-mouth' referral of peer-approved Web sites" and categorizes sites according to a user's circle of friends.
Technorati	Usually considered the premiere source of information on blogs, this site tracks blogs, allows searches, and provides an "authority" score based on rankings by community members. Also famous for its "State of the Blogosphere" reports.
BlogPulse	A service of Nielsen BuzzMetrics, this is a blog search engine that also allows users to graphically plot trends and topics in the blogosphere.
Mashable.com	One of the most popular news blogs specializing on social media on the Web. In 2009 it was listed as #5 on Technorati with an authority score of 10,112.
Twellow	Called the Twitter "Yellow Pages," this site allows users to search for key words and receive a rank-ordered list of Twitter profiles.
Twitscoop	Provides real-time updates on current tweets in a tag-cloud format. Also allows users to search for trending terms.
Alexa	The premiere Web site ranking tool. Allows users to search for a term and provides the URL, a brief description (if available), and ranking of site.
Amazon	A golden oldie, but searching Amazon for key terms and following sales ranking info can help locate authors in a field.

the types of members who will be attracted to it, the ways they can interact with it, and, more than anything else, your story has to let them see your passion.

Seth Godin, in his book *Tribes*, offers critical insight into the importance of passion by distinguishing between casual followers and "true fans." Godin writes:

> Too many organizations care about numbers, not fans. They care about hits or turnstile clicks or media mentions. What they're missing is the depth of the commitment and interconnection that true fans deliver. Instead of always being on the hunt for one more set of eyeballs, true leaders have figured out that the real win is in turning a casual fan into a true one.

[7], 33

Your passion has to come through in the story you tell and in the invitation you send. You can't fake it, you can't force it, and you don't want to try to hide it, which is why you need to be having a quality conversation with them—the significance of your community will be in the story you tell when you invite individuals to join. If you communicate your passion, you'll attract "true fans" who will help you identify hubs whom you can also contact, or, better yet, whom they will contact on behalf of your community. And therein lies the danger of hiding or faking your passion. True fans will *always* sniff out deceit or incompetence and then they will turn the power of social media against you. They will warn other influentials against you. It's for this reason you need to have your story ready and have tested it out on trusted colleagues before you start.

FOCUS ON TECHNIQUE

For more discussion of ways to shape your story, see Technique #1.

You shouldn't be afraid of social media, however, and you should expect rejections from many of the folks you contact. Exclusive communities like the one we're discussing here aren't for everyone, and rejection doesn't mean that you're not still creating significance for your community if your story is doing its job. In fact, you're probably going to be unable to recruit many technorati and major book authors when you initially contact them with your story and personal invitation to join, but your story and your genuine passion may "stick" with them. Many of these folks are already actively engaged in established communities that sustain them and enable them to do that work that got your attention in the first place. They may not have the time and energy to contribute to another community, but that doesn't mean that they won't pass your story on to others. When they're contacted by others who are true fans and who would benefit from your community, the technorati will remember your story and may decide to pass it on. If this happens often enough, then the major authors and technorati will follow. Indeed, I've often found that it takes an additional contact from another passionate member of the community to be compelling.

Open access social network

Let's shift to a different type of group with different purposes. The previous example used an invitation-only community of practice that wasn't tied to any particular organization, so in this case we'll flip some of those parameters around.

Say, for example, that you work for a large corporation and that you've been tasked with building a social network that will allow different units within your organization to form their own communities. In this case, your organization mainly wants people to have the emotional and professional support of colleagues in their own departments, to gather around the "virtual water cooler," and to share their ideas about problems they observe and potential solutions. But upper management also wants to encourage people to see what's going on in other departments in the organization so they don't feel as though they're trapped in a silo. Because it costs four times as much on average to recruit and train a new employee than it does to retain a current employee, they want to keep people in the company and want to encourage people to view their careers as moving from one department to another in the organization rather than leaving the company entirely.

Building a social network like this is obviously going to take a lot of effort on the remuneration, influence, and belonging sides; employees aren't going to want to come near the network and will starve it to death if they don't see any benefits to them of joining, if they don't believe that anything they say on the system will have an impact on the organization, and if they don't feel any commitment to the other people who are using it. However, in order to focus on how to build significance in the minds of people both inside and outside your network, let's assume that, because you've been reading this book, these other RIBS elements have already been addressed in the network's design.

Once again, we need to begin with the story you're going to use to send out messages for the network. But unlike the usability community discussed in the previous example, this time the ethos and passion of a visionary leader can't drive the story. Because the network represents the institution, the story needs to demonstrate significance through alternative means. Fortunately, Amy Shuen, in her excellent book, *Web 2.0: A Strategy Guide*, provides a useful framework for compelling people that new technologies are worth adopting [14]. Shuen uses Everett Rogers' 1962 classic study of technology adoption, *Diffusion of Innovations*, and articulates five factors that are likely to trigger adoptions. She illustrates these with Facebook and why the college student for whom Facebook was originally targeted was so successful.

These five decision triggers are tremendously helpful because they explain what highlights our story of belonging need to hit in order to be successful in recruiting new members to the network.

We faced a similar situation on the Boys and Girls Clubs of America (BGCA) project. There we were attempting to build a social network for the 35,000 people who worked in clubs throughout the world. One of our principal goals was

SHUEN'S APPLICATION OF ROGERS ADOPTION CURVE TO FACEBOOK

Relative advantage
How much better the new product is compared with the old one. Facebook allows college students to keep up with high-school friends who went to another college.

Compatibility
If a new product fits with current values and usage, it broadens the initial audience. Major changes are risky and appeal to a relatively smaller group of early adopters. For Facebook, college students represent a digital youth generation that is used to being connected wirelessly with their friends through various devices.

Complexity
Ease of use and understanding of features make adoption faster and easier. Facebook is very easy to use with information pushed to users through e-mail and RSS feeds.

Trialability
Products can sell themselves if customers experiment with them and get hooked by the personal experience. Users can try Facebook free, and the system is addictive, particularly for college students.

Observability
How visible a product usage and impact are to others. Social influence plays a role in adoption. Facebook users can easily identify who was on and using the network. The "wall" provided names, messages, photos, and videos of friends. Facebook's viral applications raised this observability to a whole new level of referral, subtle peer/friend pressure, and social influence. Not only do friends invite friends to "join the party" and play an application with them, they get constant numerical updates and reminders of how many of their circle of friends are participating.

Adapted from Shuen [14], 78-79

to retain as many BGCA professionals as possible. As an organization, BGCA wanted to encourage youth development professionals (YDP) to see their entire career stretching across BGCA's range of opportunities so that employees didn't leave the movement to pursue jobs in other fields at other organizations.

However, we couldn't tie our story simply to organizational needs; our users might be motivated to help the organization cut costs and achieve its mission of creating positive, long-term relationships between youth and adults, but we needed something more significant to them personally and professionally to compel them to become part of the network.

In order to learn what potential members of the network would consider "significant," we conducted several research studies with clubs across the country for several months, including site visits, surveys, interviews, case studies, and task analyses. We studied the communication channels BGCA professionals used, their training and professional development programs, the organizational structures of their units at both regional and local levels, and typical problems they faced and tasks they performed. Based on our research, we built a profile of the typical types of BGCA professionals (i.e., personas) and created narratives of each type's typical day or week.

We found that the typical "youth development professional" spends her day working almost entirely with kids on specific activities and programs in the clubs. She's passionate about the kids and desperate to help them and the community, but she also has very, very few opportunities to express her frustration with the often shocking emotional and socioeconomic difficulties that she tries to help her kids resolve. She's constantly seeking out new, engaging, and entertaining educational activities for the kids, as well as the physical space, supplies, and financial resources necessary for offering those activities. But she's also siloed into her club, and the demands of working with the kids rarely give her the time to "blow off steam" with another adult, much less share ideas with another YDP at another club. She does get information about the BGCA movement and takes advantage of training workshops, regional conferences, visits from regional service directors, and other opportunities to connect with other professionals in the national movement when she can, but because of the cost of travel and the disruption these events create in the club's routine, they don't have as much impact on her day-to-day working life as she would like.

Based on our research, we built our stories around the following themes:

- Learn techniques for successful programs by sharing ideas with others
- Learn about opportunities for professional development and career advancement
- Create an emotional and professional support network of like-minded colleagues
- Have greater impact on the movement by reaching other influential professionals
- Get insider knowledge about emerging trends in the movement
- Partner with other clubs to take advantage of national fund-raising activities
- Leverage resources and space in other clubs through cooperative relationships

In terms of identifying key "influentials" who would be critical in getting the network used, our research revealed that four groups would be key:

Regional Service Directors—These individuals, known as "RSDs" in BGCA-speak, were a bit like traveling minstrels or medieval bards for BGCA. Each RSD was responsible for a geographical region and personally traveled to and visited clubs in that region providing support from the national headquarters for federally funded educational programs, training programs, administrative services, etc. RSDs were critical because they not only spread messages from the national headquarters to a region, but they also spread information between clubs in a region.

National Training Staff—Like RSDs, staff who provided professional development seminars around the country were critical to the spread of information. They traveled to regional conferences, national conferences, and individual clubs offering a variety of training opportunities for every type of professional in the movement. As such, they had individually made and maintained an enormous number of personal contacts both geographically and vertically throughout the movement.

Executive Directors—Known in BGCA-speak as "EDs," these individuals were responsible for managing the club (or more often clubs) in their organization unit. EDs were responsible for personnel evaluations, financial resources, and, most particularly for us, technological resources. EDs could prohibit or promote the use of the network because they controlled how their people used their time and whether their people could access the technology to use the social network. If the EDs felt that the social network distracted their employees from more critical activities, then they could discourage its use (which is part of the reason we didn't call it a "social" network). Conversely, if the EDs used the network and rewarded employees who also used it, then YDPs were more likely to join.

Resource Development Officers—We discovered through our research that there was a group of people in the organization who, somewhat unexpectedly, were powerful influentials for us. Resource development officers had different titles depending on the unit where they worked, but they all had basically the same job—they were the people responsible for writing grants, organizing fundraising events, working with foundations, and locating donors. Because resource developers have to collaborate with each other in order to make themselves eligible for many government RFPs, it's normal for them to need to partner with another organization in order to meet the submission criteria a potential funder might request. Also, because these individuals are tasked with meeting the resource needs of club professionals, they have to develop and maintain a keen sense of what's happening in the clubs around them. As a result, we discovered that resource development personnel already had developed their own informal network so they could do their jobs more effectively. We hoped to leverage that existing network to advance the one we were building.

The RSDs, EDs, and resource developers all had their own extensive networks that they used to contact each other, but these were based primarily on the telephone. A few of them used e-mail and instant messaging to keep in touch, but mainly these individuals didn't have tremendous experience at collaborating in online environments and were unfamiliar with using groupware to collaborate on long-term projects. Consequently, in order to begin seeding our network with content that would attract the rank and file membership and to provide a core around which the network could grow, we began by offering what we called the "Advanced Leadership Certificate Program" (ALCP). The ALCP program is where we began to bring the principle of exclusivity to bear on the project because the certificates were awarded exclusively to participants in the program and individuals who wished to participate in the program had to apply and be admitted to it.

In the ALCP program we would bring in, for example, 25 RSDs at a time, house and feed them for a week, and teach them how to use a social networking suite of tools that we built in order to collaborate on long-term projects. We helped the groups identify a particular problem that four to six of them had in common and then asked them to work on that problem together for 90 days using the network; at the end of that 90-day period, we "published" their solutions in the "Exhibit Hall" of our social network. We offered nine of these workshops each year, and those projects judged to be the best were published in "Featured Booths" in the Exhibit Hall where they served as models for members of the network who hadn't gone through the training program. Also, by providing these individuals with an actual certificate at the end of the experience, they were able to obtain professional development credit, which helped them receive a raise.

Beyond the "ALCP" workshop core, we then used additional "marketing" techniques:

PREMIUM ACCESS FOR INFLUENTIALS

In order to encourage EDs and RSDs in particular to adopt the network, we offered them "premium" space and technical support services on the network. For example, we offered any executive director who wanted to host electronic staff meetings on the network privileged special accounts for all the staff and premium archiving services for any of the content generated. We also gave those units dedicated technical support personnel to help with any training or special software support they might need in order to ensure that their experience with the networking tools was positive from the get-go.

POSTER CHILD TESTIMONIALS

Out of our ALCP workshops we were able to identify particular individuals who became our "poster children" for the social network. We invited these individuals back to other workshops and had them offer testimonials to the workshop participants who followed them.

PRESENTATIONS AT REGIONAL CONFERENCES

We also sponsored the attendance of our "poster children" at regional conferences where they provided talks at those conferences illustrating and testifying to the benefits of using the social networking technology to do their jobs more effectively. When we identified regional conferences and couldn't send a member of the ALCP team, the network team, or one of our poster children, we would send the conference organizers fliers and brochures about the network that we requested they distribute.

DOCUMENTARY DVD

Next, we hired a video production team and produced a documentary-style video of the ALCP workshops and the network. Over the course of the video, RSDs, EDs, resource developers, and youth development professionals all gave testimonials in their own words how they perceived the social networking tools to be of benefit. Furthermore, we also had the president of BGCA and the president of Clemson University, as well as other respected members of the Boys and Girls Club movement, offer interviews in which they described why they supported the use of the network and promised to give full support to other BGCA employees who participated in the network. This DVD was distributed to clubs around the world and was handed out at conferences.

VIDEO THEATER

In addition to handing out the DVD at conferences, we also made the video available on the social network in what we called the "Theatre." More important than the documentary movie, however, were short video presentations made by each ALCP project team. At the end of their weeklong workshop experience, each project team gave a presentation on the project they were going to complete over the next 90 days, which we video recorded and then made available on the social network. Because of the novelty of streaming video at the time (YouTube and Hulu weren't phenomena then), participants would go back to their clubs and send others to the theatre in order to watch the videos. The peer pressure to watch the video streams made this one of the most effective tools we used.

MAGAZINE STORIES

Like most large corporations, BGCA also had existing news and information distribution channels, and we used those as well to spread the word about the significance of our social network. One of our team was dedicated to writing stories, which were published in the BGCA national magazine describing the ways a particular individual in a club or a group of individuals on an ALCP project team collaborated in order to solve problems that plagued members of the movement. We also located regional newsletters and seeded those with similar stories.

PRESS RELEASES AND RADIO INTERVIEWS

We also reached out to the public mass media and wrote several press releases that were picked up by a few newspapers describing both the ALCP and social networking projects. We were able to get a South Carolina public radio station to interview the network director and project director on a radio program that was broadcast across the state.

NATIONAL CONVENTION BOOTH

BGCA holds a national convention each year and we took advantage of that event in order to spread the word about the program. We built a booth in a prime location at the conference hotel, set up networked computers in the booth, and demoed the network to passersbys. We invited our poster children to stop by and offer demonstrations to their colleagues in many minisessions in order to lend their credibility about the significance of the project. Additionally, we were able to secure time on the conference program where we were able to provide talks about the goals of the network and tell stories about how it was being used by members who had attended our ALCP sessions.

E-MAIL BLASTS

In order to encourage members to keep returning to the network in order to participate and to give people something that they could forward to friends and colleagues, we developed a mailing list of members and sent out monthly e-mail blasts updating people on new projects and new content available on the network, which included stories that addressed two or more of the themes our research showed would be most appealing to our audience.

As this hopefully illustrates, although we built at the core of our program a strong effort to reach "influentials" in the BGCA movement who could help us, we didn't depend solely on social media marketing techniques to spread the word about the significance of the social network we were providing. We also used traditional marketing techniques through traditional marketing channels.

Building a network of this type took both time and considerable resources. In our first year of operation we only had a few hundred people, but by the third year we had several thousand members of the BGCA movement using the social network. How quickly your organization takes advantage of your network is obviously going to depend on how fluent your users are with networking technologies and on the size of your organization, but you shouldn't be misled by the term "viral." It takes a lot of time to build the infrastructure for a message to go viral. Indeed, our success was really contingent on the initial research that we did. Identifying the RSDs and other influentials in the organizations was the key, but developing profiles and stories that helped us see what their needs were and what they found significant was critical to our success.

TECHNIQUES

In the two case studies from the previous section, we've actually already discussed a number of effective techniques for helping members of your social network or community develop a sense of the significance of your system. However, below are some additional techniques or more information about techniques we've already introduced that will hopefully help you think creatively about strategies you can use to share the significance of your communities.

CHECKLIST OF TECHNIQUES
1. Provide a story that shares a vision
2. List members' accomplishments
3. Participate in influential communities to create trails back to yours

> **4.** Build your social network or community in a custom space
> **5.** Make connections with other leaders in social media
> **6.** Celebrate celebrities
> **7.** Create a contest, game, or video
> **8.** Mobilize your existing members

1. PROVIDE A STORY THAT SHARES A VISION

We've already seen the power that storytelling can have in the Belonging chapter. Dixie Goswami is a superb grant writer from a long way back, and I've been fortunate to have had her as one of my mentors. When we would go to potential funding sources to try to get the resources needed to build the BreadLoaf Rural Teacher Network (BLRTN) for K-12 teachers, one of the very first things Dixie taught me was the power of storytelling. We would meet with a grant officer from the Department of Education or the State department or some foundation, and within minutes, Dixie would have them mesmerized by telling stories about how some K-12 teacher's life had been transformed through the use of online communities. There's no doubt in anyone's mind who knows the history of BLRTN that Dixie's storytelling ability is one of the primary reasons it has been successful since the early 1980s. Like the BGCA stories about little old New England ladies serving tea and cookies to hooligans mentioned in the previous chapter or like Dixie's stories, you need to find stories about your social network or communities and how they have had an impact on others.

Like Dixie, Seth Godin is a master at telling these kinds of stories. The success of his books is based almost entirely on his ability to tell a story about a seemingly insignificant event and yet make his audience understand immediately the importance of his point. Consider the following example from his book *Tribes*:

> Scott Beal is an impresario with a long history of innovation and leadership. His company, Laughing Squid, does everything from Web hosting to T-shirts, from laser engraving to arts listings. In short, he leads an eclectic tribe.
>
> At the SXSW conference in 2008, Scott got tired of waiting in line to get into the Google party so he walked down the street, found a deserted bar, grabbed some tables in the back, and fired up his cell phone. Using Twitter, he announced "Alta Vista Party at Ginger Man." Within minutes, 8 people showed up. Shortly thereafter, 50. Then there was a line out the door.

[7], 37–38

What are we really talking about here? We're talking about a guy who started a party in a bar. It's not at all significant, but Godin makes the power of Twitter significant through this story. That's the kind of story that you need to tell about your network and its power to impact people that your users care about.

FIGURE 7.4
UX Book Club followers on Twitter.

Name UX Book Club
Location Anywhere UX people gather.
Web http://uxbookclub...
Bio Follow us for information about upcoming UX Book Club events in your area

924   1,324
following   followers

Tweets   320

Favorites

Actions
message **uxbookclub**
block **uxbookclub**

Following

DIT

View All...

RSS feed of uxbookclub's tweets

2. LIST MEMBERS' ACCOMPLISHMENTS

People develop a sense of the importance of your community or network through "social significance" [13]. If other people whom they respect are part of your community, then they're more likely to feel that your community has significance. That's why it's important for Twitter to show a list of who is "following you" in a community. If people see names they recognize among your followers, then they're more likely to follow you too. For example, Figure 7.4 shows how users can check the UX Book Club on Twitter to see if they recognize followers there who are respected in the user experience (or UX) community.

With other kinds of communities, such as listservs or Web-based forums, you can achieve the same effect by maintaining a Web page where you list special accomplishments of members. For example, in a user-experience community you might list all the books and articles your members have published within the past 5 years. This obviously is in the best interest of the members because they get their work showcased, but it also helps build the significance of the community.

3. PARTICIPATE IN INFLUENTIAL COMMUNITIES TO CREATE TRAILS BACK TO YOURS

Louis Rosenfield is doing some really interesting things with publishing. Rosenfield has abandoned the traditional book publishing model. The books that Rosenfield Media produce have communities built around them, and Louis tries to promote those. One of the ways that he does this is by finding the influential communities that already exist for his books and participating in them. When the opportunity arises for him to talk about one of his authors and provide a trail back to his own communities, he does. Leaving comments on other bloggers' posts that support the positions of the blogs by calling attention to things going on in your community or network is yet another way of accomplishing this same effort.

There is, however, a real danger here. As discussed in the Remuneration chapter, it's critical that community managers prevent people from "spamming" their members and that they prevent conversations from being siphoned off of their communities into another community. When Louis sends an e-mail message to an online community, he's careful to make sure that he's contributing to the existing conversation and supporting it by providing more information that people can pursue if they choose to. However, many messages of this type are not. LinkedIn's groups, for example, are currently being plagued by messages from members that are just "brochureware." Consultants and vendors are posting messages that are nothing but hypertext links to concept papers or white papers that advertise products and services. You should avoid these kinds of messages at all costs. Rather than enhancing the "significance" of your community, you'll simply disgust and infuriate most of the members of the community where you post. Yes, you might get a few eyeballs attracted to your site, but most people have a shock-proof, unerring spam detector when it comes to these types of posts and they don't appreciate your abuse of their community. Consequently, you always have to be sure that you're demonstrating the significance of your community by drawing attention to the *existing conversation* that's going on in the other community. In other words, make sure you're always providing support for what's going on in that community.

4. BUILD YOUR SOCIAL NETWORK OR COMMUNITY IN A CUSTOM SPACE

Google Groups and Ning Groups are readily available, and anybody can go start a group on nearly any topic of interest. If I'm interested in apple pies or quilting, I can start a group on them, but they don't have significance for most people because anyone can join them. There are hundreds of groups on those systems, and they do perform a useful, valuable function. Indeed, I find them incredibly valuable when I have a small team of people who need to share information to solve a problem and work on a project, i.e., when I need to build an adhocracy. But they're not sustainable, and they're not compelling for users because they lack significance. As Paul Gillin has also observed about such groups, "you may be surprised to find how many groups already exist. You may also be surprised at how many of them haven't been updated in months or have just a few members. Facebook lists more than 500 groups about the Apple iPhone and more than 250 that cover bowling balls, but most have fewer than 100 members. These groups generally aren't worth your time" ([5], 105).

I recently had a phone conversation with Rachel Luxemburg, a community manager for Adobe, and she made clear that when Adobe built the AUG online communities, one of the most important things that they wanted was to make sure that the forums lived on adobe.com. Adobe.com is ranked fourth among Internet Web sites, and Rachel and her colleagues wanted to make sure to take advantage of that brand to enhance the significance of their communities. It was critical for them to be able to show that Adobe supported what they were doing at the highest level. Building user groups on some unrecognized, no-name site just didn't make sense in terms of significance. Plus, from a management perspective, your community is always going to be at the mercy of another vendor's decisions. If Second Life changes its client, for example, then you have little choice but to play along. You need to work with ISPs and vendors who will allow you to develop and maintain your own domain name and control your own destiny where functionality is concerned.

5. MAKE CONNECTIONS WITH OTHER LEADERS IN SOCIAL MEDIA

Partner with other communities, vendors, or leaders in the use of social media to attract eyeballs to your community. For example, Amazon and LinkedIn have created a partnership that allows LinkedIn users to write reviews and make recommendations of books they are reading through a connection with Amazon. LinkedIn users can create a list that others in their group can follow. This allows me to see what other members in communities on LinkedIn are reading, and of course, from Amazon's perspective, encourages LinkedIn's users to want to purchase the books from them (Figure 7.5).

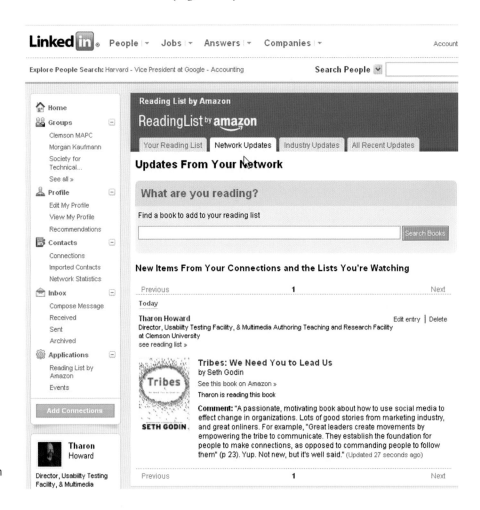

FIGURE 7.5
Amazon reading lists on LinkedIn.

Furthermore, LinkedIn's communities benefit from Amazon's name recognition. As an established leader in the online world, Amazon's *gravitas* adds credibility to LinkedIn's communities.

6. CELEBRATE CELEBRITIES

The advantages of being a member of an "exclusive" community were addressed earlier in this chapter. Members are empowered both emotionally and professionally by being the first to know, which certainly drives much of the membership in our Adobe User Group. Still, Adobe has so many products available and so many different professional interests to serve that it's still necessary to reach out to members to stimulate their interests and to help them see the significance of their community. One tried and true method is, of course, the celebrity spokesperson.

In the example given in Figure 7.6, Stacy Sison, who manages various video communities for Adobe Systems and who is a Community Manager of the USA/ Canada User Group Managers, sent the message shown to managers Adobe User Groups [15]. For those who may not be familiar with Adobe Connect, it is a powerful Web conferencing and online meeting package that allows large groups to have real-time meetings on their Web browsers.

In the screen captures from the blog site that appear in Figure 7.7, you can see examples of how the Obama administration took advantage of Connect's ability to stream live video and to allow meeting participants to conduct live chats simultaneously.

Beyond their use of the President's celebrity status and the *gravitas* afforded by the U.S. Department of State, Stacy's message and the blog site shown in Figure 7.7

From: Stacy Sison - AUG - Announce [prforums@adobe.com]
Sent: Monday, April 20, 2009 3:51 PM
To: Tharon Howard
Subject: Connect with Obama! - AUG - Announce - Adobe User Group – Announce

Stacy Sison wrote:

Hi all,

I wanted to share the following:

http://blogs.adobe.com/acrobatconnect/2009/04/government_20_powered_by_conne.html

This is fantastic - because most of you utilize our Community Connect server on a daily basis! As I have said in the past - our community currently has the largest customer account at Adobe. Which means we are first in line for upgrades, etc. Congratulations to you! :)

If you haven't already, and are interested in obtaining a Connect Pro account just like the President of the United States... please visit (read through carefully prior to submitting!):

https://[confidential URL Removed]

All types of videos featuring an Adobe product in ANY format qualify (30 seconds to 90+ minutes in length). UGM meetings, tips and tricks via YouTube, Captivate podcast, etc. More information on how to submit the video requirement will be shared next month.

Happy Monday!

FIGURE 7.6
Connect with Obama announcement to community.

Adobe Acrobat Connect Pro

Information about the product, the market, and opportunities to use Adobe Acrobat Connect Pro in your daily lives.

« Extending Connect Pro Meetings | Main

Government 2.0, Powered by Connect Pro

President Obama has paid a lot of lip service to his emphasis on streamlining government. This was further emphasized by a few announcements this weekend including his appointment of a Chief Technology Officer and Chief Performance Officer and his request for cabinet officers to find a way to eliminate $100 M from their budgets by finding new efficiencies.

But the proof is in the pudding, right? Well the U.S. Department of State, which has to be one of the most geographically dispersed organizations in the world with embassies and diplomats stationed around the globe, has been really ramping up their Connect Pro usage and to great effect.

First we told you about Secretary of State Hillary Clinton appearing in Connect Pro via a simulcast of her historic meeting with the European Parliament:

Well now we can say that President Obama himself has made his Connect Pro debut earlier this week, presenting at a Town Hall meeting during last week's visit to Turkey.

It's great to see the Obama Administration really delivering on their promises of streamlining government, openness, transparency, and a commitment to using technology to achieve these goals. And can I say that it's even more exciting for us that Connect Pro is a component of Obama's vision.

What's even better is that it's clear that the Department of State have become quite the Connect Pro experts with their snazzy layouts and extensive customization and branding.

Posted by David Yun on April 20, 2009 12:16 PM | Permalink

FIGURE 7.7
Adobe Connect pro blog story about Obama administration [18].

are important for a couple of additional reasons. First, the impact that these have on *internal* members of the community shouldn't be overlooked. Stacy's message is a celebration of the significance of those in the Connect community who had the foresight to adopt Connect before the President of the United States. In other words, not only is the message here intended to be sent to people who don't use Connect, but more importantly, it strengthens *existing* members' sense of the significance of their community.

7. CREATE A CONTEST, GAME, OR VIDEO

This is a technique that's been around probably since marketing began. Basically, in order to raise consciousness about a social network or community, you give something away as a winner of a contest or as a reward for playing a game in order to raise consciousness about or show the significance of your social network or community. For example, Google, when it first started, offered a $1 million prize to one randomly selected Google user; the more you used Google, the more likely you were to win $1 million.

Girl Scout troops give away prizes to the girl in the troop who sells the most cookies and raises the most money for the troop. In my son's WoW guild, members who attend every raid that the guild has for a month earn gear distribution points that they can use in order to obtain new equipment, armor, and weapons during raids. The manager of an HR department might offer her employees a gift certificate to a local restaurant for the member who recruits the most new employees to their online community.

Finally, one of the most successful techniques is to post a humorous video that calls attention to some funny, workplace incident that's happened. We've all seen these viral videos of people in a workplace setting experiencing crazy, funny events. For example, CHEEKSDOWN.com created a "Best Office Prank Ever" video, which has been viewed 3.2 million times on YouTube [4]. The video shows how a team went in and walled up a hallway to office space in a business complex and then the reactions of the perplexed employees and managers as they attempted to understand what happened to their work environment. Embedded in the clip is a not-so-subtle marketing teaser that says "if you like this prank, support us by visiting cheeksdown.com." Of course, as the CHEEKSDOWN.com video also suggests, there is a danger here if the videos aren't done tastefully, you can actually damage the significance and reputation of your community either by socially inappropriate material or by overtly heavy-handed commercialization. However, a successful video of this type can go viral and provide tremendous marketing potential and payoff with little cost.

8. MOBILIZE YOUR EXISTING MEMBERS

Mary James and Marissa Hederson of the Morgan Kaufmann publishing division of Elsevier are beginning to experiment with social media marketing techniques and community building in order to provide better support for their books

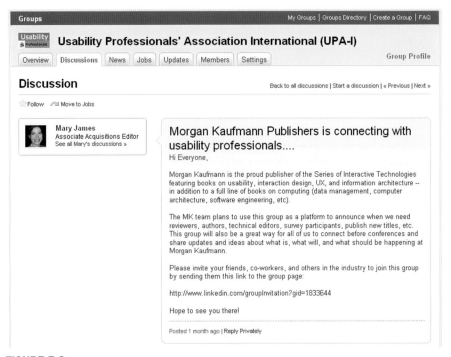

FIGURE 7.8
Mary James' LinkedIn.

and their authors. Mary has begun a Morgan Kaufmann group on LinkedIn in order to find "reviewers, authors, technical editors," and others in the Usability Professionals' Association International community who can benefit from a relationship with Morgan Kaufmann Publishing (see Figure 7.8).

In the message shown in Figure 7.8, Mary is trying to mobilize members of the UPA community to use the Morgan Kaufmann group in order to help both communities benefit from the publication of human computer interaction (HCI) books [9].

In the e-mail message shown in Figure 7.9, Mary's colleague, Marissa Hederson, is not only attempting to mobilize the community of authors who publish at Morgan Kaufmann [8], but she's also using some of the other traditional marketing techniques discussed in order to raise consciousness about HCI.

As Marissa's message explains, she's inviting members of the community of the HCI MKP authors' community to write reviews of other members' books in exchange for free copies of those books. Marissa is creating a win–win situation where all parties benefit. Through this program, she's creating significance by calling attention to the quality of the authors and the work created by this community.

From: Hederson, Marissa (ELS-BUR) [xxx@Elsevier.com]
Sent: Thursday, March 19, 2009 5:36 PM
To: Tharon Howard
Subject: Invitation to join the MK HCI author book club

Dear Tharon,

The Morgan Kaufmann Human Computer Interaction list includes extraordinary authors such as:

o Bill Buxton, author of *Sketching User Experiences*
o Ginny Redish, author of *Letting Go of the Words*, and
o Jeff Johnson, author of *GUI Bloopers, 2.0*

As Morgan Kaufmann HCI author -- you're in good company. You're part of a robust community that thinks deeply about cutting-edge concepts and actively seeks to share knowledge. Have you ever wondered what your colleagues are writing -- ever wanted to read one of *their* books?

Well here is your chance and we'll help you do it for **free**!

As you might know, online bookstore such as Amazon.com and bn.com tend to be more influential than ever in driving sales. A good review on these sites is an invaluable sales tool. We'd like to invite you to become part of a program of "**authors-helping-authors**." And you'll get to read one of the exciting books written by your colleagues--for free-- in the process. Here is how:

We are creating the MK HCI book club to help you:

• Gain more recognition as an expert in your field
• generate more reviews for your book
• increase sales for your book
• Explore some of the exciting HCI books

Are there MK HCI books that you have been dying to read but haven't gotten around to yet? Here is your shot!

HOW IT WORKS...
• I've included a list of titles that you can request at the bottom of my message with links to view the title info and Table of Contents
• Send me the book that you would like to read along with your mailing address – I will not share this info with anyone else
• This book will be absolutely free for you and you get to keep it!
• Post a review to Amazon.com and bn.com for the book you have reviewed and send me a little note when it is posted
• Please also post the reviews on your personal blog/website if you have one!
• If there are any other MK HCI books that you have already read please post a review!

This is a great opportunity to read an incredible book while helping grow sales for your community...

FIGURE 7.9
E-mail to HCI authors.

CONCLUSION

This chapter discussed how you can use elements of both social media and traditional marketing techniques to create a sense of significance about your networks and communities. We discussed the paradox of exclusivity and how you can use people's desire to obtain social capital. People's will and desire to use social capital to distinguish themselves from the others can be used to create an enhanced sense of significance for your community. We also discussed how understanding that certain "nodes" in a social network have more importance than others and how you can exploit those "influentials" in order to spread your message of significance through both social and traditional media.

As always, the techniques I've offered here are by no means inclusive or comprehensive. However, now that you're familiar with social capital, influentials theory, and the five factors in Rogers's adoption curve, it is hoped that you'll be able to use these suggestions as jumping off points for helping both members within your network and those in surrounding communities to develop a sense of the significance of your own systems.

WORKS CITED

[1] Be the First to Know. Organizing for America. 11 May 2009. http://my.barackobama.com/page/s/firsttoknow.

[2] Bourdieu, P. Distinction: A Social Critique of the Judgement of Taste [Nice R, Trans.]. Cambridge, MA: Harvard University Press; 1984.

[3] Crane, D. Invisible Colleges: Diffusion of Knowledge in Scientific Communities. Chicago: University of Chicago Press; 1972.

[4] Cheekdown.com. Youtube—best office prank ever. YouTube – Broadcast Yourself 11 May 2009. http://www.youtube.com/watch?v=q0XdthbOkMU.

[5] Gillin, P. Secrets of Social Media Marketing. Fresno, CA: Quill Driver Books; 2009.

[6] Gladwell, M. The Tipping Point: How Little Things Can Make a Big Difference. Boston: Back Bay Books; 2002.

[7] Godin, S. Tribes: We Need You to Lead Us. New York: Portfolio; 2008.

[8] Hederson M. Invitation to join the MK HCI author book club. E-mail to the author. 19 Mar 2009.

[9] James, M. Mogan Kaufmann publishers is connecting with usability professionals. LinkedIn. 7 May 2009. http://www.linkedin.com/groupAnswers?viewQuestionAndAnswers=&gid=717&discussionID=2122851&sik=1241886045064&trk=ug_qa_q&goback=.ana_717_1241886045064_3_1http://www.linkedin.com/groupAnswers?viewQuestionAndAnswers=&gid=717&discussionID=2122851&sik=1241886045064&trk=ug_qa_q&goback=.ana_717_1241886045064_3_1.

[10] Levine, R. Christopher L, Searls D, Weinberger D. The Cluetrain Manifesto: The End of Business as Usual. New York: Basic Books; 2001.

[11] Lomas, R. The Invisible College: The Royal Society, Freemasonry, and the Birth of Modern Science. London: Headline Books; 2002.

[12] Mirel, B. Product, process, and profit: The politics of usability in a software venture. J Comput Doc 2000;24(4):185–203.

[13] Shirky, C. Here Comes Everybody: The Power of Organizing Without Organizations. New York: Penguin; 2009.

[14] Shuen, A. Web 2.0: A Strategy Guide. Sebastopol: O'Reilly Media, Inc; 2008.

[15] Sison, S. Connect with Obama - AUG Announce. E-mail to the author. 20 Apr 2009.

[16] Thompson, C. Is the tipping point toast? Duncan Watts—Trendsetting Fast Company. FastCompany.com—Where ideas and people meet Fast Company. 28 Jan 2008. 11 May 2009, http://www.fastcompany.com/magazine/122/is-the-tipping-point-toast .html.

[17] Weinschenk, S. Neuro Web Design:What Makes Them Click?. Berkeley, CA: New Riders; 2009.

[18] Yun, D. Adobe Acrobat Connect Pro: Government 2.0, powered by Connect Pro. Adobe Blogs 20 Apr 2009. 11 May 2009 http://blogs.adobe.com/acrobatconnect/ 2009/04/government_20_powered_by_conne.html.

CHAPTER 8

Technology Changes Rapidly; Humans Don't

HOW LESSONS FROM COMMUNICATION TECHNOLOGIES OF THE PAST CAN INFORM OUR FUTURE

SYNOPSIS

Previous chapters looked closely at each element of the RIBS heuristic in order to better understand how to design sustainable social networks and online communities. This final chapter takes a step back in order to afford network architects and community designers a slightly longer view both of RIBS and of external forces in the social media landscape. The chapter begins with the observation that those of us who are fortunate enough to serve as community managers and/or who have the opportunity to engineer networking systems wield a double-edged sword that the RIBS heuristic alone may not help us address.

Social networks and online communities have the potential to effect economic, political, and social changes far beyond the expectations of their designers, and that kind of "success" can ironically threaten the sustainability of a community. When social media begin to impact larger institutions, such as the election of government officials, intellectual property laws, religious institutions, educational settings, and other established institutions of literate cultures, then a battle for control ensues.

The issues resulting from such clashes can destroy those communities whose leaders lack a means of understanding and anticipating the conflicts. Consequently, we will look at four areas of the future that history suggests are likely to be the social networking battlefield of the future. These four areas are:

1. copyrights and intellectual property
2. disciplinary control vs individual creativity
3. visual, technological, and new media literacies
4. decision-making contexts for future markets

Ultimately, the chapter concludes with the observation that human mental bandwidth will be the scarce commodity of the future. Communities and networks of the future will need to market themselves based on their ability to help members make more creative and better-informed decisions rather than the size of their user base. The quality of user experience will replace quantity of connections as the measure of success, which will bring us full circle back to RIBS, as RIBS is intended to help designers produce positive social networking and community experiences for members.

THE POWER OF SOCIAL MEDIA TO EFFECT CHANGE

Any fundamental shift in the ways that human beings are able to share information has the potential for extraordinary sociopolitical impacts. And looking at the history of the Internet, we've certainly seen evidence to suggest that new social media are, as Jeff Jarvis puts it in *What Would Google Do*, "going to change everything" ([7], 27). Over 20 years ago now, even though the traditional news organizations were initially unable to report what was going on in Tiananmen Square, those of us on the Internet were reading reports from Chinese students about the atrocities there within minutes of the events. Back then we claimed that the way Chinese protesters used the networking technologies and the Internet to bypass restrictions imposed on traditional mass media was going to change the world. More recently in 2009, Iranian protesters, enraged by allegations of massive fraud in the country's national elections, used Twitter to share information about the extraordinary protests taking place in the streets of Tehran while traditional media outlets were, once again, struck dumb by government oversight and censorship.

Young Iranians, like their Chinese counterparts 20 years before in Tiananmen, used proxy servers to bypass government attempts to block their messages, and they shared their stories, observations, images, and cell phone videos with the world. They used Twitter's ability to create "feeds" through the use of "hashtags" to connect with one another and organize their protests. As Figure 8.1 shows, one adhocracy created on the social network for this purpose was a group known as the "#gr88 hashtag."

Using RIBS to understand the dynamics of a community

The tweets shown in Figure 8.1 are truly astonishing for the power they represent; at the same time, we can use them to illustrate how all of the RIBS principles work together to heighten the experience of the group's conversation. Consider for example the first tweet shown. In this tweet, an American is answering a question about why the news media in the United States wasn't reporting what was happening in Tehran, and yet, on Twitter, nearly all the Americans using the #gr88 hashtag had changed their profiles to a green tint in order to show

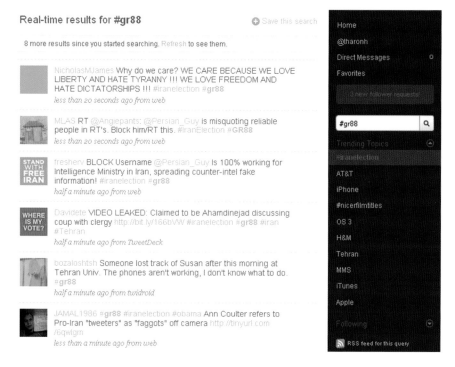

FIGURE 8.1
Sample Twitter messages about 2009 Iranian election protests.

their support for Iranian protesters. To illustrate their sense of belonging, many Westerners chose to make their accounts look like the Iranians' accounts in order to make it harder for Iranian officials to identify Iranian protesters. Indeed, non-Iranian participants in the #gr88 hashtag were even instructed to change their computer's clocks to Tehran's time zone, and manuals were posted on Web sites providing instructions on how to use proxy servers so that it appeared that posts were originating from servers in Iran.

HASHTAG PROTOCOL

Hashtags on Twitter are used to create ad hoc groups. Any Twitter user can simply type a # at the beginning of a word to create a hashtag. Using the format #*groupname* evolved from users who were familiar with an older technology called IRC channels where topics available for group discussion were also designated by the #*topic* format. Twitter users discovered that using the hashtag in front of a group's name made it easier for others on the system to find the group's messages (aka, "tweets") using Twitter's search tool. In fact, the site Hashtag.org was created explicitly for the purpose of allowing users to find and follow hashtags.

Legend has it that the hashtag protocol (which is, by the way, an example of a belonging protocol) really began on Twitter during the 2007 California wildfires that threatened many

(Continued)

HASHTAG PROTOCOL—CONT'D

San Diego residential areas. Because Twitter limits messages to 140 characters, it is ideal for cell phones and mobile devices. This made Twitter a perfect choice for people dealing with the fire to send and receive information about its spread. According to legend, the first hashtag was #sandiegofire and it was created to allow people to obtain emergency information about the fire. Although this wasn't actually the first use of a hashtag as the legend suggests, use of the #sandiegofire hashtag during that 2007 emergency is extremely well documented and it did popularize hashtag use. So while it's not clear who created the #gr88 hashtag during the Iranian election protests, the precedent for using hashtag adhocracies on Twitter in order to disseminate real-time information needed to organize groups during an emergency was well understood years before it was used to organize and share information about the protests.

Westerners' outpouring of signs of belonging and solidarity was so overwhelming that it led Iranian protesters to ask why the Americans on Twitter went to such lengths to show how much they cared when neither the U.S. government nor the U.S. media were commenting on the election fraud or the uprising at the time. The response, illustrated by the first tweet in Figure 8.1 and many others not shown, was that the American people, as individuals, did care. The response by NicholsMJames is compelling because it gives us an opportunity to see the RIBS principle of influence at work. After all, how often does an individual American have an opportunity to speak directly to and show support for protesters in another country who are clearly shaping the history of that country? In a sense, and particularly during these early days of the protest, this kind of communication gave individual Americans and other Westerners an opportunity to have the kind of influence and to speak in a voice of support that is typically reserved for State Department officials speaking to journalists.

The next two tweets are also fascinating because they show how dissidents sought to protect themselves from capture and arrest. Someone using the Twitter account @Persian_Guy was sending out "retweets" or "RT's" as they're known on Twitter. Retweets on Twitter are critical because they are often the only way that users can keep up with the massive flow of information. To give you an idea of how fast the information was coming, Mashable.com reported that, at one point, there were 221,744 tweets in a single hour just on #iranelection hashtag alone [9]. More tweets were being delivered than could be usefully displayed on a typical monitor. In other words, when a user refreshed his or her Web page on Twitter in order to receive the new tweets that had been sent, more new messages were being delivered than could be read. This means that, unless a tweet is repeated several times (i.e., retweeted), the information is likely to be missed.

Retweeting is an important part of how people demonstrate they are part of a group on Twitter; it's a way of having influence and of making a contribution even if you don't have anything new to contribute. However, in addition to using retweets to provide influence to members, we can also see the principle of belonging at work here. There's a sort of an unwritten protocol on Twitter that says that users are expected to review information coming in, assess its value, and then retweet what is important. In this way, "noise" and useless information are filtered out, and over time, users monitoring the retweets will be able to see a consensus emerging on what members of the group think is important information at that moment. Retweeting is, thus, essential to Twitter's success. It's what allows Twitter users to see what are called "trending topics" in the data stream. And of course, "trending topics" is one of the ways of demonstrating the significance of conversations happening on Twitter.

When someone abuses retweeting, that's a serious breach of one of the protocols of belonging. The person using the account @Persian_Guy was accused of retweeting messages from leaders in the Iranian protest movement. Normally, his retweeting was something that the group would find valuable and a behavior that would be interpreted as saying, "I'm a member of this collective and I want to help support the goals of this adhocracy by retweeting critical information." Normally, his retweeting would be a sign of belonging. The problem was, in this case, @Persian_Guy appeared to be modifying and editing the retweets in ways so that people using the information would inadvertently reveal their identities to the Iranian authorities. Once it was suggested that the account @Persian_Guy was attempting to pervert the basic social contract of the group and had violated the trust other members placed in retweeting, the ire and outrage expressed was astonishing. Watching the kinds of tweets shown in the second and third tweets from Figure 8.1 was the 21st century equivalent of watching a virtual community stone a pariah to death. As a user experience, it was frightening, compelling, and, above all, riveting, which, of course, was part of the remuneration obtained by participants.

The tweet by bazaloshtsh is also a particularly compelling story for anyone with imagination and empathy. Those who followed the #gr88 hashtag knew that there had been a protest rally at Tehran University, organized at least in part on Twitter as well as on specific Google groups. However, someone named Susan went missing in the chaos of the protest rally. This plaintive cry for assistance in attempting to locate Susan and the soul-wrenching line "I don't know what to do" are incredibly moving. Anyone who has worried about a friend or loved one during a crisis can't help but recognize the extraordinary human connection we share with bazaloshtsh. And it was the hundreds of tweets like this one that produced incredible outpourings of support. People around the world voluntarily set up Web sites listing the names of those who, like Susan, had gone missing. They provided information about those who were reported as having been arrested, killed, or admitted to hospitals. Indeed, the desire to help was so strong that the U.S. State Department asked Twitter to delay shutting down the service for a scheduled maintenance event in order to continue to allow Iranians to continue to share information on the system—testimony again to both the significance and the influence participants in the #gr88 hashtag were experiencing, as well as the remuneration the protesters obtained as a result of being able to use Twitter to become organized and share information about events [8].

The explanatory power and scope of RIBS

Collectively, the RIBS principles, as I hope this #gr88 example illustrates, offer useful explanatory power for anyone who needs to be able to observe and respond to events like those shown in Figure 8.1. In other words, not only can the RIBS be used in isolation to brainstorm techniques that can be used to design social networks as discussed in Chapters 4–7, the elements can also be used to analyze and interpret conversations taking place in your community. When all four of the RIBS elements are taken into consideration at the same time, they reveal how rich and complex those interactions can be. Indeed, in successful, healthy communities, all four elements combine and coalesce in order to create a user experience that satisfies your members' intellectual, economic, and emotional needs in ways that bring them back frequently and for a sustained period of time.

On a pragmatic, practical level, you can use RIBS as an analytical tool on existing communities in order to assess the health of your community's interactions. Are members' influence needs being met? Are the protocols and symbols members use to signify belonging clear and easy to use or, as shown earlier, are there protocols such as "retweeting" that you need to help new members understand clearly so that they are able to participate fully? We could keep going asking questions about the other RIBS elements, but you probably get the point, i.e., now that you know what RIBS are and what they mean, you can use them to ask questions about a community so that you can identify when a critical component—like your members' sense of significance for example—is missing from a community.

And yet, while RIBS is a powerful tool for planning and analyzing social networking designs, there are uses that are beyond its scope. Of course, that's a hard thing for me to admit having just written a whole book about RIBS. I'd love to tell you that RIBS is the panacea when it comes to all things involving social networking, but obviously it's not. RIBS will get you most of the way toward building a sustainable social network and designing communities that thrive, but factors outside your community and beyond the internal influence of RIBS can impact the future of your community.

Ironically, one of the most dangerous things that can happen to your network is the kind of success Twitter enjoyed as a result of the Iran election protests. Evan Williams, one of the co-founders and CEO of Twitter, remarked in a February 2009 TED talk that he and his colleagues "never anticipated the many, many uses which would evolve from this simple system," a system that Evans explained was merely designed to let friends share 140-character-long updates with their friends. Williams described his surprise when San Diego residents and local fire departments used Twitter to keep track of and to share information about the October 2007 California wildfires raging in their area [13]. However, if that event surprised Twitter's managers, imagine how it must have felt to have Iranian protesters use your social network to stage a popular uprising that, for a time, threatened to topple the government.

Still, while Twitter gained a lot of popular press for the role it played in the Iranian election protests, what consequences will flow from the fact that Twitter was asked by the U.S. State Department to change its normal practices and keep it servers up so the protesters could use it?

The point here is that social networks and online communities have the potential to affect economic, political, and social changes far beyond the expectations of their designers, and that kind of "success" can ironically threaten the sustainability of a community. When social media begin to impact larger institutions such as the election of government officials, intellectual property laws, religious institutions, education, and other established institutions of literate cultures, then a battle for control ensues. There are forces outside social networks that can destroy those communities whose leaders lack a means of understanding the conflicts.

Consequently, in the few pages remaining in this chapter, I propose to speculate about issues that future managers of successful communities can anticipate. What kinds of potential issues will we need to confront and overcome to sustain our social networks and online communities? What does the future hold for social networking?

TECHNOLOGY CHANGES RAPIDLY; PEOPLE DON'T

Considering our society's experiences with online communities and social networks during events such as Tiananmen Square, the Howard Dean fundraising campaign, the Obama presidential election, and the Iranian protests, it's easy to claim that the Internet, social networks, and online communities are going to "change everything." It's easy to understand why so many find the future of social networking and online communities so compelling. We understand when Charlene Li talks about how social networks in the future are going to be "like air," suggesting that they're going to be ubiquitous, pervasive, and omnipresent. In fact, I'm just not sure that the assertion that social networking will be "like air" in the future really goes far enough. I think it's a pretty safe bet that we're already there.

If you look at the history of online communities and social networks, this revolution in communication technology has been happening since the early 1980s. Starr Roxanne Hiltz and Murray Turoff in their visionary book, *Network Nation*, saw the potential for online communities and social networks to have a profound impact back in the 1970s. In 1974 during the Nixon administration, Turoff worked in the president's office of emergency preparedness to build what many researchers regard as the first viable computer conferencing system, which was called EMISARY. Designed as a crisis management and strategic planning tool, this first online community connected economic advisors from states all around the country and enabled officials in local governments to have input into the creation of federal policies that would protect the national economy from the runaway, double-digit inflation of the day. Later in 1976, the same technology received National Science Foundation funding, and Hiltz expanded its use among a variety of online groups, conducting empirical studies on what Turoff and Hiltz would come to call the "Electronic Information Exchange System" or EIES. In 1978, Hiltz and Turoff used their combined experiences to make a few general observations in the preface to *Network Nation*, observations worth repeating here because they are startlingly prescient. They wrote:

- Computerized conferencing will be a prominent form of communications in most organizations by the mid-1980s.
- By the mid-1990s, it will be as widely used in society as the telephone today.
- It will offer a home recreational use that will make significant inroads into the TV viewing patterns.
- It will have dramatic psychological and sociological impacts on various group communication objectives and processes.
- It will be cheaper than mails or long distance telephone voice communications.
- It will offer major opportunities to disadvantaged groups in the society to acquire the skills and social ties they need to become full members of the society.
- It will have dramatic impacts on the degree of centralization or decentralization possible in organizations.
- It will become a fundamental mechanism for individuals to form groups having common concerns, interests, or purposes.
- It will facilitate working at home for a large percentage of the work force during at least half of their normal work week.
- It will have a dramatic impact upon the formation of political and special interest groups.

[5], xxv

In hindsight, Hiltz and Turoff's predictions were mind-bogglingly prophetic. They foresaw the advent of YouTube and Hulu 3 decades ago. They recognized, even then, that we would reach a day when the average American household would have more computers than televisions. Their predictions about e-mail vs "snail mail" and Skype vs long distance telephones were spot on. And of course, they clearly saw that political campaigns such as Howard Dean's or President Obama's would be able to take full advantage of the power of social networks and online communities in order to vault their candidates into the national limelight.

Why were Hiltz and Turoff so prescient in their predictions? Technologies are notoriously unstable, and it's hard to predict a technological future 3 years out, much less 3 decades from now in, say, 2040. So why were Hiltz and Turoff so visionary?

The simplest answer is that most predictions about technological innovation are driven by the particular and contingent factors in the marketplace rather than looking to general, abstract principles drawn from historical and sociological analyses. Put another way, Hiltz and Turoff were thinking *strategically* rather than tactically. They based their predictions on a sociological understanding of the history of communication technologies and on deep-seated understandings about fundamental social needs rather than technological possibilities.

It's worth remembering that while technologies may change rapidly, human beings don't. If we look back to the communications revolutions of past, then the communication revolution we're currently experiencing is not all that different, which is why I've been arguing that we've been "breathing the air" from these systems for a long time. And what worries me is that we'll repeat the mistakes of the past if we overinvest in these hopeful predictions about the impact these technologies will have on the future. What worries me is that we may not have learned the lessons of the dot com bubble of 2001 and that we're setting ourselves up for a social network apocalypse of 2015.

LOOKING BACKWARD TO LOOK AHEAD

So what do the communication technologies of the past tell us about the social media of the future? Why are Hiltz and Turoff looking at the cost of computer-mediated communication compared to the telephone? After all, isn't that a tactical issue rather than strategic? It turns out that it's not. History teaches us that when you reduce the cost of sharing information, you can have profound effects on a society's literacy rates and on who is allowed to control what kinds of information can be distributed in a social system. Let's briefly consider what happened when Gutenburg's printing press reduced the cost of publishing books and then consider what lessons this has for social networks.

Reducing the cost of media production

Before the invention of the printing press, if you wanted a book, you had to get medieval scribes to copy it for you. Because the scribes were almost exclusively ordained clergy, this virtually ensured that your book's subject was going to be limited to a religious, state-sanctioned text. There are a number of reasons for this, including the fact that a clergyman couldn't be expected to copy a heretical or seditious text. However, the subject matter of the book was also considered part of the cost of copying, as part of the "remuneration" the scribes expected to receive for their labors was their service to the church and the spread of religious knowledge. Furthermore, because vellum was the material of choice for the pages used in books of the highest quality and because vellum is made from animal skins, a single volume could easily require the harvesting of 200 farm animals—or the equivalent of the entire annual output from a feudal lord's estate.

Imagine the impact this would have if books today cost as much as the annual output of a modern farm. And yet in medieval times, this cost merely reflects what was required to produce the raw material for the book. Extensive tanning, stretching, drying, and other labor-intensive processing of animal skins were also required to prepare the vellum for use in a book. Small wonder that ownership of a book of any sort was an extraordinary status symbol and a testimony to the wealth and power of the owner. Indeed, books were so expensive that they were often chained to the podiums on which they were placed.

> **THE COST OF LIBRARIES**
>
> The cost of creating copies of what books were available virtually ensured that only the rich and powerful could afford to make copies of books. Peter Yu points out that, "when Bishop Leofric took over Exeter Cathedral in 1050 AD, he found only 5 books in its library" and in 1424 AD, "the Library of Cambridge University had a remarkable collection of 122 books" ([15], 7).

The cost of literacy

The extraordinary cost of books and the fact that only the uber-wealthy could touch them meant that literacy itself was cost-prohibitive. After all, why bother to become literate if your access to reading materials was so severely limited? The invention of paper and the invention of the printing press obviously changed that dynamic. With the reduced costs of materials in the production process that resulted from rag papers, it was no longer necessary for whole herds of animals to be slaughtered and their skins turned into vellum. What's more, with the invention of the printing press, the labor needed to produce books was not only reduced, but it also meant that it could be performed by laborers other than monks and priests, thereby opening up the range of potential subjects for books to nonreligious and unsanctioned texts. Called "stationers," these early printers didn't have to be paid in the lucre of sacred texts as had the scribes who preceded them. They were more entrepreneurial in their motivations and, as such, were more amenable to printing texts on subjects that could generate a return on their investments.

Of course, we're seeing the same thing happening with the Internet and online communities. It's extremely inexpensive and extremely easy to set up online communities with tools such as Shutterfly, Flickr, Ning, and Google groups. Furthermore, we're seeing the same explosion in who can publish. Today, videos that used to require the resources of a television news crew to video, edit, produce, and distribute can be created by an Iranian college student armed with a cell phone camera and a connection to YouTube. Indeed, that is precisely what the Iranian protesters did. According to statistics he collected on Trendrr, a social media trend tracker, Mashable blogger Ben Parr found that over 3000 videos on the Iranian protests were published on YouTube between June 16th and 17th at the height of the unrest [9]. These videos, were produced by amateurs and were the primary source of information coming from Iran for several days during the unrest. Mass media channels such as CNN, MSNBC, and the *New York Times Online* all ended up having to use Twitter and links to videos and images posted on Twitter by eyewitnesses in order to "report the news."

Except that news media outlets weren't "reporting the news" any longer. Like the stationers who followed the scribes, amateur videographers were willing to go places where professionally trained journalists could not or would not go and document subjects that journalists could not or would not document. Television news crews who would have provided "coverage" of the news have, like medieval scribes, undergone rigorous "disciplining" in order to become members of the professional journalist community. As we all know, they have a code of ethics regarding what they will and will not report. They are trained to adopt an outsiders' perspective in order to observe the "object" of their report "objectively."

But the people *living* the Iran protest are the subject of the videos, images, and tweets they report. They have a decidedly *insider* perspective and are unabashedly "subjective" as a result. From their perspective, they report what they see—even if it offends an outsider's delicate sensibilities. One amateur video widely distributed on the Internet captured the shocking and tragic death of Neda Agha-Soltan, which eventually did make it to CNN and the BBC because it became a trending topic on Twitter under the hashtag #neda and had gone viral on the Internet. But there were many such videos posted on YouTube and announced on #gr88 that were never and will never be shown by mass media news outlets because they provided images that "objective" and disciplined mass media journalists won't carry. Images from hospital admissions rooms where a man is lying on a gurney with an enormous gash in his side exposing his chest cavity or images of blood-covered woman being transferred from a vehicle so that she can receive medical treatment for gunshot wounds to her chest. Images that are so horrible that they can't be displayed in this book or on CNN, MSNBC, and BBC World News. Images that are so threatening to the established authority that to give the authors of the video credit for them might put them at risk of imprisonment.

THE ORIGINS OF COPYRIGHTS

Okay, so if you're thinking that the point of all this is that less expensive and more accessible communication technologies mean that people can post gross, shocking, and disturbing images we don't want children to see, then you're right—but you're also thinking tactically. The more important, strategic issue here has to do with how social institutions respond to and evolve from the loss of control. When the discipline that journalists brought to bear on what information was reported breaks down, how does that impact our social institutions? If you're the manager of a social network such as YouTube or Twitter, what would you do? One way to get some perspective on that question is to look at what happened when scribes were replaced by the stationers.

Free speech vs agents of the state

What did less expensive books and the printing press give us? It definitely improved literacy (and as shown later, social media is having the same effect on new kinds of literacies). We've already discussed why, when one book cost more than an entire herd of sheep, it simply was not possible for the explosion of knowledge that took Western culture from the Dark Ages into the Renaissance to have happened had it not been for the printing press. But less expensive printing and increased literacy also brought about the Protestant Reformation. Not a bad thing for today's Protestants, but throughout the 1500s this was a seriously disruptive cultural influence if you were someone like Phillip of Spain or Mary Tudor or some other monarch whose ability to rule was dependent on the disciplining of your subjects provided by the Catholic church.

Martin Luther could not have done what he did without the printing press and the ability to distribute paper copies cheaply. If Luther had really nailed his 95 theses to the door of All Saints' Church in Wittenberg and left it at that, the movement he started wouldn't have gotten outside Wittenberg. It was the ability to make and distribute inexpensive copies, combined with higher literacy rates made possible by the new technologies, that allowed Luther's theses to spread. Before that technology, the Catholic church was able to maintain its monopoly on the interpretation of religious texts because it was able to control the means of production, i.e., the disciplining of the scribes. As the Iranian election protests on Twitter illustrate, the future of social networks and online communities promises similar kinds of change. Mass media outlets and well-disciplined journalists can no more withstand the kind of pressures that inexpensive, easy-to-create social networks and online communities are going to have on controlling access to information than could the Catholic church control and respond to the Protestant Reformation.

In the early 1500s, the convergence of inexpensive production technologies, higher literacy rates, and alternatively disciplined producers of information meant that new materials (such as Luther's) began to be produced that were no longer restricted by the interests of the state or the church. Texts that Mary Tudor and Phillip of Spain regarded as subversive and inappropriate for the eyes of children and the general public appeared on the markets. So in 1556, Mary and Phillip granted the Stationers Company a royal charter granting the stationers the exclusive right to profit from the books they printed in exchange for censoring inappropriate material. In short, the social institutions responded to the loss of control by inventing the institution we call "copyright."

To modern eyes, the Stationer's Charter is surprising clear about its purpose. In its preamble it states that the charter was issued in order "To satisfy the desire of the Crown for an effective remedy against the publishing of seditious and heretical books" ([2], 384). The Stationers' royal charter co-opted publishers by playing on their desire to "protect profit by prohibiting unlicensed competition" ([2], 383). The charter "limited most printing to members of that company and empowered the stationers to search out and destroy unlawful books" ([10], 23). In so doing, the monarchy effectively reestablished the state's control over what books could be published. It gave the Stationers exclusive rights to copy and to profit from "appropriate" texts in exchange for regulating the publishing industry in much the same way that scribes had previously done. It turned the Stationers into agents of the state.

By analogy then, one of the issues that community managers and social network designers need to monitor carefully in the future is what will happen to *us* as more and more governments recognize the power of social media? In a sense, those of us who manage communities and administer social networks occupy the same role that the Stationers once held when the printing press was the new technology threatening established order. As such, we need to be considering how *we* will respond when states attempt to turn us into their agents in order to maintain control of their citizens who happen to be using our networks or communities to challenge the status quo.

If you're thinking that there's no way that what happened in benighted medieval times could happen in to us in the enlightened 21st century, then you need to look at legislation such as Illinois' "Social Networking Access Restriction Act," which was introduced in February 2009. Just as the Stationer's Charter turned the stationers into agents of the state and forced them to protect the state's views of "seditious texts," Illinois bill HB1312 "Provides that operators of a social networking website must allow the parent or guardian of the minor [who has an account on the site] unrestricted access to the profile webpage of the minor at all times." What's more, this cost-prohibitive piece of legislative coercion "Provides that an owner of a social networking website must also verify the status of the parents or guardians who have granted permission to a minor to host a social networking website" [6]. In short, this legislation turns owners of social networking sites into agents of the state of Illinois so that parents in Illinois can keep their kids from accessing sexually explicit and seditious content.

Whether you live in the 15th or the 21st century, the point here is that our role in shaping the ways that people communicate exposes you to major social institutions and at levels the average person would never consider. The Internet is global, so not only can the state of Illinois come after you, but think how would you respond if, as happened to Twitter during the Iran protests, the U.S. State Department contacted you about the ways foreign nationals were using your network? Indeed, what if the Iranian government had, simultaneously, asked Twitter to shut down or to at least cut off its citizens' access to the system in order to stop the unrest and end the violence in its country? How would you choose between the two requests? What about China and accommodating Chinese users on your network and in your communities? China is already famous for its aggressive policies regarding search engines and censoring information (whether pornographic or political) that it doesn't want its citizens to obtain and yet China has more Internet users than any other country in the world. So can you afford *not* to have a relationship with China?

And don't think you're immune from this issue just because your social network operates on a more local level—what if your company has a censorship policy limiting employees' ability to post messages that are in any way critical about the company? Is reporting to management on potential abusers of this policy any different than providing the United States, Iran, China, or any other government with information about your users that would allow them to, say, track and identify terrorists, protesters, or dissidents? Is it any different than what Illinois is trying to force social network administrators to do with users on our sites who happen to be 17?

Unfortunately, at this point, there isn't a clear way to answer these questions. But at least in looking back at the Stationers' experiences with their new technology, we can see that one of the future battlegrounds we will have to face as community managers and network administrators is legislation and policy making, which shape our roles as agents of states or institutions. As our industry grows, it's likely that we will need to organize ourselves and to create professional organizations that can help determine what are the best practices and ethical codes of conduct that professional community managers should use in such situations. We probably also need such organizations to serve as watchdogs and lobbyists who can protect us from frivolous legislation. Indeed, the past has also shown that until we use our own networking and community-building technologies to organize ourselves, we will, ironically, remain vulnerable.

Intellectual property and content ownership in social media

In addition to revealing our vulnerability to becoming agents of the state, the history of intellectual property has more to teach us in terms of thinking about the future of social networks and online communities. It's also important to recognize that the origins of copyright law did nothing to recognize or establish the rights of authors. Copyright protected publishers. Intellectual property law has always protected the system, but it didn't protect the individual author. As we go forward into the future, the legacy of that division will revisit itself upon us. In fact, we can see that it's already beginning, and it's happening because of what we have already observed about the distinction between journalists' "disciplined" approach to reporting the news and the public's new ability to share original content in social media.

Consider the fact that, as professionals who have a contract with a news organization, journalists are operating under a work-for-hire arrangement. The content that journalists generate is, thus, owned by the news organization that paid the journalist to produce the work. The old intellectual property institutions work fine under such an arrangement. But like the social systems that supported the scribes before the introduction of the printing press, modern intellectual property laws and customs creak and groan almost immediately when they are put under the pressure of content generated by everybody.

Imagine, for a moment, that one of the videos an Iranian protester uploaded to YouTube suddenly became marketable for millions of dollars. Imagine that someone figured out a way to use that video so that people were willing to pay large sums of money to see it displayed on a system other than YouTube—maybe as part of a video game let's say. YouTube management wouldn't wait long before they were demanding a piece of the pie. However, what about the person who shot the video in the first place? What about this person's claims on the video as its original creator? You're probably thinking that the protester who posted the video gave up the right to make any claims against its use when he or she agreed to YouTube's terms of use policy in order to create their account in the first place; you're probably assuming that YouTube claims to own the video once it's uploaded to their site. That is, after all, a pretty good assumption to make given the legacy of the Stationer's Charter and the fact that it protected publishers but not authors.

Actually, however, part of YouTube's success in the emerging social networking economy can be attributed to the fact that they get the Influence part of RIBS. They understand that their users demand some measure of control over the content they provide as a condition of their participation. YouTube's terms of service have evolved and changed over time, but as of June 2009, their terms state that if you upload a video "you retain all of your ownership rights in your User Submissions" [14]. Of course, YouTube does claim the right to distribute, royalty-free, the videos its "users" uploaded to their site after stating that users still own their content.

It's at this point, however, where individual ownership of the content gets confused with YouTube's. In the next sentence, the terms of service go on to state that

> …by submitting User Submissions to YouTube, you hereby grant YouTube a worldwide, non-exclusive, royalty-free, sublicenseable and transferable license to use, reproduce, distribute, prepare derivative works of, display, and perform the User Submissions in connection with the YouTube Website and YouTube's (and its successors' and affiliates') business, including without limitation for promoting and redistributing part or all of the YouTube Website (and derivative works thereof) in any media formats and through any media channels [14].

There's a lot embedded in this sentence, but in short, our imaginary Iranian protester would be hard pressed to prevent YouTube from profiting from a video game's use of the material. Effectively, our hypothetical protester has lost the ability to control whether the video can be used by any company YouTube decides to sell a sublicense.

My point here isn't that YouTube is wrong to expect to profit from this sort of sublicensing. If the video hadn't been distributed on YouTube's service, then it's likely that it wouldn't have gotten noticed and become marketable. So YouTube certainly has a logical claim. The point here and the future battle we face is how we, as community managers, can protect the influence and control that RIBS tells us our members require in the face of copyright laws designed to protect institutions rather than individuals.

Ownership and control of virtual identities

Control of an individual's virtual identity is yet another example of this future intellectual property battlefield. In this book, I've talked a lot about Blizzard's extraordinarily successful game, World of Warcraft (WoW). I've talked about how WoW players have an incredible investment in the avatars they create. Players spend months, years even, creating their avatars, collecting different weapons, armor, articles of clothing, and so on by playing the game. And, as shown in Chapter 6 with the character Justus, WoW players invest a lot of their real identities in the characters they create. For most of them, that avatar belongs to them; they made it and they invested significant resources in its creation. This is also true for users of the social network Second Life. They also identify with their avatars so strongly that users are living a "second life" through those avatars as well as the spaces they create. For WoW and Second Life users, their avatars are *their* virtual identities. So if these users want to share an image of their virtual selves with others, they should be able to do so, right?

Wrong. They can't share their virtual identities because (1) screen captures are considered "derivative works" and (2) because Blizzard owns World of Warcraft and Linden Labs owns Second Life. Blizzard had hundreds of artists, designers, and programmers create the armor, weapons, clothing, and mounts that players collect. As a result, they own the game and any derivative works that come from it. If a player wished, for example, to create a line of t-shirts and posters with her avatar on the front that she would sell through, say, Café Press, then Blizzard could sue for copyright infringement. And again, this makes sense from Blizzard's perspective, as the company provided all the artwork and software required to derive that particular avatar's configuration. But from the player's perspective, the avatar is her virtual self; it's who she is in that world. In the real world, she might wear Lee blue jeans to work every day; that doesn't mean she has to give Lee a cut of her salary or, to carry the analogy further, that Lee has the right to tell her she can't go to that particular job because she's wearing jeans they designed.

OWNERSHIP OF PURCHASING IDENTITIES

Beacon was an application that would tell other users on Facebook what products and services an individual was purchasing. The idea, presumably, was that knowing what videos your friends were renting, what movie tickets they were purchasing, and what video games they were buying would encourage you to make similar purchase decisions. However, the loss of control over the information being revealed about a user's Facebook identity infuriated large numbers of Facebook users who brought a class action lawsuit against Beacon, Blockbuster, Fandango, Overstock, Gamefly, Hotwire, and a small number of other companies who had partnered with Beacon to provide the service. In this case, the virtual identity wasn't an image or an avatar, it was the ability to control the story or picture of an individual that emerged through his or her purchasing decisions. The virtual identity in this case may be less tangible than an avatar, yet users' need to own and control it is no less passionate.

Summary of future copyright issues

If we look at this issue through the perspective afforded us in the history of the scribes, the Stationers' Company, and Luther's reformation, then it's easy to see how this is a bomb waiting to explode in the middle of our social institutions.

As more and more content development is located in the hands of the public rather than a disciplined professional (such as a scribe, a journalist, or a book author), we're going to see the same challenges to what is considered "appropriate" content and legitimate subjects for discussion emerge. As future social network and community managers, we all need to be planning for the changes this will bring. We need to be preparing for the "Internet-free speech" legislation of the future.

Equally important, however, is the emotional energy that the idea of controlling a "virtual identity" will have on our social institutions. Even though social networking and online community users may not have avatars like those found in WoW and Second Life, there is already a growing sense that an individual has a virtual identity or an electronic footprint in the network "cloud." Indeed, you can see how Apple is already trying to tap into that construct with their "MobileMe" products. Other companies are also developing products to help users manage and control their virtual identities. As a community manager or social network designer, there's an opportunity here to out-innovate existing systems by offering users this kind of control of their identities' use. However, it also means that we all need to be preparing for the legislative, legal, and moral changes that we can expect, particularly in countries with strong participatory democracies. In these countries, it seems likely that the passion of citizens to have control over their virtual identities and the electronic footprint created by the content they produce will ultimately lead to new social institutions designed to monitor the tension between the systems' need to produce and distribute information on the one hand and the individual authors who create it on the other.

THE DILEMMA OF CONTROL VS CREATIVITY

So far in this consideration of future external forces that may derail the sustainability of social networking systems, we've only considered issues stemming from intellectual property. A second area where history shows us we can expect future friction is the classic binary between social control and individual creativity.

If we look at how political power, economic capital, and hegemonic cultural practices have been sustained, we can see the same pattern of inventing institutions of control being repeated historically. In feudal systems, ownership of the land was essential to the control of power. These were agrarian economies, and land was essential to produce crops; hence, social structures such as the concept of nobility were invented to support the landed gentry. In the industrial age, ownership of the means of production was the method for controlling power. If you were a pencil manufacturer and you owned the pencil-making machines, then you were going to ascend to the ranks of the bourgeoisie. During the information age of mass media, as Mark Poster has observed in his 1990 book *The Mode of Information*, it has been ownership of the mode of information dissemination that earned access to power [11]. Simply put, the ability to control how knowledge is produced and who can access it has been strategic to obtaining access to power and capital in modern information societies.

The impact of social capital on disciplinary institutions

In thinking strategically about the future of social networks and online communities, it's certainly the case that social networks and online communities participate in the economics of knowledge production. Studies have shown that creative problem solving, for example, can be attributed to an individual's membership in a number of different communities. Ronald Burt, Hobart W. Williams Professor of Sociology and Strategy at the University of Chicago's Booth School of Business, describes how people who are given problems to solve but who also only belong to one type of community are less creative in their ability to generate solutions than people who belong to multiple communities. In his article, "The Network Structure of Social Capital," Burt observed that

> Information can be expected to spread across the people in a market, but it will circulate within groups before it circulates between groups. A generic research finding is that information circulates more within than between groups—within a work group more than between groups, within a division more than between divisions, within an industry more than between industries [3], 6.

In other words, what Burt is saying is that people tend to get "siloed in" and are inclined to communicate with others in the same silo rather than reaching across what Burt calls "structural holes" in a network. People tend not to talk across the "gaps" between silos and don't discuss ideas with people in other silos. However, in his empirical studies of organizational cultures, Burt has found that there are a few individuals who do bridge the structural gaps in a network in order to obtain "social capital" that (as we also saw with Bourdieu in Chapter 7) is "a kind of capital that can create for certain individuals or groups a competitive advantage in pursuing their ends. Better connected people enjoy higher returns" ([3], 3).

TIP

Similarly, the Wright brothers were able to create the first powered airplane because they understood how bicycles worked. The same chains and gears that they used to manufacture their bicycles successfully were used to create the Wright flyer.

Burt's empirical research validates the observation that "better-connected people" or people with more social capital are better problem solvers. Historically, we see evidence of this all the time. To use the printing press as an example, yet again, Guttenberg was only able to invent the printing press because he was a goldsmith. In other words, the techniques from one disciplinary silo (in this case, a goldsmith's knowledge of how to create highly detailed metal shapes) are applied to a problem in an entirely different silo (how to spread ink on a page without the ink creating a gooey mess) in order to come up with a creative solution (the reusable metal type in the printing press). Hence, Guttenberg's knowledge of how to create finely detailed metal shapes learned from making gold jewelry enabled him to produce metal type thin enough to print fine lines of text and durable enough to be used over and over again.

The ability to see how something obvious in one field (such as bicycle chains) can be applied to a problem in another field (such as how to transfer power from an engine to a propeller) is often how new knowledge is created. Membership in multiple communities enables that.

Disciplinary turf wars

However, it's precisely this observation and the fact that ownership of the modes of production are what give access to power in information economies, which will militate against social networks and online communities becoming "like air." As we saw in Chapter 7's discussion of exclusivity, people recognize that invisible colleges and "smoke-filled rooms" are a means of achieving power. Power isn't given away for nothing. Power is given to people who can pay for it or to people who give you something in return. This is why universities continue to give college degrees to graduates. It's why priests have to be ordained, why doctors are licensed, why lawyers pass the bar, and why professionals are certified. It explains why we describe certain fields of knowledge as "disciplines." You have to be disciplined in order to become a member of certain kinds of communities. And that's done in order to make sure that not everyone can have access to the knowledge that a particular community produces.

The future, therefore, doesn't lie in everybody being connected to everybody. I don't agree with those who see us headed toward a single, flat, monolithic culture where we all share the same values and the same literacies and sense of purpose. The tension between the need to control access to information so that certain groups can profit from it on the one hand and the need for creativity and improved problem solving that comes from enhanced connectivity on the other is going to be the engine of major governmental change and economic policies. We probably don't need to fear, as some do, that Google will take over the world or that single sources will control everything because of this dynamic. Just as the monopoly of the church was broken by Martin Luther as a result of the new information technologies and as our Tiannamen Square and Iran election protests also illustrate, the ability to have social networks and online communities on demand will further fragment and chip away at hegemonic practices of a monolithic culture. It doesn't really seem to matter whether we're talking about Eastern or Western cultures. Regardless of religious, economic, or political practices—where once there was tremendous homogeneity from a single voice of authority, now there is polyphony of authorities. If I don't like the religious truths, the political truths, or the cultural truths that I'm pressured to swallow in one community, then I can go find a community of people who do share my version of truth and my values.

Now many people will read that last sentence and cheer. Social networking will change everything and put an end to tyranny—in terms of both large political structures and large corporate structures. Top-down is broken; resistance isn't "futile;" rather, it's inevitable. However, the fact that I can create my own community in protest if I don't like the mainstream community isn't necessarily desirable. Burk has shown us that homeostasis, or getting siloed in to my small collection of comfortable communities, doesn't help me grow intellectually. That's going to have an impact on our society that we need to consider. The question here will not be whether we really want anybody to be able to create communities that can undermine established social, religious, governmental, and economic structures, but do we really want to create (or indeed, have we already created) the babble of polyphony? We have already created an anti-intellectual and intolerant mass media where, if I'm a right-winged conservative, I don't have to listen to National Public Radio and come to terms with the news and information from that source because I can go to Fox and get the ideologically saturated spin that I find more digestible. Do we really want to create communities that make us even more intellectually fat and lazy, that make us less willing to even listen to voices of dissent?

Currently, social networking enjoys extraordinary popularity because the pendulum of public opinion is swinging in favor of Burk's observations about social capital and the ways that membership in multiple communities enhances individual creativity and problem solving. Companies are rushing to build social networks and to take advantage of crowd-sourcing and increased productivity. But we're already seeing the pendulum beginning to swing the other way. Books such as Mark Helprin's *Digital Barbarism* [4] or Mark Bauerlin's *The Dumbest Generation: How the Digital Age Stupifies Young Americans and Jeopardizes Our Future* [1] are just the first salvos in an antisocial networking backlash that I believe the future holds. It hasn't happened in the mainstream yet, but over the next 5 years, we can expect a public debate to erupt during which there will be a serious backlash against the social networks and online communities that we design.

We can expect the political pundits and many in higher education to claim that our social networks and online communities are actually counterproductive and that we are merely producing intellectual ghettos for our members. They will argue that what we're doing in online environments is no different than what happens in real urban environments where a significant percentage of a population hasn't learned English, as all the people in their particular neighborhood speak, say, Spanish or Korean. The argument against us will be analogous to the one used by the English-first proponents. People in non-English-speaking neighborhoods aren't pressured to deal with English, and so the argument goes, they become victims of their ability to speak the dominant language of their society.

This has the potential to become a huge threat to the social networking industry because many traditional organizations already have the perception that employees are "wasting time" on systems such as Facebook, MySpace, Second Life, and/or YouTube. Indeed, many companies already prohibit and/or actively block these and other similar sites on their corporate LANs. If executives already believe that social networks may be wasting their employees' time, then the argument that social networks and online communities silo them into intellectual ghettos and fail to improve their creativity is really going to push them over the edge.

To prevent this trend in the future, online community managers need to show that the English-first or intellectual ghetto metaphor is based on a bogus analogy and on retrograde thinking. Real ghettos require an individual's physical presence in them. Real neighborhoods have physical and spatial limitations that prevent me from being in multiple neighborhoods at once. Yet as those of us who design them know, online networks and communities don't suffer from these limitations. There's absolutely no reason why I can't be in multiple communities at the same time online. And if I can inhabit multiple communities at the same time, then I am able to take the same kinds of transdisciplinary views that Guttenburg and the Wright brothers used. Hence Burk's observations about social capital leading to more creative problem solving still obtains, but only if corporate executives, managers, educators, and policy makers encourage their charges to become members of multiple communities. As community managers, this is the type of argument we must be prepared to use to defend our work and the value we bring to the workplace, education, and society.

INVESTING IN FUTURE LITERACIES

A third area for the future is to recognize that—just as there was an explosion in the growth of new literacy as a result of the printing press—we are already seeing a similar explosion in new media literacies beyond the simple reading, writing, and arithmetic of our parents' generation. Researchers are predicting that the Internet will be 50 times larger in 2015 than it was in 2006. Much of that growth is going to be coming from new users who are getting online. But even more growth is predicted to come from the additional storage and bandwidth capacity required by video and other media.

Visual literacies are already far outpacing the ability of educational institutions and professional development programs to keep up. The people growing up digital today aren't members of "Generation X" or "Generation Y," they're the "Eye Generation." Their literacies and the culture upon which those literacies are based are no longer dominated by the hegemony of print. They produce knowledge visually as well as verbally. We can already see this in the forms of digital scholarship being produced. The online journal JOVE.com, the *Journal of Online Visualized Experiments*, is already taking advantage of this move toward visual scholarship and knowledge production (Figure 8.2).

JOVE takes biological experiments and rather than producing them in the extremely obscure, highly technical language of biology, it publishes them as video clips. The videos certainly make JOVE's material more accessible, but that's not what makes JOVE so interesting in terms of our discussion. The other thing that JOVE does, which is critical to its success, is that its publishers and editors provide a template for video scholars to use to produce their experiments. Their format demands that contributors start the video off with an abstract that will last a particular length of time. Then it has the research questions that the study tries to address, followed by explanations of the experimental methodology.

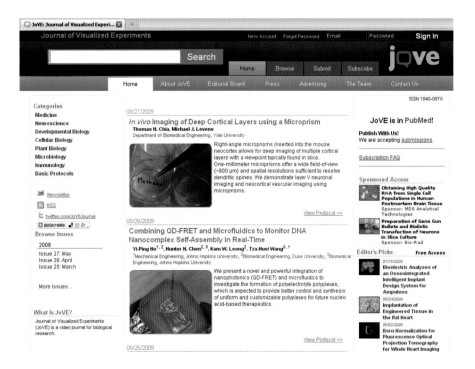

FIGURE 8.2
Video scholarship at JOVE.com.

The format also determines how long the overall video can last. It describes how the subtitles should appear in the video. In short, JOVE's publishers describe the literacies necessary to produce these videos. Compliance with their video template ensures that users of the JOVE.com site will enjoy a consistent, high-quality user experience.

Although it doesn't invest in the literacies of its users the way JOVE does, SlideShare is an example of another service positioning itself to take advantage of the emerging visual literacies and new modes of knowledge production. Today, the peer-reviewed, scholarly article that drove and continues to drive the "publish or perish" models at universities is under attack from these multimodal means of knowledge production such as SlideShare. This will no doubt seem ironic coming from a Rhetoric professor who is writing a book (although in my defense, we built an online community around issues raised in the book). Still as a rhetorician who is interested in effective techniques of persuasion, it's easy to see that if someone wants to have a broad impact on today's business and industry practices, then they need to create digital videos such as Michael Wesch's viral videos, "Web 2.0: The Machine is Us/ing Us" or "A Vision of Students Today." Universities simply can't ignore the ways that Wesch used his literacy in the new media to revitalize interest in the relatively obscure field of anthropology and in the use of ethnographic research methodologies. Instead of discouraging untenured assistant professors by refusing to recognize digital publications, university administrators need to encourage faculty to get one of their presentations uploaded on TED Talks or GoogleTalks or they need to reward faculty who create SlideShare presentations with visual arguments, as well as audio delivery of the material. The days of writing an editorial for a newspaper or, worse, publishing in a peer-reviewed print journal aren't dead but they are fading.

Again, we can look to analogies in the past for instruction here. Consider that the only kinds of books anyone had seen prior to the printing press were those that had been copied by hand. As a result, when Gutenberg created his first Bible, the font he used looked like handwriting. It took nearly 200 years before printers realized that the fonts they used to produce books didn't have to look like they were handwritten. Social network designers and online community architects need to be thinking of ways to get in front of these new visual literacies. We need to begin asking questions like what "makes for a good video scholarship?" What makes for an effective video-based presentation? In an age where it's already possible to create streaming videos from a cell phone, how can I ensure that participants in my social network are able to not merely upload those videos, but upload quality videos that other members of the network and community are going to want to see?

Beyond the audio/visual media that we see, we also need to be looking for other kinds of literacies that are emerging from the collectives. For example, radio-frequency identification tags and global positioning systems are a new kind of literacy that is evolving these days. As Howard Rheingold has shown in his book, *Smart Mobs*, there are potential uses for mobile networked devices and global positioning systems that we're really only just beginning to understand because we've not yet developed a means of understanding and talking about these modes of information sharing [12].

DECISION-MAKING CONTEXTS WILL DOMINATE THE MARKETPLACE

The final observation I would like to make about the future is one that will ultimately bring us back, full circle, to RIBS. The point I want to make here is that the scarce resource and the principal commodity in the future will be attention. The ability to connect everybody to everybody isn't going to sell the network for much longer. Being "like air" isn't going to be perceived to be a good thing when there are only so many minutes in a day. The *time* needed to give attention to anything is a fundamental condition of reality. You can't make more time, and we humans only have so much attention. Mental bandwidth rather than network bandwidth will be the limitations of the future. Consequently, building networks and communities that are huge and require tremendous investments in attention from their users aren't likely to succeed. Instead, what the users of the future will look for is decision-making contexts.

What I mean by "context" is that what future networks and communities will have to sell is a quality user experience for knowledge production. When I look for a community of the future, I'm going to be looking for a community that's going to help me make decisions in the new multimodal media that are available to me. I'm not going to want to go to YouTube and see thousands of hours of juveniles making faces at the webcam. I'm not going to get on Twitter and follow Angelina Jolie in order to find out that she just exited a trendy restaurant.

I don't mean to get down on Twitter because Twitter is very good for certain kinds of things. I use Twitter to send updates to my clients from my cell phone or iPod about usability studies that I'm conducting. My staff and I use Twitter to share information about projects that we're working on in real time. I can ask a question about how to create a cascading style sheet style that will achieve a particular kind of effect on a Web site and get an answer almost immediately from one of my staff members who happens to be working at home that day. As we've seen with the Iranian protests, Twitter is great for adhocracies and for exchanging information in real time about rapidly emerging events. But again, it's the context of use that makes the difference. If I'm in a community that allows messages to be posted about Angelina Jolie's daily activities and if I don't particularly care about that, then that community is the equivalent to spam to me. It sucks my attention away from more productive information, and attention is one of my most precious commodities.

As a result, in the future, I'm going to look for communities and social networks that create a context for smart decision making. These communities are going to use technologies that require literate uses of video productions. Because of the community's design, the members are only going to be producing high-quality videos, smart verbal messages, compelling slide shows, and persuasive visual arguments. I'm not going to worry that I'm wasting my time on dreck in these kinds of communities. Instead, just as restaurants sell atmosphere and attract certain kinds of customers as a result, online communities and social networks that attract the kind of contexts that produce the kinds of knowledge and information that I'm seeking are what I'm going to "buy." To use the analogy of choosing a university rather than a restaurant, universities are also primarily selling contexts—that's one of the reasons why the parents of high school seniors dutifully take their children on the "campus tour." Intuitively we know that campuses are basically communities of scholars, and they produce context for production of knowledge. Some of them are better at that than others. The context provided by the Harvard Business School is perceived to have more value than business courses at Podunk technical college.

So what is it then that the social network and online community of the future needs to sell? We're not selling technology. Technologies change. We're not selling connections to everybody. Six Degrees tried to do that, Friendster tried to do that, Classmates.com tried to do that, and they all failed because *people didn't want to be connected to everybody else*, they wanted to be connected to people that help them make the kinds of cultural and meaningful choices that they wanted. They wanted to be part of the "in" crowd, and the insider crowd isn't where "the everybody crowd" is. To put this another way, Charlene Li is absolutely right when she says that social networks are "like air." It's just that the issue for the future of social networks and online communities will be about which communities provide their users with the cleanest and best air quality.

What online communities of the future have to sell is the promise that they will enhance the literacies of their membership—the promise that they'll provide their members with the disciplining necessary to be successful. What this book has been arguing is that the way designers provide that disciplining is through RIBS. You make sure that the remuneration is there, i.e., that the attention that your members invest in your community or network is remunerated. You make sure that the scarce resource of the future—attention—generates a return on investment. You make sure that your users have influence and that the governance of the community is set up so that they can be literate because you can't be influential if you're not literate. You make structures that make people feel like they belong. You tell stories of origin that help them become literate with the values and discursive practices of that community. And you build significance so that members are proud to be part of the community and motivated, because of that pride, to join and to participate. In short, you create the context through which your community will thrive with RIBS.

WORKS CITED

[1] Bauerlein M. The Dumbest Generation: How the Digital Age Stupefies Young Americans and Jeopardizes Our Future (or, Don't Trust Anyone under 30). New York: Tarcher; 2008.

[2] Beard J. The copyright issue. Annu Rev Inf Sci Technol 1974;9:381–411.

[3] Burt R. The network structure of social capital. July 2000. http://faculty.chicagobooth.edu/ronald.burt/research/NSSC.pdf.

[4] Helprin M. Digital Barbarism: A Writer's Manifesto. New York: Harper; 2009.

[5] Hiltz SR, Turoff M. Network Nation—Revised Edition: Human Communication via Computer. MIT Press; 1993.

[6] Illinois 96th General Assembly. HB1312. Illinois General Assembly Website. 18 Feb 2009. 29 August 2009 http://www.ilga.gov/legislation/96/HB/09600HB1312.htm.

[7] Jarvis J. What Would Google Do?. New York: Harper Collins; 2009.

[8] Parr B. U.S. government asks Twitter to stay up for #iranelection crisis. 16 June 2009. Mashable: The Social Media Guide. 18 June 2009. http://mashable.com/2009/06/16/twitter-iran/.

[9] Parr B. Mindblowing #iranelection stats: 221,744 tweets per hour at peak. Mashable: The Social Media Guide 17 June 2009. 18 June 2009 http://mashable.com/2009/06/17/iranelection-crisis-numbers/.

[10] Patterson RL, Lindberg SW. The Nature of Copyright: A Law of Users' Rights. Athens, GA: University of Georgia; 1991.

[11] Poster M. The Mode of Information: Poststructuralism and Social Context. Chicago: University of Chicago Press; 1990.

[12] Rheingold H. Smart Mobs: The Next Social Revolution. New York: Basic Books; 2003.

[13] Williams E. Evan Williams on listening to Twitter users. TED: Ideas Worth Spreading. Feb 2009. 12 August 2009. http://www.ted.com/talks/evan_williams_on_listening_to_twitter_users.html.

[14] YouTube. Terms of service. YouTube–Broadcast Yourself 19 June 2009. http://www.youtube.com/t/terms.

[15] Yu P. Of monks, medieval scribes, and middlemen. Michigan State Law Rev 2006;1(2006):1–31.

Index

Note: Page numbers followed by *b* indicates boxes; *f* indicates figures; *t* indicates tables.